Achievement

Achievement

Gwen Bradford

OXFORD
UNIVERSITY PRESS

OXFORD
UNIVERSITY PRESS

Great Clarendon Street, Oxford, OX2 6DP,
United Kingdom

Oxford University Press is a department of the University of Oxford.
It furthers the University's objective of excellence in research, scholarship,
and education by publishing worldwide. Oxford is a registered trade mark of
Oxford University Press in the UK and in certain other countries

© Gwen Bradford 2015

The moral rights of the author have been asserted

First Edition published in 2015

Impression: 3

Published in the United States of America by Oxford University Press
198 Madison Avenue, New York, NY 10016, United States of America

British Library Cataloguing in Publication Data

Data available

Library of Congress Control Number: 2014952719

ISBN 978-0-19-871402-6

Printed and bound by
CPI Group (UK) Ltd, Croydon, CR0 4YY

Acknowledgments

This project began as a paper on the intrinsic value of games that I wrote in Thomas Hurka's seminar, which I took in my penultimate semester as an undergraduate at University of Toronto. He suggested I pursue my games topic, writ large as achievements, for my dissertation, which subsequently grew to become this book. And so I find myself back on the road of philosophical inquiry I had begun as an undergraduate, and, it seems, from which I might not stray for some time. I owe him many thanks for his encouragement and support.

I am deeply grateful for having the Socrates incarnate Shelly Kagan as my dissertation advisor at Yale, who guided me along the path of inquiry that has finally culminated in this book. To paraphrase of one of the other so-privileged few, Shelly went far beyond the call of duty, although he himself would not think such a thing were possible.

Parts of the book have appeared in other incarnations. Chapter 4 draws from "The Value of Achievements," which appeared in *Pacific Philosophical Quarterly*, 94 (2013): 204–24, and the discussion of evil achievements in Chapter 5 draws from "Evil Achievements and the Principle of Recursion," which appeared in *Oxford Studies in Normative Ethics*, iii (OUP, 2013) 79–97. The manuscript was completed with support from the Humanities Research Center at Rice University, and final revisions were polished while I enjoyed a Faculty Fellowship at the Murphy Institute at Tulane University. I'm very grateful for this support.

The runners, gourmet cooks, mountain climbers, bodybuilders, musicians, billiards players, chemists, golfers, treasure-hunters, shoelace-tiers, and philosophers in my life have inspired and supported me in innumerable ways, and I thank you all.

Finally, my happy thanks to my parents. Their gentle natures and subtle encouragement allowed my wily will to flourish in this most imprudent and improbable direction.

Contents

Contents

1

Achievements
They're Great—But What Are They?

If you're reading this now, it's probably safe to assume that you are, in some way, a philosopher. Perhaps you are a professor: someone who has succeeded in academic achievements enough to make a career out of it. If this is the case, no doubt you have worked very hard and struggled to overcome a great many obstacles to finally find yourself with a position coveted by so many. But, we might stop and wonder, what's so great about all this? Why bother? Why should we think our lives will be so much better if we devote them to philosophy, and better still if we do well in our philosophical pursuits?

Now, I suspect that there are those among us who secretly (or not so secretly) congratulate themselves on thinking that we have devoted ourselves to *the* superlatively worthwhile pursuit. No doubt there are philosophers who think that the philosophical life is truly the best life, and philosophical achievements the best toward which any human can aspire. Alternatively, there are others with more pluralistic leanings who think that we might have fared just as well having chosen to devote our lives to some other pursuit, and subsequently enjoyed just as much good in our lives as we do from our philosophical pursuits. These philosophers among us think that we would have found just as much satisfaction and meaning in being a concert violinist, a professional hockey player, the owner of a successful business, or a politician.

Regardless of our views on this particular issue, even the "philosophy elitists" among us would agree, I think, that, not only are philosophical achievements valuable, but *many* achievements, from many domains, can *meaning-providing*

be valuable, and can fill our lives with meaning and significance. It is a commonly held view, among both philosophers and non-philosophers alike, that achievements of one kind or another are one of life's greatest sources of meaning, and that dedicating ourselves to a worthy pursuit is precisely what we should aim for if we want to have a worthwhile and meaningful life.   *pursuit/believe.*

But why should we think that this is the case? Why should we think that achieving—either in philosophy, or another domain—is a worthwhile endeavor, worthy of our sacrifice and efforts, and significant enough so as to bring real meaning and value to our lives? Further, why, as some of us think, are some pursuits and accomplishments more worthwhile than others?

More fundamentally still, what if anything do these valuable endeavors share in common? That is, what is it that makes something that we have done an *achievement* at all?

Curing cancer, for example, certainly would be a significant achievement, perhaps (at least in part) because it would have an enduring impact of saving millions of lives. But not all remarkable achievements *intrinsic* have instrumental value of such significance. Running a marathon in *value* record-breaking time, for instance, or climbing Mount Kilimanjaro are *necessary* · valuable achievements even if they result in no further good beyond their own accomplishment. Moreover, if a radioactive meteorite crashed into the earth and had the effect of curing cancer, while we might be happy with this valuable effect, it doesn't seem right to call the natural event of the meteorite crash an *achievement*.

We might then start by wondering whether all achievements are *diffi-cult to* accomplish: running a marathon, climbing Mount Kilimanjaro, and curing cancer are all difficult. If I tie my shoelaces, it does not constitute an achievement for me, whereas for Jim, who has only one arm, tying his shoes presents a unique challenge, and accomplishing it does seem to be an achievement—and for him to master the skill would be even more impressive. Yet we might balk at saying that *all* difficult endeavors are achievements. After all, planning and carrying out a large-scale project to massacre millions of people would be remarkably difficult, but I think that many would hesitate to say that, for instance, the Holocaust was an achievement, let alone one that endowed the lives of its participants with positive value.

Moreover, some endeavors may be typically difficult, but not difficult for someone who is particularly gifted. A virtuoso violinist easily tosses off a stunning and flawless performance of the Mendelssohn violin concerto with barely any effort. Now consider the hard-working amateur who toils for hours every week to accomplish his dream of performing the same concerto, and after months of intense practicing, manages to scrape out a decent but much less artistically impressive performance. The virtuoso has contributed an impressive artistic accomplishment, but it was all in a day's work for him and required little in the way of effort, while our amateur has produced a much less impressive performance, but given real effort and accomplished something of special meaning and significance in his own life. Are both performances achievements, or not?

If both the virtuoso's effortless performance and the amateur's successful struggle *are* achievements, we might then wonder which one is a more valuable achievement. One plausible thought is that the difficulty overcome by the amateur makes the achievement more significant in the life of the amateur—the more difficult the achievement, the more valuable within the context of the life. Yet it might not seem that difficulty tells us the whole story of the value of the achievement. I take it that inventing the telephone was a great achievement. Now imagine that the process of inventing the telephone was made much, much more difficult by the interference of a malicious villain. Would this have made Alexander Graham Bell's invention of the telephone more valuable?

Other inventions present us with further puzzles. In 2004, the South Korean scientist Hwang Woo-Suk claimed to have cloned the first human embryo. Later, it was revealed that Hwang had falsified data, along with a number of other not so nice things, and had not, in the end, managed to clone any human embryos. Hwang had, however, generated embryos by parthenogenesis—a remarkable achievement in its own right, which could have effects similar to cloning in the world of stem cell research. Yet consider that Hwang failed to recognize what he had accomplished and its significance. Should Hwang's innovation confer meaning and value to his life?

Moreover, we might ask, does Hwang's deceit alter the good of the achievement? If deceit is enough to color the value of his otherwise impressive achievement, we might wonder what other factors can change the value of achievements. Controversy in baseball over the use of various performance-enhancing substances not only cast a shadow over Barry Bonds' all-time home run record, but also called into question the merit of whole seasons' worth of wins and the value of team efforts. Why do the latest technology in special equipment and training count as legitimate contributions to an achievement, but certain technological advances, in the form of performance-enhancing drugs and treatments, seem to be cheating?

Looking over the questions we have just begun to puzzle, we can see that we can categorize these questions into two groups: questions that concern the nature of achievements—what makes something an achievement *at all*?—and questions that concern the *value* of achievements—given that something is an achievement, is it more or less valuable than some other achievement, and how much value does it confer to the life of the achiever? This seems to me to be a natural way, then, to divide the tasks of this investigation: we need an investigation into the *descriptive* nature of achievements, and we need an investigation into the *value* of achievements.

Of course we might say that in some sense every instance of accomplishing an aim, even a small one, is an achievement—every little accomplishment, starting with getting out of bed, making breakfast, taking out the garbage, and so on, might count as an achievement in this wide sense. But these aren't the sorts of achievements that we strive to shape our lives around. Rather, it seems to be the case that there is a special class of achievements, which are particularly worthy of our efforts. There is special significance to exceptional endeavors. We might put it this way: there is a sense of the word "achievement" in which every little thing we do, every aim we accomplish is an "achievement." But there is another sense of the word "achievement," which seems to be reserved for exceptional accomplishments—those endeavors that are particularly noteworthy in some respect, and evoke a sense of awe, admiration, and of being impressed. It is achievements in this latter sense that we aim for in our lives.

These specially significant achievements—achievements with a capital A, as it were—seem to be so much more valuable than mundane accomplishments that many would say that one successful achievement is worth more than many mundane accomplishments. Moreover, we might even think that achievements are *so* special relative to mundane accomplishments that even if a life dedicated toward the pursuit of a single significant achievement results in failure, it might be more worthwhile than a life filled with many mundane successful accomplishments. Dedicating one's life to trying but failing to find the cure for cancer might be a more worth-while choice than a life filled with nothing but successfully tied shoes and peeled bananas.

Now, it seems like a reasonable question to ask what these capital-A achievements have in common, apart from being especially valuable. Perhaps there are some characteristics that they share, and perhaps it is in virtue of these shared characteristics that they are particularly valuable. Maybe it's the case that these characteristics are *different* characteristics from the mundane accomplishments. This, then, is the hypothesis under which my investigation here will proceed: that there are some characteristics that these particularly valuable achievements have in common, which ground their special value.

It could turn out, that, like any hypothesis, my hypothesis is false, and there are no characteristics shared by achievements. Or, it might turn out to be the case that, even if achievements have some characteristics in common, they are not valuable *in virtue* of these characteristics, and that, while they are all valuable, they have nothing in common in virtue of which they are all valuable—their value, that is, comes from diverse sources.

I suppose that one of these alternatives could be true. But in order to get a grip on just what it is for something to be an achievement *at all*, I will proceed to determine what these common characteristics are, if there are any at all, in the hope that working in this way will be the most illumin-ating method for uncovering what it is that makes specially significant achievements more valuable than their mundane counterpart. As my investigation progresses, I will of course return to these issues, and we may indeed find that the difference is not in kind but only in degree of value, or that some other alternative is the case.

For now, then, I will proceed with the hypothesis that there are descrip-tive characteristics shared by especially significant achievements that ground their superlative value. It seems to be a reasonable approach, given that it at least seems to be true that some achievements have significantly more value than others, to ask what makes this the case by looking into what descriptive characteristics they share that make them distinctive, and to see if these descriptive characteristics shed light on what makes them particularly valuable.

Of course, a completely isolated descriptive study of achievements would be an overly forced and unnatural approach and so I will often draw from intuitions about the value of achievements in order to help inform the investigation into the descriptive side of things. I'm not going to go Cartesian and lock myself in a room with nothing but my descriptive investigation about achievements; rather, I will often visit intuitions about the value of achievements in order to guide the descriptive investigation.

In short, then, this is how I will proceed: I will first work toward a *descriptive* account of the nature of achievement, answering the question *what is an achievement?* Subsequently, I will turn to the value-theoretic question: in light of the descriptive account of the nature of achievements, *why are achievements valuable?*

What should we expect from a comprehensive descriptive account? The highest expectations for a comprehensive descriptive account would be for a list of necessary and sufficient conditions of achievement. Or, if the notion of achievement is one that doesn't lend itself to this kind of analysis, we should be able to see why this is the case, and then tailor our expectations accordingly. At least, then, we should hope for an account of the core features of achievements. A good descriptive account should also capture most of our common-sense intuitions about what counts as an achievement and what does not. Additionally, a comprehensive account of achievement should stretch across the various domains of activity where achievements are accomplished: athletic achievements, artistic achievements, intellectual achievements (such as inventions or scientific discoveries), and so on.

I should be clear that I don't take the aim of the project to be an account of how we use the *term* "achievement." Rather, I take myself to be in the business of sorting out some of the true key features of *achievements*, and, although we would expect use of the term to track these features for the most part, I am more interested in the nature of achievements themselves rather than the use of the term. Of course, how we talk about achievements is sometimes good evidence, and so I will appeal from time to time to things that we might naturally say about them.

Concerning the value-theoretic question, we might think that asking about the value of achievements is asking about the role of achievement in wellbeing—what is the value of achievement *to* the person whose achievement it is? Alternatively, we might be asking about the value of achievement in a broader sense—what is the *intrinsic value* of an achievement? It is this latter question that will be our concern here. Achievement may or may not play a role in wellbeing. But the question is broader than the role of achievements in wellbeing. I think we would be inclined to say that curing cancer is a tremendously valuable achievement, even if it doesn't contribute at all to the wellbeing of the researchers who develop the cure. Insofar as your achievements are a part of your life, it is a natural thought that their value shapes the value of your life. But this isn't necessarily because they play a role in your wellbeing. So it is this question concerning the intrinsic value of achievement that is the focus of the investigation.

Before we begin, we should take a look to see what ground has already been covered. The apparent significance of achievements has been acknowledged in philosophical literature. It has led many philosophers to opt out of the experience machine, and reject mental state theories of wellbeing.[1] Classic formulations of the objective list include achievements, and perfectionists also give them a central role.[2] Some theories make attaining goals a constitutive element of wellbeing.[3]

Yet, in spite of this acknowledgment of significance, much of the discussion of achievements has been cursory.

In accounts of wellbeing that give achievement of one's aims a constitutive role, the focus in most discussions is not on capital-A achievements, but on wide, mundane achievements. The appeal of such accounts is generally to capture a subjective element where what makes one's life go well has something to do with one's own choices or preferences, yet block certain objections to which desire-satisfaction views are susceptible, by holding that only those desires that are satisfied by (at least in part) one's own success are relevant for wellbeing. However, these accounts are generally concerned with achievements in the wide sense—achievements in the sense that every little thing we do is an achievement, even peeling a banana, and not achievements in the capital-A sense.

Joseph Raz's account, for example, is that one's life goes well when we achieve the goals that we have good reason to pursue. The more of these

---

[1] The classic instance: Robert Nozick, *Anarchy, State, and Utopia* (New York: Basic Books, 1974), 42–5.
[2] Cf. Derek Parfit, *Reasons and Persons* (Oxford: Clarendon Press, 1984), 499–501; Thomas Hurka, *Perfectionism* (Oxford: OUP, 1993); George Sher, *Beyond Neutrality: Perfectionism and Politics* (Cambridge: CUP, 1997).
[3] Joseph Raz, *The Morality of Freedom* (Oxford: Clarendon Press, 1986), 288 ff.; T. M. Scanlon, *What We Owe to Each Other* (Cambridge, MA: Harvard University Press, 1998), 121 ff.; Simon Keller, "Welfare as Success," *Noûs*, 43 (2009): 656–83.

goals that we attain, the better our life goes for us. If getting into art school will help Jane get a job, and she aims to get a job, then she has good reason to have getting into art school as a goal, and her life goes better if she reaches this goal.[4]

Ultimately, however, Raz's account is unhelpful as far as the nature of achievements goes. Raz's notion of achievement concerns achievements in the broad sense, so that even the most trivial undertaking can constitute an achieved goal, such as successfully brushing one's teeth. Moreover, he does not provide a thorough account of just what an achievement *is*, apart from having a goal and reaching it; nor does he dig particularly deeply into what it is to reach a goal. To be fair, much of Raz's discussion concerns the *value* of attaining goals, and which goals are valuable to attain. To this extent, then, his discussion sheds light on which goals are more worthy than others. Apart from this, it is not illuminating as far as the nature or value of the achievements themselves is concerned.

Moreover, Raz's view generates what I take to be a seriously counterintuitive answer to key cases. Consider his example of Jane going to art school in order to get a job. Raz says,

> If it turns out that getting a job is not a good thing to do then Jane's well-being is not adversely affected by failing to get admitted to art school. Her pursuit of this goal was premised on the belief that it is.[5]

So, to be precise, the view is as follows. Suppose that A believes that goal x is helpful for attaining her other goal, y. A adopts goal x on the basis of this belief, and pursues it. A fails at her attempt to succeed in x. It turns out that x is not, in fact, helpful for y. So A's belief was false. A's failure to succeed in x is *not* bad. That is, A's goal of x is valuable *only if* x is helpful for y. For Jane, the goodness of her goal of going to art school is conditional on its being related to her getting a job.

This doesn't seem obviously implausible. It means that it's actually not good if Jane gets into art school, if it's also true that it doesn't contribute to her getting a job. Perhaps some people might be inclined to see that as plausible. But here is something less plausible. If Jane *succeeds* in getting into (and going to, presumably) art school, but her belief about jobs and art school is false, her success in art school *is not valuable*. More generally,

---

[4] Raz, *Morality of Freedom*, 300 ff.   [5] Raz, *Morality of Freedom*, 301.

suppose again A believes x is helpful for attaining y, and adopts x as a goal on this basis. A succeeds in x. But A's belief is false. So A's success in attaining x has no value. This would be true even if A never comes to realize that her belief is false.

This is problematic. It implies that virtually all scientists currently working on cures for cancer do not make their lives better in attempting their goals. Presumably they adopt the goals of their current research because they believe that these goals will facilitate their further goal, namely curing cancer. Most research of this nature, sad but true, does not lead to the cure for cancer. On Raz's view, goals are only valuable if beliefs about their connection to further goals are true. So the scientists' current research projects are not in fact valuable.

We might be able to accommodate this example by stipulating that the scientists' current goals are such that they would want to toil away on their current projects even if what they are currently doing has no relationship to curing cancer. But even if this were true of some scientists, I suspect it is much more likely that many deeply want to be working on something on the condition that it contributes to the actual cure. Regardless, I don't think we would want to say that the goals of those who have their current goals conditionally have no value, which is precisely what his view would entail: that it is absolutely worthless for these scientists to strive for their goals.

Furthermore, it's quite likely that most people are like these scientists, including philosophers. Suppose that many philosophers work under the assumption that philosophical progress is possible, and believe that their work is in some way related to this. Suppose that there are some optimists who only have the goal of doing philosophy if this is indeed the case. Imagine one such optimist with an incredibly successful philosophical career, who publishes a great many interesting books and articles and is a successful teacher. Would we want to say that this philosopher's goals and successes had no value, since her beliefs about their relationship to the progress of philosophy was false? Surely not.

Moreover, we can imagine that most people in their various jobs have their goals—both large- and small-scale—under the supposition that these goals are connected to achieving some higher, significant goal, such as attaining meaning in life, or being a part of something larger than themselves, or somehow making a lasting difference. Indeed, it's plausible that many people have these beliefs in such a way that if they came to believe that their careers or other goals and activities had no bearing on these larger aspirations, then they would change them. In other words, many people's aims seem to be entirely conditional on being connected to some larger purpose. But suppose these beliefs are false. Most people's activities are futile with respect to these larger aspirations. Rather, most people's endeavors resemble more the farmer who raises pigs so he can buy more land so he can raise more pigs.[6] Raz's view implies, then, that most people, since their goals are contingent on serving some larger purpose, have no value in their lives. So Raz's account of the value of achievements has implausible implications.

Another account that gives achievement a central role is from T. M. Scanlon. His view is that "success in one's rational aims" is one of the constitutive elements of wellbeing.[7] He adopts several aspects of Raz's view, such as the notion that attaining goals that are more "comprehensive" and "shape a large part of one's life" are more important for wellbeing than more trivial ones.[8] Scanlon's view of achievements is similar to Raz's in its appeal to mundane, wide achievements—trivial undertakings nonetheless are relevant for wellbeing and are achievements. Similarly, Scanlon's analysis does not extend to investigate just what it is for someone to attain a goal, since his focus is on the rational side rather than the aiming side.

Something achievement-like also has an important role for Bernard Williams. Ground projects, as he calls them, play an integral role for agency, and for giving life meaning.[9] Ground projects are large-scale endeavors, projects with an interconnected "nexus" of plans that span over significant parts of life and give meaning and purpose to agency. No doubt many ground projects would be achievements. But not all valuable achievements are ground projects. Some valuable achievements are relatively short chapters in our lives, such as hiking across Europe. Although it might be a source of value if all our projects and achievements were related to each other, it is not an essential feature of achievements that they be interconnected to our other projects. So while Williams' account

---

[6] The example is from David Wiggins, "Truth, Invention, and the Meaning of Life," *Needs, Values, Truth* (Oxford: Clarendon Press, 1998), 100.

[7] *What We Owe to Each Other*, 118.   [8] *What We Owe to Each Other*, 122.

[9] Bernard Williams, "Persons, Character and Morality," *Moral Luck* (Cambridge: CUP, 1981), 1–19.

of ground projects seems relevant, it is not an account of achievement per se.[10]

So, although it may appear that achievements have been thoroughly discussed in the literature, it turns out that extant discussions so far don't really dig the depths of the nature and value of achievement. But these are not the only philosophical discussions of achievements. There are others who have looked directly at the nature of achievements in the capital-A sense. I will take up these approaches as the elements of my view come together.

I will kickstart this descriptive leg of my investigation with a preliminary observation about *all* achievements—that is, achievements in the broad sense, not just capital-A achievements. Achievements, it seems, aren't the sort of thing that just pop into existence, *ex nihilo*. Rather, they are the result of some process. So it seems achievements have this particular structure: there is a *process* and a *product*, we might say. The process *culminates in a product*. In some cases, such as building a house or publishing a novel, the product is something that is separate and distinct from the process, while in other cases, such as dance performances, the process and product are one and the same thing. In any case, the process and the product need to be related in a certain way in order to count as an achievement: the process culminates in the product, whether this culmination be the execution of the process itself, or something distinct from the process. The successfulness of an achievement, in a typical case, is the production of the product, such as the finished painting, or the completion of the dance performance. For clarity, then, when I refer to the "process" or "product" of an achievement, this is the distinction that I have in mind. This structure, being comprised of a process and a product, seems common to all achievements—both the mundane sort, and momentous, capital-A achievements.

Now we might ask, what, if anything, do these especially significant ("capital-A") achievements have in common?

[10] A similar notion of ground projects or personal projects is further developed by Monika Betzler, but again the notion of projects is broader than achievements, which need not be life-shaping, expansive endeavors. Cf. Monika Betzler, "The Normative Significance of Personal Projects," in Michael Kühler and Nadja Jelinek (eds), *Autonomy and the Self* (Dordrecht: Springer, 2013), 101–26.

A Preliminary Sketch of the Account

Consider Jim, our one-armed friend who successfully ties his shoes. Why does this count as an achievement for Jim, but tying my shoes with both my healthy hands does not count as an achievement for me?

One feature that appears to distinguish his achievement—and, I will contend, all achievements—is that it is *difficult*. If tying my shoes presented a particular difficulty for me to overcome, as it does for Jim, then my success might count as an achievement too. If writing a novel were so easy that anyone could do it, we wouldn't think of it as an achievement. Finding a cure for cancer is turning out to be difficult task. Writing a dissertation, running a marathon, or even smaller scale achievements, such as winning a game of chess, baking a soufflé, or cultivating a bonsai—all of these achievements are difficult to do.

Were it the case that any of these activities were easy, we wouldn't think of them as achievements. Reaching the summit of Mount Everest only seems to count as an achievement if it is difficult. We could accomplish the same result—getting to the top of the mountain—by taking a helicopter, but surely the getting to the summit by helicopter would hardly be an achievement, whereas reaching the top at the end of a challenging climb would be. This suggests that difficulty is a necessary component for achievements. Counterexamples will no doubt come to mind, and I will address putative problems as we go along. In any case, the relevance of difficulty seems to be the point that Raz and Scanlon overlooked in their accounts. There is more to achievements than simply realizing some aim. Achievements, properly speaking, are difficult.

So it seems to be a plausible starting point, then, to think that achievements have at least this characteristic in common: that they are difficult. But is it the case that being difficult is *sufficient* for achievements?

The answer appears to be *no*. Consider the following example, inspired by an example by Simon Keller, one of the few contemporary philosophers who have written explicitly about achievements.[11]

Joan and the Politician. There is a local law prohibiting overnight parking in the town where Joan lives, and she has the goal of having this

---

[11] Simon Keller, "Welfare and the Achievement of Goals," *Philosophical Studies,* 121 (2004): 27–41.

law changed. She has the crazy idea that standing on her head for three hours a day will have the effect of changing the law. She does this. As it happens, the law does get changed, but, of course not as a result of anything Joan does. Rather, a local politician buys a new car and needs a parking space.[12]

Joan's activity is difficult, but the change in the parking law doesn't count as an achievement for Joan. There needs to be a connection between Joan's difficult activities and the outcome that the activity is aimed toward. There must be some *contribution that Joan's efforts* make to the outcome. It seems that, in order to count as an achievement, it must be achieved at least in part *through one's own efforts*. According to Keller, that achievements come about by one's own efforts *just is* a matter of the meaning of the word "achieve."[13] I think that Keller is right about this—at least part of what it means for something to count as an achievement for a person is that it comes about by way of their efforts. We might say, then, that the agent's difficult activities need to be a *cause* of the achievement.

We observed earlier that achievements have a particular structure: there is a process that culminates in a product. Now we need to clarify that by *culmination* we need to understand some kind of *causation*—that is, the process needs to *cause* the product. So according to the account so far, to count as an achievement, the process that results in the product must be difficult, and the product must obtain in such a way that the difficult process causes the product.

But I think that there is still more to be said, and if Keller intends his gloss of achievements to be comprehensive, it is not. Merely having a difficult activity cause a goal to come about is not sufficient to constitute an achievement. Consider this example.

Buried Treasure. Lucky Lon comes to believe that there is treasure buried somewhere in the area, and embarks on a vigorous but hare-brained

[12] Keller, "Welfare and the Achievement of Goals," 33. In Keller's example, Joan chants the word "widget" over and over again, rather than stand on her head. However, given the account of achievements that I have sketched so far, difficulty is a necessary feature of achievements, and chanting the word "widget" is not particularly difficult. At this point we need an example of a difficult activity and so I have altered the example accordingly. Moreover, I should mention here the further point that Keller fails to discuss difficulty as necessary for achievements. It's unclear whether or not he intends his sketch of achievements to be a comprehensive analysis, however.

[13] Keller, "Welfare and the Achievement of Goals," 33.

research plan involving magic 8-balls, ouiji boards, séances, and dowsing wands. Suppose that Lon's research program is, in spite of its questionable reliability, quite difficult for Lon to carry out and requires a great deal of effort. He eventually settles on what he believes is the precise location of the treasure, digs for days, and lo and behold! there just happens to be treasure buried in this exact spot.

Lon's hare-brained activities were difficult for him, and his activities cause the discovery of the buried treasure. But I doubt we would be happy calling Lon's discovering the treasure an "achievement" for Lon. A lucky turn of events, but not, it seems, an achievement. So just difficulty and causation are not jointly sufficient for achievements. Rather, we need the process to cause the product in a certain way—in a *non-accidental* way. Consider a different example:

> *Deserving Discovery.* Diligent Don has been conducting a research project and has good reason to believe that there is treasure buried in the area. He systematically scrutinizes various historical documents and maps, and conducts land surveys, and once he has pinpointed the location of the treasure, uses a metal detector to find it. He digs and, lo, the treasure! just where it was expected.

Now Don's discovery is an achievement, whereas Lon's is not. Where Lon's hare-brained plans by chance lead him to find the treasure, Don's research makes his discovery of the treasure much less surprising, leaving much less to chance than Lon's approach. Lon's discovery is accidental whereas Don's discovery is not. This feature of being non-accidental that characterizes Don's activities, but not Lon's, helps to explain why Don's discovery counts as an achievement, which suggests that being non-accidental may be necessary for achievements.

But what does it mean for the success of an achievement to be non-accidental? Lon's activities are more reasonable, it seems, and Don's discovery of the treasure is more likely than Lon's. Had the treasure been buried in a different location, and circumstances had been slightly different, it's likely that Don would still have found the treasure—the various historical sources would have still indicated the correct location, Don would follow maps, and the metal detector would pinpoint the location. But had Lon's treasure been buried in even a slightly different location it would be very unlikely that Lon would find the treasure. Perhaps, then, this is what makes up the difference: Don's activity makes the success of the outcome more likely—it's a better way of finding treasure because this way is more *reliable*, we might say.

One plausible and popular way of characterizing reliability is in terms of possible worlds, where a reliable process is one that would produce similar results under similar conditions in a sufficiently high percentage of nearby possible worlds.[14] There may, of course, be other plausible accounts of reliability, but let's begin with this one.

By using the same methods he uses to discover the treasure, would Don discover treasure in nearby possible worlds, say, in worlds where the treasure is buried in a slightly different location? The answer seems to be yes—historical sources would indicate the rough location of the treasure in these worlds, and Don's metal detector would help him to find it. In contrast, in worlds where the treasure is buried in a slightly different location, Lon would *fail* to find the treasure. His dowsing wand and ouiji board would be of no real help. So this *reliabilist* account of achievement (or let's call it that) seems to be off to a promising start.

But one might object that appealing to reliability is not a helpful approach for other cases. Many achievements are the sort of thing that are *one-off* achievements, such as inventing the telephone or decoding the platypus genome. Once an achievement such as an invention or discovery is completed, it's not the sort of thing that can be reproduced, let alone be reproduced reliably.

I think, however, that this objection confuses reliability with its similar cousin, *repeatability*. That some process reliably produces its product could lead you to think that the product could be produced again and again in similar circumstances and of course this can't happen in the case

---

[14] Epistemologists who worry about a roughly analogous problem of accidentally true beliefs counting as knowledge appeal to the reliability of the process by which the beliefs were formed. According to these *reliabilist* accounts of knowledge, true beliefs that are justified via a reliable process count as knowledge, where a reliable process is one that would produce similar results in a sufficiently high percentage of the relevant nearby possible worlds. Many versions of this view are developed in the literature. A seminal statement of the view is given by Alvin Goldman in "What Is Justified Belief?" in G. Pappas (ed.), *Justification and Knowledge* (Dordrecht: Reidel, 1979). Alternative accounts appeal to *ability*, which is likewise characterized as producing similar results in a sufficiently high amount of the relevant nearby possible worlds. Cf. John Greco, *Achieving Knowledge* (Cambridge: CUP, 2010). I address these accounts directly in "Knowledge, Achievement, and Manifestation," *Erkenntnis*, forthcoming.

of an invention, which, in virtue of being an invention, is the sort of thing that only gets done once. But reliability isn't a matter of repeating the similar results in the actual world. Rather, it's a matter of producing similar results in nearby possible worlds, and possible worlds don't really care about whether or not you could repeat it in the actual world. Depending on the circumstances of the invention, it could be the case that the same method repeated in nearby worlds would have the same results, and so the method of the invention might indeed be reliable. That is to say, even if conditions had been slightly different, it's still possible that someone trying to invent the telephone would eventually figure out how to make a telephone. So the process of inventing the telephone could, on this account, be characterized as reliable.

However, as promising as the reliabilist account may look so far, there are other cases where it goes awry. For instance,

Close Race. A and B are two race car drivers of virtually equal ability to win racing against each other. Conditions are such that neither A nor B is favored over the other.

Winning the race would be an achievement for the winner. But in how many nearby possible worlds would the winner achieve the same results? About half. Recall that, to develop the reliabilist account, we need to determine how high a percentage of nearby possible worlds with success is sufficiently high to capture non-accidentality. So if the reliabilist is going to capture the win of Close Race as an achievement, the reliabilist will need to say that success in *half* of the nearby worlds is sufficiently high. So far so good. But what if there were three equally capable drivers in the race? The win would still count as an achievement for the winner. So the reliabilist would have to revise his view once again, and say that success in a *third* of nearby worlds is sufficiently high.

But we can soon see that even setting the bar at a third is too high. Even if there were five or even a dozen comparably capable drivers in the race, the win would still be an achievement for the winner. In fact, it seems that no matter how many comparably capable drivers are in the race, the win is an achievement. In order to capture this, the reliabilist will have to say that the required percentage of possible worlds with success is actually quite small. But to make this move is to abandon the proposed view. The reliabilist account characterized non-accidental success as success in a sufficiently high percentage in nearby possible worlds. But now we see that non-accidental success is compatible with a very *small* percentage of success in nearby possible worlds. So looking at percentages of success in nearby possible worlds is not helpful for distinguishing non-accidental successes from merely accidental ones. A fortiori, an account where reliability is analyzed in terms of chances of success in possible worlds can't be what we are looking for either.

Now, a reliabilist could respond by providing a different account of reliability—perhaps an account of reliability that is not cashed out in terms of possible worlds. But regardless of the account of reliability developed, it just doesn't seem like it's a good way to characterize the win in Close Race. No matter how you slice up reliability, it's just false to say that, in a race with a hundred equally capable competitors, the winner's win is *reliable*. So we need a better way than reliability to characterize the non-accidental feature of achievements.

I suggest a more promising approach is to appeal to the competence of the agent and his activity. We credit Don with his achievement, but we do not credit Lon for his discovery because Don's search for the treasure was executed competently, whereas Lon's was not. Don knows how to find treasure—he has an understanding of what he is doing and what a good way to do it is.

Similarly, in Close Race with many drivers, since all the competitors are comparably competent drivers, no matter who wins, the winner's process not only caused his win, but caused it competently. Even though it is false that the winner would win in many nearby possible worlds, his activities are linked to his success competently, and this element seems to do the trick in explaining why, in spite of the lack of "reliability" in his methods, winning the race is still an achievement for the winner. It seems that we credit the success to the winner in virtue of his being competent. Without competence, even if there is success, there is no achievement—as in Lon's discovery of the buried treasure.

There is, to be sure, a great deal more to say about the nature of competence. But for now my goal is simply to get the basic elements of achievements in place, and later I will return to fill in the details of our account.

Now the sketch of the account of achievements is beginning to take shape. Achievements have these features: (a) a difficult process; (b) the process causes the product; (c) the process is executed competently. In short, we could say that achievements are comprised by a difficult and competent process, and the product in which this process culminates.

Objections to the Account: Candidates for Further Components

All the cases that we have covered so far indicate that these three conditions—the difficulty condition, the causal condition, and the competence condition—are necessary for achievements. But surely these three conditions aren't yet sufficient. Is it the case that all culminations of difficult, competent processes are achievements?

First we might worry about whether or not we need an *agential* condition. I haven't yet stipulated the somewhat obvious feature of achievements that they are done by people—or agents, more generally. A painting, for example, must be the result of somebody painting it, in order to be an achievement. If a painting just emerges miraculously from a swamp, it is not an achievement—a miracle perhaps, but not an achievement. Perhaps, then, we need to add an agential component—this component would require that, in order to count as an achievement, the process must be done by an *agent*. — competence

But with the competence requirement, we get what we need for free. The process must be executed sufficiently competently, so only beings that can do things competently are eligible to be the authors of achievements. Swamps cannot be competent. So as long as we have a competence condition of some sort, we already understand the process to be one that is done by an agent of the relevant sort. One might wonder if this means that animals can achieve. Would it be an achievement for a dog to learn a complicated task? This would seem to be a possibility, so long as the process is sufficiently difficult and demands competence.

Still, there are further objections. Recall Don, from Deserving Discovery, here in a different scenario, which, as you will see, is something of a practical Gettier case.

Shallow Benefactor. Don embarks once again on his vigorous and competent research project, examining maps and historical sources, all of which indicate that there is treasure buried in the area. Unbeknownst to Don, by some fluke course of events undetectable by historical research, there is in fact no treasure, although it is reasonable to think that there could be. However, also unknown to Don, Benefactor has spotted Don at the library, and, finding him an attractive guy, she decides to plant some treasure for him to find in the location where he thinks it's buried. So, when Don goes to dig, lo, treasure! From all Don can tell, he has discovered the treasure he has been vigorously searching for. Of course, the treasure he has found was from Benefactor, and not the treasure he had been researching.

Now, although Don finds the treasure, his discovery is not an achievement. What's missing? Don's activities were difficult, and they were executed competently. Additionally, his activities are a cause of the product—albeit indirectly: after all, Benefactor sees Don at the library while he is conducting his research. Had Don not been conducting his research project, Benefactor would not have seen him, and would not have planted the treasure for him to discover. So Don's activities are part of the causal chain resulting in the discovery of the treasure.

It seems that we need to add a further component to the analysis. Don's activity is competent, and it causes the product. According to the account so far, it should count as an achievement. But the intuition is that the discovery is not an achievement for Don in this case.

Since Shallow Benefactor is something of a practical Gettier case, it looks like we need to add an anti-Gettier condition to the account. Just as it is not enough to have a belief that is justified and true, it is also the case that, for achievements, it is not enough that the process is competent and the product comes about. There needs to be a further condition that links up the process and the product in the right sort of way. We have already established that the process must *cause* the product, and the process must be competent. Now it looks like we need to be more specific: it must be the case that the *competence of the process causes the product*. That is, it's not enough that the agent's activities be (a) competent and (b) cause the product: in achievements, the competence must cause the product.

Yet a further example shows that this is not enough still.

Rewarding Benefactor. Don is embarking on his vigorous research, and again, unbeknownst to Don, the treasure is not buried in the area after all. And once again, Don has been spotted in the library. This time, however, Benefactor, is struck not by Don's handsome appearance, but by his perseverance and hard work which she thinks should be rewarded. So she decides to plant treasure for Don to find in the location where he has most reason to believe it is buried. When Don digs, he finds Benefactor's treasure, once again thinking that it is the historical treasure.

Now Don's competence causes the treasure to be found. But, it seems, this is still not enough to make the discovery an achievement for Don. Rather, Don's competence must cause the treasure to be found *in the right way*. It's not enough that Don's property of being competent, or the activity's being competent, is the cause of the treasure being discovered. This is true even in Rewarding Benefactor. Don must not merely cause the discovery with his competent activities; rather, in order for it to count as an achievement, he must *competently cause* the discovery.

What this means is that, to count as an achievement, not only must Don cause the discovery to come about, but he must do so *in a certain way*. His competence must cause the discovery in "the usual way," as philosophers sometimes like to put it. It is not enough for Don's competence to be just one link in the chain of causation that results in the discovery; rather, his competence must cause it in the way that we usually expect competence to cause discoveries—such as knowledge of the methods for figuring out the most likely locations, and so on.

As a result, it is more accurate to say that there are not two separate components at work here, but *one*. The two features that we have been discussing, causation and competence, don't really operate independently after all. It's not that the agent is (a) competent and (b) causes the product. Rather, there is *one* component here that has features of both. The component is a causal component, but it requires causation of a certain specific sort. So I propose that these two components are best understood folded into one component, which I will dub *competent causation*. This approach provides a solution to our Gettieresque problems without stipulating an additional anti-Gettier condition; quite the opposite, in fact, I have decreased the number of conditions, rendering the account even more theoretically parsimonious. Of course, there is more to be said here to fill in the details of this component of competent causation, but this is something I take up later.

Refining the Account

So achievements, so far, have not three, but two necessary features. To be clear, the account now picks out two features of an activity. Difficulty is a feature of the activity itself, and competent causation is a relation between the activity and the product that it causes. These two components, I have argued, are necessary for achievements.

But are these necessary features also sufficient? The obvious counter-examples indicate an initial no: these are cases of *evil achievements*. Many people would, reasonably, balk at accepting an account that called the Holocaust an achievement. But surely the process was difficult, and the result was competently caused by the difficult process.

However, in some respects, the Holocaust is a bad example because it ultimately failed. The goal, after all, was the mass extermination of *all* Jews, and the institution of the Aryan race as rulers of the world. So it can't be an achievement, since it failed—at least, it failed according to the goal that it had set for itself. But this needn't deter us from considering it as an example. Imagine that the Holocaust *had* succeeded.[15] So then the question is, does this "success," such as it was, count as an achievement?

I think most of us would balk at this. Surely the Holocaust is not an achievement, we might say, and any account of achievements that says it is must have taken a wrong turn. So my account must be incomplete.

Here's a plausible suggestion: the product of an achievement must not be of negative value. I will refer to this as the *value condition*. Achievements, we have seen, necessarily have a certain structure, a process culminating in a product. The account so far gives us a condition of the process (it must be difficult) and a relation that connects the process to the product (causal competence). The value condition, now under discussion, is a condition of the product. The value condition would stipulate that the *product* component of the achievement must not be of negative value. This addition to the account of achievements has the nice advantage of giving the account some theoretical symmetry.

Yet there is a worry about introducing a value condition: if there is a condition that requires that the product be of a certain value in order for something to be an achievement, then the questions of whether and how achievements are valuable are *trivial*. After all, we would just be building the value into the achievement, leaving nothing interesting for the investigation.

But this would not be the case. Even if the products of all achievements must be of a certain value, this leaves open the possibility that

---

[15] There is also a sense in which the Holocaust, as it was, succeeded at something. Even if the ultimate goal of an achievement is not successfully attained, getting part of the way there can itself be an achievement.

there is *more* to the value of achievement than the value of the product. The value of the product need not be all there is to the value of the
achievement. As a result, requiring the product to be of a certain intrinsic value would not imply that all achievements are valuable *overall*, nor
would it imply that achievements are valuable *as such*. So there is no
concern that a value condition would render the investigation into the
value of achievements trivial.

However, there are further problems with a value condition. I have said
that the value condition would require that the product of an achievement
not be of negative value. It might be thought that the value condition should
require that the product be of *positive* value. But this is too strong. There
is no positive value in standing on top of a mountain or stepping over a
finish line. Yet these can be the products of genuine achievements. So the
most it is plausible to demand is that the value condition require that the
value of the product not be negative, and so it suffices if it is neutral.

Still, there may be cases that suggest that the value of the product can
be negative. We may have, I think, started on the wrong foot by considering such an extreme example as the Holocaust as a candidate for being an
achievement. Our intuitions may be intense and difficult to read. I think it
is more fruitful to consider some evil achievements that are less horrific, in
order to get a more tempered reading of our intuitions.

Consider practical jokes, for instance, that involve elaborate and difficult planning, and have as their goal some minor pain. I think most people would have the intuition that pulling off a very elaborate and difficult
practical joke counts as an achievement. An account that frowns on practical jokes as too evil to count as achievements would, I think, be overly
moralistic.

Yet I think it is too soon for me to worry that my account is heading in
this schoolmarmish direction. The product of a practical joke isn't *just* the
minor pain—the goal, after all, isn't to cause some pain, but to cause some
laughs. Assuming, then, that in a successful practical joke the positive
value of the laughs outweighs the negative value of the minor pain, then it
will satisfy the value condition. If the planning and execution of the joke
is elaborate and difficult enough, and competently causes the punch-line,
as it were, then the other two conditions are satisfied as well, and practical jokes can be achievements on this account. So we need not reject the
neutral-and-up version of the value condition.

There are, however, other examples that also appear to be achievements, yet really do have products that are of a small negative value: a witty insult, for example. Here the product is disvaluable, but the skill, panache, and composure required, let's assume, are difficult enough for the insult to be an achievement, and it seems silly of the account to reject it as such. So the value condition runs the risk of excluding petty evil achievements.

Further, there are other examples of what seem to be achievements that have evil ends that are not merely petty evils. Consider, for instance, an elaborate art heist. The heist involves months of planning, extensive research into security systems, physical training and endurance, intense mental concentration and calmness to successfully pull off. The product of the heist is, of course, to steal, which let's assume is disvaluable. It seems to me that a clever and elaborate plan, pulled off with skill and panache, evokes the same sense of awe and astonishment that we have for noncontroversial achievements in other domains. When we ratchet down the evilness, we find that we have a similar reaction to (relatively less) evil deeds as we do to noncontroversial achievements: a sense of admiration, wonder, and even respect.

Note that there may be murkiness in our sense that the art heist is an achievement: our reactions to petty evil achievements may be mixed. We don't have the same unqualified respect and admiration for art heists as we do for violin solos. But this doesn't, I think, take away from their status as achievements. The sense of awe and admiration for these deeds seems to be precisely for those features of these deeds that are common with noncontroversial, non-evil achievements. We are impressed with the elaborate and clever plan that is difficult to carry off, and the creativity, effort, and intelligence of the achiever. That is to say, the respect and admiration that we have for evil deeds is qua achievements. But we may not have a sense of respect and admiration for the evil achievement on the whole. Our respect is tempered, it seems, by disapproval of the evil end.

But bear in mind that the purpose of my investigation so far is to determine the nature of what counts as an achievement, and *not* whether or not or by how much any particular achievement is valuable. That is, the question here is not what counts as a *valuable* achievement, but just what counts as an achievement at all. It seems to me that it would be overly fastidious and moralistic to say that the art heist is not an achievement. Whether or not it is overall of positive value is another matter, but it does seem to be an achievement. An account that excludes it would be an overly stingy account of achievements.

So I suggest an alternative is that there *is no* value condition for achievements. Let's call this new, inclusive approach the *inclusive* view of achievements, and the more restrictive, moralistic one the *exclusive* view. According to the inclusive view, the sole conditions of an achievement are the difficulty and the causal competency conditions. Although it lacks the nice theoretical symmetry of the account with the value condition, it gains the theoretical parsimony of having only two components rather than three. And while it gains the unfortunate downside of including very evil deeds as achievements, it gains the plausible upside of including impressive, less-evil deeds such as art heists and insults.

However, the downside of the inclusive view is considerable. If the products of achievements may be evil without limit, then the inclusive view must have an explanation for why we find it so difficult to call extremely evil deeds, such as the Holocaust, achievements.

One explanation is that we typically reserve the term "achievement" for achievements that are of great positive value. Recall the point that I made earlier, that there is a sense in which every little thing that we accomplish—brushing our teeth, taking the dog for a walk—is an achievement, in the broad sense of the term. We typically don't refer to these broad achievements as "achievements," but reserve the term to pick out what I called capital-A achievements. Since most capital-A achievements are of great positive value, we have come to think of the term as picking out only achievements that are of great positive value.

My investigation, however, is not in the business of giving an account of the use of the term, but of the nature of achievements themselves. So the contention of the inclusive view, then, is that, while we typically do not use the term "achievement" to refer to evil achievements, evil achievements nonetheless have the traits necessary to make them achievements. It sounds funny to call them that, since we don't usually refer to evil achievements in this way.

But there is a further objection: didn't I start out this investigation by claiming to investigate only "capital-A" achievements, which just are the class of great achievements—that is to say, the class of achievements of great value? If this is the case, then my account of achievements has taken a seriously wrong turn by including achievements that are of negative value!

To be clear, however, my investigation is into *great* achievements. This may or may not be the same thing as achievements that are of *great value*. I think that retaining this distinction between magnitude of achievement and value of achievement is very important. It is a substantive question whether or not value tracks greatness. The ground of value of achievements, after all, may extend beyond the features of achievements themselves. So it's possible that there could be great achievements that are of considerable negative value. In subsequent discussion of the value of achievements these claims will be elaborated and defended, and we will see that it is indeed the case that value and greatness come apart. There can be achievements of large magnitude that are nonetheless of negative value.

So, since the exclusive view excludes too much, and the potentially counterintuitive implications of the inclusive view will be resolved in later chapters, my account favors the inclusive view. There is no value condition for the value of the product of achievements.

This, then, is the sketch of the account of achievements that I propose, which can be summarized thus: achievements are comprised by a process and product, where the process is difficult, and competently causes the product.

To be clear, my view is that achievements have two *parts*—the process and the product—where one of these parts (the process) is difficult, and competently causes the other part (the product). Thus I don't accept any particular metaphysical view where strictly speaking the achievement is simply the process, or is simply the product. Rather, my view is that the achievement is comprised by *both* the process and product. (Nonetheless, as you will see, it's often more convenient to help myself to locutions that suggest that achievements are strictly speaking one or the other of these things. So in what follows, I hope you won't find my use of such locutions misleading, since my view is that achievements are comprised of *both* parts.)

2
Difficulty

In the previous chapter, I arrived at an account of achievements. Achievements, it turns out, are competently caused by difficult activities. Now it's time to get down to business and fill in the details of these two components: difficulty and competent causation. Once the details of these components are articulated in greater detail, and the account has a better-defined shape, I will be in a good position to discern why and in what ways achievements are valuable. Along the way, there are some avenues of exploration that turn out to be interesting in their own right. The first avenue I explore is the nature of difficulty. I present a full account of difficulty—not only an account of necessary and sufficient conditions, but an account of that in virtue of which a thing is difficult. But before I develop the details of the account, I will first take up a challenge according to which there is another distinct kind of difficulty. First, however, a few words about difficulty in general.

Difficult Things

We often talk about *things* that are difficult—crossword puzzles, math problems, recipes, and so on. Other times we talk about activities being difficult—shoveling the driveway, building a house, writing a dissertation, running a marathon. Difficulty, then, is primarily a quality of *activities*, and when we talk about *things* being difficult, this is derivative from the difficulty of corresponding activities: these things are *difficult to accomplish*. We wouldn't, for example, classify a math problem as difficult if it were easy to solve—there is no property of the math problem itself independent from the process required to solve it that makes it difficult.

Rather, difficulty is a property of the process of solving the problem, and so difficult things, are, strictly speaking, things that are accomplished via a difficult process.

We are familiar, I assume, with *people* who are difficult. Difficult people have a variety of character traits, such as being picky, persnickety, disagreeable, stubborn, and so on. Similar to things that are difficult, there are corresponding difficult activities involving difficult people: difficult people are difficult to get along with, or difficult to placate, and so on. In this respect difficult people are difficult in the same way that math problems are. So it is primarily *activities* that are difficult—and if we are calling things or people difficult, in either case the difficulty invoked is the difficulty of the activity corresponding to the thing or person.

The Relativity of Difficulty

Let's make a second preliminary observation, and notice that difficulty is always *relative*. Something may be difficult for me, but not for you. Something may not be difficult for me today that was very difficult for me last year. Something may not be difficult for one very talented person that is difficult for the average person. So when X is difficult, it is either difficult *for* some particular agent, or X is difficult for a typical agent from the relevant class.   *Independ on skill-level (flow)*

You might think that there is a sense in which something can be difficult *simpliciter*. Getting a perfect score on the LSAT, for example, seems to be difficult in this absolute sense, regardless of how much effort it would require from any particular agent, or from an agent of some relevant class.

Yet I think that this quality of absolute difficulty is merely apparent. Difficulty is always relativized. Even if the difficulty is relativized to the class of human beings, it is still relative. For whatever allegedly difficult *simpliciter* activities, we can imagine a race of alien beings for whom these activities are quite easy. So even if we say that there are indeed difficult *simpliciter* activities, they will only be difficult relative to our abilities as human beings. So there is no real way in which anything is difficult in an absolute sense.

We do, of course, say that some things are difficult full stop, without having in mind any particular agent. Scoring perfect on the LSAT is such

an example. In these cases, we are making use of this class-relative difficulty. Getting a perfect score on the LSAT would be (we can imagine) difficult for a typical member of the class of test-takers.

To clarify, then, something is difficult *for* a particular agent just in case
it is difficult for that agent to do it. Something is difficult (*sans* "for") just in
case it *would* be difficult for some typical member of the relevant class of
agents, were the typical agent to engage in the activity.

The relevant class of agents for any particular instance of difficulty is
determined, I think, fairly straightforwardly. Like many things of this
nature, it is determined by context. Whatever activity we are interested
in evaluating, it seems that we can quite easily pick out the relevant class
of agents for whom it may or may not be difficult. The default may be the
class of adult human beings, but of course many activities are difficult for
four-year-olds, but not for the typical adult. Whatever class it is that is
relevant for the evaluation of whether or not some activity is difficult is
generally apparent from the context of the activity, or can be discerned or
stipulated without much controversy.

Now that these preliminary distinctions are out of the way, I will move
on to defend my positive account of the nature of difficulty.

Difficulty: Expending Effort

Here is the view. Something is difficult in virtue of requiring some sufficient degree of *effort*. Things require effort in virtue of having certain *features*. Different activities require effort in virtue of various features that
they have. Some activities require effort because they are very physically
demanding, others require effort because they make use of multiple skills,
or a lot of diverse knowledge. There is no class of features, however, such
that everything that requires effort requires effort in virtue of these same
features, nor is it the case that there are some features such that they always
require such a degree of effort that they are always difficult. So the one
common feature of all difficult things is requiring effort.

We often identify activities as difficult on the basis of features typical of
things that require effort—for instance, activities with many complicated
steps usually require effort. As a result, even if there is no particular agent
currently engaged in this complicated activity for whom the activity is difficult, we can properly classify it as difficult, since were the relevant sort of

agent to engage in the activity, it would take effort, and thus be difficult for this agent.

It might appear that there are some things that are difficult even though they don't take effort at all, such as winning the lottery, seeing a shooting star, or catching malaria in Connecticut. But what we really mean when we describe something like winning the lottery as "difficult" is that it is *unlikely* or very improbable. To be sure, if you *tried* to win the lottery or to catch malaria in Connecticut, it would indeed probably take a lot of effort. One can imagine buying up all the lottery tickets one could afford, or researching lottery numbers or bribing the lottery officials. This would indeed take considerable effort.

Complexity

One might think that there is something else that's relevant for difficulty: *complexity*. One might think that there is a distinct kind of difficulty, where effort is irrelevant. This is the difficulty of complexity.

I do not think that complexity is necessary for difficulty, nor is there a separate kind of difficulty, and any apparent advantages of a complexity approach can also be incorporated by my view, which has additional theoretical felicities that a complexity approach lacks. But before I argue for these conclusions, first I will present the case for difficulty as complexity, since it is indeed a compelling one.

Something is complex, roughly speaking, when it has many parts, and the parts are organized. The more parts there are, and the more organized they are, the higher the degree of complexity.[1] The kinds of things that make up the parts, and the kinds of relations among them according to which they are organized, can vary. Complexity, then, is a matter of the *form* or structure of something. Much more could be said about the nature of complexity—what, for instance, are the relevant parts, and the relations that organize them?—but this brief sketch should be adequate for my discussion here.

According to the Complexity account of difficulty, then, things that have a complex structure are difficult in virtue of this structure. They have

---

[1] For a detailed and thorough account of the nature of complexity, see Thomas Hurka, *Perfectionism* (Oxford: OUP, 1993), esp. ch. 9.

what we will call "C-difficulty." Since complexity admits of degree, there will be some sufficient degree of complexity that is required for difficulty. Moreover, there may be some complex things that are C-difficult but do not require effort, and some effortful things that are not complex. The idea is that C-difficulty is a different *kind* of difficulty.

Not just anything that is complex is difficult. Ecosystems, robots, digestion, and snowflakes are all complex, but they just don't seem to be difficult—calling an ecosystem or a robot difficult is a category mistake. But *building* robots is difficult. The Complexity account of difficulty, then, pertains to only certain kinds of complex things: agential activities. Not just *any* complex thing is difficult, but complex agential activities are difficult. What makes an activity an agential one need not be that it is done by a *moral* agent, since it seems that small children and possibly also animals can engage in activities that are agential in the relevant sense. So the Complexity account of difficulty holds that complex agential activities are difficult.

Moreover, since complexity admits of degrees, not just *any* tiny degree of complexity is enough for difficulty—tying your shoes, after all, is *somewhat* complex, but it's not difficult, other things being equal. So the Complexity account of difficulty claims that *some sufficient degree* of complexity is what makes an activity difficult.

So far, this seems like a plausible approach: it seems that there are many cases of difficult activities that are complex, so it's not unreasonable to think that there is a kind of difficulty that is constituted by complexity. Building a robot, making a canoe, solving a difficult math problem are agential activities, typically made up of many parts, where the parts are interrelated with one another—as steps in a plan, or as factors that shape and influence the progress of the activity as it unfolds. These activities are all complex, and all difficult.

Next, I will present the case for the Complexity account, first by appealing to (alleged) pure complexity cases, namely, examples of difficult things that are complex but do not require effort.[2] Then we turn to two tests of

---

[2] I say "alleged" here because, of course, my view is that complexity is not sufficient for difficulty, and so there are no genuine pure complexity cases. Shortly I will provide an explanation for how effort is involved in these "pure" complexity cases. I will grant, however, that in pure complexity cases, effort is *not* involved on the part of the particular agent engaged in the activity. In this respect, then, these cases really are "pure." But as I will explain later, the correct understanding of how it is that they are difficult still involves an appeal to effort.

support, the Degree of Intensity test and the In Virtue Of test, which aim to show that difficulty is constituted by complexity in pure complexity cases. These tests are designed as necessary criteria for seeing if one thing is constituted by another. Although passing the tests is not sufficient to show constitution, it is a necessary condition and so provides some support. In what follows, I show that Complexity passes these tests, but I will argue that it is not constitutive of difficulty nonetheless. Even though complexity appears to clear the bar, the effort view that I present can provide an explanation for this appearance, and it can give a more streamlined account of difficulty overall.

Pure Complexity Cases

Virtuoso. Heifetz, the great violin virtuoso, effortlessly tosses off a flawless performance of the complex Paganini caprices.   *by def. we use effort.*

The Paganini caprices are famously difficult to play, but since Heifetz is such a genius at the violin, he plays them effortlessly. Heifetz does something difficult but without effort, so Virtuoso is a case of difficulty that is complex but effortless—a pure complexity case. Here complexity appears to be sufficient for difficulty—no effort required. This appears to be a pure complexity case, and so complexity appears to be sufficient for difficulty.

A proponent of the Complexity approach can also argue that complexity is constitutive of difficulty by appealing to the two following tests of support, the Degree of Intensity test and the In Virtue Of test, which we turn to next.

Degree of Intensity

On the Degree of Intensity test, when some feature A is constituted by some other feature B, as the degree of intensity of B increases, the degree of intensity of A increases. This correlative change in degree of intensity suggests that the two features don't merely obtain coincidently, but correspond in a deeper way. B's constituting A can be one way in which this deeper correspondence obtains. As a result, correlative change in degree of intensity shows that one feature may be constituted by the other. If the degrees of intensity of the two features can vary independently of one another, this is evidence that B is not constitutive of A.

This test can be applied across variations on the *same* thing (i.e. by increasing the intensity of a feature in different instantiations of the same thing) or by comparing two different things that have similar features but of different intensities.

Increased complexity corresponds with increased difficulty. The same complex activity, when made more complex, is more difficult. For example, Julia is a highly gifted chess player, who plays a very advanced game with very little effort. She plays a solid game against a grand master as effortlessly as she does against a novice. Playing against the chess master is far more complex than playing against the novice: the master player has long-range plans, and each move the master makes is integrated into her overall strategy. The novice, on the other hand, simply moves the pieces according to the rules, with an eye to winning, but without the complexity of strategy. Playing against the master player, accordingly, requires much more forethought and strategy than playing against the novice—it's more complex, and accordingly more difficult.

Similarly, Peter is a highly gifted chef who prepares a complex and elaborate meal as effortlessly as he makes Kraft dinner out of a box. Kraft dinner is simple and easy, but cooking an elaborate meal with many courses is far more complex, and accordingly much more difficult.

Moreover, between two different complex activities, it seems that the more complex is the more difficult. Julia is also gifted at tic-tac-toe, which is quite different from chess. Playing chess is more complex than playing tic-tac-toe, and it is also more difficult. Peter is also a virtuoso tobogganer. Cooking an elaborate gourmet meal is more complex than tobogganing down a snowy hill, and it is also more difficult.

In Virtue Of

It counts as some evidence that some feature A is *constituted by* B when A obtains *in virtue of* B. As a result, if we find that we are willing to say that A obtains in virtue of B, this counts as some evidence that A is constituted by B. To be clear about the strength of this test: the in-virtue-of relation can obtain for many different reasons, so there may be reasons other than B's constituting A that explain A's obtaining in virtue of B. But A obtains in virtue of B in all cases where B *does* constitute A. Passing the test, then, is necessary but not sufficient for A's being constituted by B. So if it is not the case that A obtains in virtue of B, this is conclusive evidence that B does *not* constitute A. Passing the test provides some positive support, but not conclusive evidence for A's being constituted by B, and failing the test is conclusive evidence that A is not constituted by B.

Not only does increased degree of complexity correspond to increased difficulty, it also seems that the increased difficulty arises in virtue of the increased complexity. Playing chess against an experienced player is more difficult than playing against a novice *in virtue of* the increased level of complexity: playing against the advanced player is difficult because it requires holding multiple strategies in mind, anticipating multiple future moves, and making decisions informed from the various strategic elements. Playing against a novice requires far less complex forethought and strategy. Making a fancy gourmet meal with many courses seems to be difficult in virtue of its complexity as well: it requires multiple diverse skills, planning ahead, attention to detail, and complex multitasking. Kraft dinner is easy to prepare in virtue of its simplicity.

So complexity passes both of these tests. As a result, we have support for the view that difficulty is constituted by complexity. From this observation, the proponents of the complexity account draw the conclusion that complexity constitutes a distinct kind of difficulty, C-difficulty, which is distinct from the difficulty of effort.

Complexity Rejected

However, it's my contention that there is no such distinct kind of difficulty. I agree that complexity passes both tests of support: there are cases where increased difficulty corresponds to increased complexity, and things may be difficult in virtue of their complexity. But recall that the tests of support are necessary but not sufficient for constitution. The Effort account can provide an explanation that accommodates complexity passing both the Degree of Intensity and In Virtue Of tests without being constitutive of difficulty in the way that the complexity view claims.

But the bigger threat to the Effort account are alleged cases of pure complexity, which appear to indicate that complexity can suffice for difficulty.

I will argue that the effort view can explain these cases just as well, and with better theoretical implications. I turn to this shortly.

First, however, I will take up a clear shortcoming of the Complexity view: cases of complex nondifficult activities. The possibility of such cases indicates that complexity is not sufficient for difficulty. So the complexity account must be *wrong* in saying that complexity is sufficient for (a kind of) difficulty.

Complex Nondifficult Agential Activities

Here is an example of a complex but nondifficult activity: communication. Carrying on an ordinary conversation in English (or whatever your native language might be) is incredibly complex. It is as at least as complex as playing a game of chess: there are multiple components, complex rules, anticipating future moves, and so on.[3] English in particular is one of the most complex languages in the world: its complicated grammatical rules are rife with obscure exceptions, pronunciation is hardly straightforward, and the number of different words is extensive. Apart from using the language itself, reading body language and facial expressions adds a further layer of complexity, not to mention observing complicated rules of etiquette. Grasping the conversational context, and anticipating the future direction of the conversation, and the background knowledge that your conversation partner has, add further layers of depth, complexity, and even strategy and planning. Even the most simple interactions can be so intricate that they have been the subject of study for sociologists and anthropologists for as long as those disciplines have been around.

Simple communication, then, is complex, but if you're a native speaker under ordinary circumstances, it's just not difficult to carry on a casual conversation. So it appears that complexity is not sufficient for difficulty.

---

[3] I'm certainly not the first person to remark on the similarity between language and games. There are goals, there are rules, which once accepted determine the context, making participation possible. There are further rules which may be followed in order to improve success at participation. Of course, there are also important differences as well: it is a characteristic of games for the easiest means to achieving the goal to be ruled out, whereas such intentional inefficiency is not always a feature of communication. These are matters for another discussion, however. All that needs to be seen for the time being is that communication can be at least as complex as a game of chess.

The proponent of the complexity account can respond to this example on two fronts. First, although communicating is complex, it's not sufficiently complex to be difficult. Second, even if we do grant that communicating is sufficiently complex, it's not the right kind of activity: only complex *agential* activities are difficult. I will show that neither of these responses succeeds.

The first response of the complexity account is to say that, in order for an activity to be difficult, not just any amount of complexity will suffice, but some sufficient degree of complexity is required for difficulty. Communication is complex, but it's not complex enough.

This response can be shown to be false simply by appealing to a noncontroversial complex difficult activity that is difficult yet less complex than communication. Here's one: putting together a jigsaw puzzle. A jigsaw puzzle with a large enough number of pieces is difficult to put together, and it seems plausible that the difficulty of putting together a puzzle is a matter of C-difficulty. But it hardly seems to be the case that putting together a jigsaw puzzle is *more* complex than communicating.

According to the second response, communication is not an *agential* activity. The complexity account only classifies activities of a certain kind as difficult, namely, agential activities. Agential activities, goes this proposal, must be consciously intentional. The proponent of the complexity account could propose these three possible criteria for conscious agential activities: steps in the activity must be either (1) consciously endorsed; or (2) have been at one time consciously endorsed (e.g. in a planning or learning stage); or (3) the kind of step that *could* be consciously endorsed.

Communicating in one's native language fails to satisfy these criteria for being a properly agential activity. It's clear that we do not consciously endorse each step in the process of our communicating. Second, learning to communicate in your native language is, if memories of my own experience are a good indication, hardly something that is the result of conscious effort. Finally, it seems that if we tried to stop and consciously reflect on and endorse each minute step involved in carrying on a conversation, we would find ourselves completely tongue-tied. So even the third criterion fails as well. As a result, the proponent of the complexity account concludes, communication in one's native language is hardly agential—it more closely resembles digestion, or some other natural process, than it does playing a game of chess or some other genuinely agential activity. Not only do we not think about each step or word or element when we communicate, but we *have never* thought about each step or element, and we *couldn't* think about each step.

It's very plausible—likely, in fact—that we have never explicitly and consciously entertained each step of our communicating, and it certainly seems to be the case that if we did stop to consider each thing we do when we speak to one another, we would find ourselves tongue-tied and paralyzed as we struggled to identify the steps in a process we take entirely for granted every day. So it appears that communicating fails to be agential.

But this response would only show that communication is not relevantly agential if these are indeed good criteria for being an agential activity. It seems that they are not. There are good examples of activities that I think we should classify as genuinely agential but fail to satisfy these criteria. Gifted musicians can perform impressive, intricate feats in a manner that would fail to be genuinely agential according to the proposed criteria. A talented musician can play in a spontaneous manner that comes naturally and unreflective to them as carrying on an ordinary conversation does to anyone else. These musicians hardly consciously reflect on what they're doing at the time, nor, it seems *could* they: they would become just as paralyzed and bogged down as an ordinary person would when trying to consciously reflect on every aspect of communicating. Moreover, it's common to hear musicians say things like "overthinking" their performance in fact hampers it. Better success in performance comes to them if they concentrate not on the individual steps of what they're doing, but just lose themselves in the music, as it were. [4]

So the proposed criteria do not correctly capture agential activities. As a result, then, there are complex nondifficult agential activities, which shows that complexity is not sufficient for difficulty.

---

[4] This phenomenon is common both to music performance and also to athletic endeavors. The Zen-like state of losing oneself in the moment is explored as it pertains to sports performance in a popular book by a former tennis player W. Timothy Gallwey, *The Inner Game of Tennis* (New York: Random House, 1974), and again with respect to both music and sports in Barry Green and W. Timothy Gallwey, *The Inner Game of Music* (New York: Doubleday, 1986). In some respects, the phenomenon of overthinking in music and sports performance resembles the paradox of hedonism, insofar as aiming for a goal renders its successful achievement less likely or impossible. I'm sure that others have remarked on this similarity as well. Railton draws a similar comparison between concentration in sports and the paradox of hedonism in "Alienation, Consequentialism, and the Demands of Morality," *Philosophy and Public Affairs*, 2 (1994): 144.

Explaining the Tests of Support

But if this is true, then why is it that complexity passes the tests of support? Doesn't this provide some evidence that difficulty is constituted by complexity?

Recall that at the introduction of the tests of support I emphasized that passing these tests is necessary but not sufficient for one thing's constituting another. This alone should be enough to dismiss the issue here. Yet passing the tests deserves some explanation, and explaining why complexity passes the tests of supports will only further strengthen my own account.

According to my account of difficulty, something is difficult when it requires sufficient effort. Things require effort in virtue of having certain features. These effort-requiring features can vary from activity to activity, so what it is that difficult activities have in common is that they have features which themselves have the feature of requiring effort. In this respect, my account of difficulty is something of a buck-passing account of difficulty: being difficult is having features which are such that they make the activity require effort.

Now, among effort-requiring features is complexity. It is indeed true that many complex things require effort in virtue of their complexity—we've seen many examples of these kinds of activities so far: playing chess, cooking elaborate gourmet meals, playing the Paganini caprices, and so on. Since it turns out that difficulty is a matter of requiring effort, and these things require effort in virtue of being complex, if we say that playing chess is difficult in virtue of being complex, we skip a step, as it were. As I suggested earlier, we are identifying chess as difficult on the basis of its having features that typically require effort. We take the "in virtue of" chain to behave transitively: the basis of the difficulty, if you go down far enough, is complexity.

If we do adopt an account that holds that there is a distinct kind of difficulty constituted by complexity, there is no good reason to deny the view that there are distinct kinds of difficulty corresponding to *each* feature in virtue of which activities can require effort. That is, there are many different features in virtue of which things can require effort in addition to complexity, such as requiring precision, knowledge, special skills, physical endurance, and so on. If we take this to indicate that there is a distinct kind of difficulty constituted by *one* of these features, then there is no reason to deny that there are distinct kinds of difficulty constituted by each of the other effort-requiring features. In fact, it seems that allowing even just one further kind of difficulty would require others, in order to be consistent. This wouldn't be such a bad implication of the theory were it not the case that a good alternative theory that avoids this issue is readily available.

My view, on the other hand, can avoid overpopulation of kinds of difficulty. I can nonetheless retain the implication that things are difficult in different ways and in virtue of having different features, and do so without risking a population explosion, as it were, of kinds of difficulty. Even better, my view provides a nice, unifying feature in virtue of which all things are difficult. So my view provides a unifying and parsimonious account of difficulty that still captures every aspect of difficult activity that we have seen so far.

Pure Complexity Cases Explained

Still I need to explain the strongest apparent counterexamples that the complexity view presents against my view, namely, pure complexity cases. After all, if there *are* pure complexity cases, complexity would appear to be sufficient for a distinct kind of difficulty. But my position is that there is no such distinct kind of difficulty. So now I will explain the apparent existence of pure complexity cases.

Recall that difficulty is always *relative*. Something may be difficult for one agent, but not for another. X-ing may be difficult full stop insofar as it would be difficult for a typical agent of a relevant comparison class to X. According to my view, this means that X-ing would require effort either from some particular agent, or it would require effort from a typical agent from the relevant class.

In Virtuoso, the Paganini caprices are difficult *for* the average violinist. In fact, they are difficult not only for the average violinist, but they are difficult even for the most outstandingly talented of violinists. Yet playing the caprices is not difficult *for Heifetz*—he does it quite easily. But since it *is* difficult for the typical violinist to play the caprices, we can still say that playing the caprices is difficult—just not for Heifetz. So Virtuoso fails to be a compelling counterexample to my account, even in the absence of appealing to any particular account of difficulty—Heifetz is simply doing something that is difficult for others but not difficult for him.

What it means for something to be difficult is that it requires effort—either from some agent, or from a typical agent of some relevant comparison class. Insofar as playing the caprices doesn't require effort from Heifetz, it's not difficult *for* him; insofar as playing the caprices does require effort on the part of a typical violinist, it's difficult to play them. As a result, there are no pure complexity cases. Cases that *appear* to be pure complexity cases are rather not difficult for the particular agent who is undertaking the activity, but would be difficult for a typical member of the relevant class.

Difficulty is therefore a matter of expending effort. What, precisely, does this mean?

Effort

I gather that effort is familiar to everyone. The phenomenon of exerting effort is something that virtually everyone experiences every day: from something as basic and mundane as getting out of bed in the morning, to more elaborate and intensive ventures, such as running a business, or completing a marathon (you may be exerting it right now as you force yourself to read this!). Being philosophers, our impulse is to analyze everything that comes our way. Yet I will take effort as *primitive*. I'll remain neutral as to whether or not it actually *is* a primitive. If I or anyone else hit upon a further analysis of effort, then I imagine we could make use of it here. My attempts at a further analysis of effort have led me to think that it is indeed primitive, but, in any case, I will simply take it as such for the purposes of this project without further argument. So I will proceed on the assumption that effort is primitive, and with the hope that nothing I go on to say would be undermined by a further analysis. I think that effort is a familiar enough notion that I need not go into great detail explaining it, so I will leave it at that.

Difficulty, as we've seen, is a matter of expending effort. Something is difficult when it requires some sufficient degree of effort. So we should ask, then, how much effort is enough? This question is really two questions: (1) how is it determined how much effort is expended overall? and (2) what amount of effort is sufficient to count as difficult? To be precise, then, suppose that the amount of effort for an activity, a, is $E(a)$. A natural proposal would be that a is difficult provided that $E(a)$ meets or exceeds some threshold, d. The initial schema, then, for determining whether a is difficult is:

a is difficult just in case E(a) ≥ d ┤ *Unsthield*

The first main goal of this section, then, is to establish the right way to measure effort, which is to say the right way to calculate E(a), the function that calculates the amount of effort expended for activity a. The second goal is to establish the threshold d. First, however, I will discuss how the schema for difficult yields further schemas for assessing and comparing degrees of difficulty.

But before I turn to develop these calculation methods, let me first set aside skepticism about quantitativeness of effort. There might be some temptation to think that effort just isn't the sort of thing that can be added up or measured at all. To dispel this worry, I appeal to an argument similar to one deployed in other areas of value theory. It seems fairly clear that we can make rough ordinal comparisons of effort: something can require *more* effort than something else. It also seems fairly clear that we can make rough cardinal comparisons: something can be roughly, say, *twice* as difficult as something else. Such rough cardinal comparisons are sufficient to ground the kinds of quantitative measurements that need to be done here. We need not be able to make precise measurements—rough ones suffice for the view. I will proceed in what follows as if we *can* make precise measurements, in order to simplify the discussion. But in fact for the view to hold together such measurements need not in fact be precise.

Even granting the quantitativeness of effort, a second skeptical worry arises. Until now I have been proceeding as if effort is homogeneous, one might say. But a skeptic might think that there are different *kinds* of effort—physical, mental, and so on—and, while each of these different kinds can be measured quantitatively, they are incommensurable across each other.

But even if there were different incommensurable kinds of effort, this would not be a problem for my account. The same calculus that I will propose for calculating total homogeneous effort could be used for one kind of effort and then the other, and then so long as the sufficient degree of either has been attained, we could say that the activity is difficult. So even if we *can't* commensurate different kinds of effort, it doesn't matter for my account. Regardless, it seems plain that we *can* commensurate—no one finds it particularly puzzling to say that writing a dissertation is more difficult than playing hopscotch. So whether or not there are kinds of effort that are homogeneous, we can apparently measure effort, and that is what matters for my account.

Now that these skeptical worries are out of the way, I'll turn to the assessment and comparison schemas. The proposed schema for determining the difficulty of a,

a is difficulty just in case E(a) ≥ d

yields the following way of assessing and comparing degrees of difficulty. The *degree* of difficulty—that is, how difficult something is—is a matter of how far E(a) is from d. That is, the greater that E(a) is than d, the greater the difficulty of a. If E(a) is close to d, it's moderately difficult, and so on.

In *comparisons* of difficulty, the basic comparison schema is this:

a is more difficult than b just in case E(a) – d > E(b) – d

For now, let us assume that d is the same in both comparates, and so it can be dropped.[5] Hence the simpler comparison schema is this:

a is more difficult than b just in case E(a) > E(b)

This schema implies that it's possible for a to be more difficult than b but neither of them to be difficult. And indeed, we make comparisons of this kind all the time with other properties that come in degrees, such as height. A may be taller than B, but neither A nor B need be tall at all. So this is a virtue of the schema.

The schema so far conceived compares the difficulty of individual instances of activities: this particular instance of board-game playing with that one. That is, the schema compares the difficulty of *tokens*. But it can also be used to compare the difficulty of *types* of activities. Types are compared by comparing the effort that would be required for an average instance of the type. In making comparisons of types of activities, then,

---

[5] In spite of such useful terms as *analysand* and *analysandum*, *definiens* and *definiendum*, there doesn't seem to be a commonly used philosophical term for a thing being compared to another. I use "comparate" as the term with this meaning. This is an extension of the meaning of "comparate" according to the *Oxford English Dictionary*, but it doesn't seem to be commonly used in philosophical discussions.

we compare the effort required for an average token of the type of activity, performed by a typical member of the relevant class of agents.

Now that these preliminary points are out of the way, and I've established that effort is indeed something that we can measure, and given a way to quantitatively compare it, let's turn at last to determine how these measurements are done. Effort (like pleasure) comes in varying degrees of strength, or *intensity.* A natural thought is this: the way to measure expended effort is a matter of the strength of intensity of the effort expended. This seems to make sense insofar as it seems that the more intensely we try to do something, the more effort we put into it. I'll call the view that holds that the amount of effort is calculated simply in terms of intensity of effort the *Intensity* view. According to the Intensity view, when an agent exerts effort above a certain threshold of intensity, his activity is difficult.

To facilitate the quantitative discussion, just as the hedonists introduce a unit of pleasure, I will propose a unit of intensity of effort, the *eff*.[6] So Intensity holds that when the amount of effs an agent exerts, f_a, for some activity a, is above some d, his activity is difficult. This implies, given the schema, that the amount of effort, $E(a)$, is calculated by this function:

$$E(a) = f_a$$

So accordingly

a is difficult just in case $f_a \geq d$

Yet Intensity is clearly inadequate. After all, it fails to capture duration, which clearly matters for amount of effort. Surely if Lucy toils at an intensity level of 10 effs for an hour she has expended more effort than Bob who has expended 10 effs for only five minutes. So Intensity does not give us the right function for calculating effort.

We might consider moving to an account that says that measuring effort is a matter of *total* effort: this account measures effort by multiplying intensity by duration. Like a hedonistic calculus for pleasure, this approach measures effort by multiplying intensity by duration—in

---

[6] My view that difficulty is a matter of effort is supported by Shelly Kagan's observation that sufficient effs result in something being eff-ing hard.

this case, the number of effs expended by the duration for which effs are expended at this level. This approach can incorporate duration, where the Intensity view failed. After the now-classic name for such methods of calculation of wellbeing, I'll call this the *Total* view. According to the Total view, then, roughly speaking,

$$E(a) = f_a t_a$$

where f_a is effs and t_a is time, in minutes, for activity a. To be more precise, when different levels of intensity of effort are expended during the same activity, we sum the products. So

$$E(a) = \sum f_n t_n$$

when $\sum f_n t_n \geq d$, a is difficult. d now will be in eff-minutes, rather than effs. To be even *more* precise, since in real life it seems more likely that the effort expended will not be in step-wise levels, but more accurately captured by a smooth curve, the Total view calculates the amount of effort expended as the area under the curve.

Yet before we get too comfortable with the Total view, there is a compelling objection to consider. Using the Total method of measuring effort by multiplying intensity by duration misses the effect of the *narrative structure* of the effort on our intuitions about how much effort was expended. We tend to think that, for example, it is more impressive to expend a great effort at the end of a slow expenditure of effort at a lower level than it is to expend a very low level of effort after a short burst of high intensity. Consider a foot race: it's more impressive and difficult to sustain a fairly quick going pace and a strong kick at the end than it is to amateurishly run quickly to exhaustion and walk. Call this objection that the increased effort of the narrative structure is not captured the objection from the *bonum variationis* (which is to say, more or less, the good in variety). There appears to be a bonus, as it were, of effort in cases where there is a variety of different levels of effort, arranged in a certain order.[7]

---

[7] The inspiration here is Brentano, whose principle of the *bonum variationis* is that the order or combination of parts of something may increase its value. See R. M. Chisholm, *Brentano and Intrinsic Value* (Cambridge: CUP, 1986), 70.

But *would* the total effort be the same in this case? I think that we have this intuition because it *requires greater effort* to structure our expenditure of effort in a certain way. It takes more discipline and knowledge to plan and know how to pace yourself in a race, and then to run the race accordingly.

But is this the case in all such instances of effort expended according to this kind of temporal structure? I think that, typically, if you have been doing something for a while at a moderate pace, requiring a moderate level of effort, and you then increase the pace, or intensity, it typically *does* require additional effort to increase to the higher level. Doing something for a long time typically requires more effort as time passes, even if the pace of the activity itself is unchanged. Similarly, if you've been exerting some moderate effort for some time, and then move to do something that typically takes only slightly more effort, the previous exertions may mean that the next phase of activity requires more effort than it usually does.

To elaborate, we may be confusing the output with the intensity of effort required to produce that output. Take the *output* of an activity to be the results generated from the agent's activities, not limited to the product of the achievement, such as how fast the agent is running, how many notes per minute he is playing. Consider activity A, which produces low-grade output for duration of ten minutes, followed by high-grade output for ten minutes. Contrast activity B, which produces high-grade output for the first ten minutes, followed by low-grade output (Figure 2.1). The intuition is that A requires greater effort than B—this is the intuition that led us to consider the *bonum variationis*. It requires more effort to perform activities with this sort of narrative structure. But the explanation for this is that the intensity of effort required to produce the higher-grade *output* after already producing the low-grade output for ten minutes *is a greater intensity* than the effort required to produce the high-grade effort starting fresh, when t = o, as in activity B (see Figure 2.2). We have the intuition that activities structured like A require greater effort than activities such as B because they typically *do*, and the Total method of calculation does succeed in capturing this, and the explanation I just gave explains why we may be intuitively confused about it. So the Total view would indeed capture the greater effort in A.

Activity A *A*

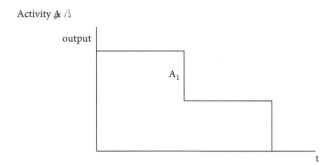

Activity B *A*

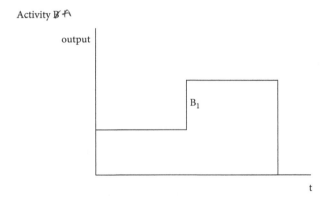

(The area of A_1 equals the area of B_1.)

Figure 2.1

What if we consider a case where the effort really *is* the same—that is, where the area under the curve is truly equal in both instances? That would just be a case where there is some high intensity effort following low intensity effort, contrasted with high intensity effort coming first. Here now the Total view will tell us that the same amount of effort has indeed been expended. But is this so counterintuitive? We might incorrectly give more weight to the last thing that the person does—if they have just stopped running very fast, and are at the last moment very tired, we might confuse this with their having expended more effort overall. But this of course is misleading. Consider front-end loading

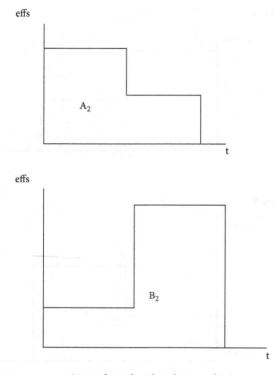

(Area of A_2 is less than the area of B_2.)

Figure 2.2

the work on a project—that is, getting the hard parts done first. Does it mean that you've expended less effort? Not at all: just that you expended more effort earlier, rather than later.

So the *bonum variationis* objection is merely apparent. In instances of activities of this general narrative structure, it typically requires more effort to structure one's activity in this way. So it is simply false that in the intuitive case the effort used (according to this method of calculation) is the same. The intuition that led us to consider the *bonum variationis* objection is nonetheless captured by the Total view: activities with a narrative structure like activity A may still be *more difficult* in a typical case. And this difference can be captured by the Total view.

The Ridiculous Conclusion

However, the Total view of effort calculation, like the Total view of well-being calculation, is subject to a far worse objection: an objection that is analogous to the repugnant conclusion.[8] An extremely minimal amount of effort expended over a very, very long time comes out as *more* effort than an extremely intense effort expended for a shorter time. As a result, for any intensely effortful activity of finite duration, there is always an activity of extremely minimal intensity of effort that requires *more total effort*. That is,

$$\Big\{\; E(\text{minimal}) > E(\text{intense})$$

(where "intense" and "minimal" are the intensely effortful and extremely long minimal activities, respectively). This means that according to the comparative schema I introduced earlier, the activity of extremely long minimal intensity is *more difficult* than the intensely effortful activity.[9] The long minimal intensity activity is more difficult than the very intense activity *even if the very intense activity is very difficult!* Although the intuition is that the very long minimal intense activity is *not* difficult at all it comes out as *more* difficult than the very intense activity. This seems implausible—ridiculous, in fact. It's not quite appalling enough to be repugnant, as the analogous argument in wellbeing calculation is, but it is unreasonable enough to be silly, so I'll call this the *ridiculous conclusion*. In short, the ridiculous conclusion that is entailed by the Total view is that, for any very difficult intensely effortful activity of finite duration, there is a very long activity of extremely minimal intensity of effort that *is more difficult* than the intensely effortful activity of shorter duration. This is illustrated

---

[8] The now-canonical Repugnant Conclusion, originally brought to light by Derek Parfit, is an entailment of the Total account of calculating wellbeing. Accounts that measure wellbeing by totaling are committed to the following: "For any possible population of at least ten billion people, all with a very high quality of life, there must be some much larger imaginable population whose existence, if other things are equal, would be better, even though its members have lives that are barely worth living." Derek Parfit, *Reasons and Persons* (Oxford: Clarendon Press, 1984), 388.

[9] It is surprisingly difficult to imagine such a case in real life. It seems to be the case that even activities requiring a minimal intensity of effort, when performed for long enough, become horribly tedious. Simply tapping one finger, if done for long enough, could require incredible effort and perseverance. Nonetheless, it suffices that we can *imagine* that there could be such an activity of minimal intensity.

in Figure 2.3, in which activity A is of high intensity, but shorter duration than activity B. Yet the duration of B is sufficiently long that the duration of B times its intensity yields a higher total effort. The main challenge for the correct approach of the effort calculus, then, will be to avoid entailing this conclusion.

A good response to the ridiculous conclusion is to move to calculating effort by appealing to the *average* intensity. On the *Average* view, then, to calculate E(a), add the eff-minutes, and divide by the total time. Average holds that

$$\left\{ E(a) = \sum f_n t_n / t_a \right\}$$

That is, sum total effort at each level of intensity, then divide by time. When $\sum f_n t_n / t_a \geq d$, a is difficult. Now d will be a matter of effs, once again, rather than eff-minutes.

But the Average approach misses duration. The degree to which this is problematic can be easily seen by considering two activities, ϕ-ing and ψ-ing, with a uniform intensity of effs—say 10. ϕ-ing is done for 10 minutes, ψ-ing for an hour. Since the intensity is the same in both activities, the average intensity is the same. But surely it seems that ψ-ing required more effort than ϕ-ing. In fact, we earlier agreed that this

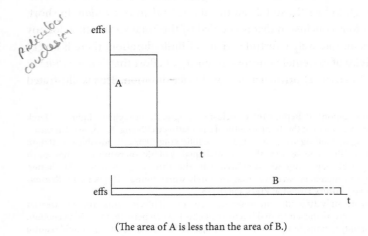

(The area of A is less than the area of B.)

Figure 2.3

would be the case, which led us to reject Intensity. So Average should also be rejected.

The Threshold of Minimum Intensity

Duration matters for amount of effort, and so does degree of intensity. We need a method of calculating amount of effort that captures intuitions about these elements, but does so while avoiding the ridiculous conclusion.

One way that we might do this is to institute a threshold of intensity below which effort expended is irrelevant to whether or not the activity is difficult. Effort expended below this threshold of minimum intensity (TMI) does not count toward the effort calculus of total effort that is relevant for difficulty. Only effort above the TMI is relevant for determining whether or not an activity is difficult.[10] Note that on this approach, we can still calculate total effort overall, even below the TMI—but it is only the effort that is above the intensity threshold that counts toward determining whether or not the activity is difficult.

In effect, then, I am now rejecting the original schema for determining difficulty. At the beginning of this section, I proposed a schema for determining difficulty which was this: a is difficult just in case E(a) ≥ d, which is to say for an activity a if the amount of effort required for a is above some threshold, d, then a is difficult. But now, it turns out, determining whether or not a is difficult is not a simple matter of the amount of effort required. It's a matter of how much effort over a certain level of intensity is required for a. We might put it this way: a is difficult when a requires a certain amount of intense effort.

The simplest way to capture the amount of intense effort is to calculate the total effort expended when effs exceed the TMI. If we graph the intensity on the y axis and time on the x axis, the TMI will be a line such that y = TMI (Figure 2.4). We then can graph the intensity of effort of the activity over time. To measure the difficulty of the activity, the amount of intense

---

[10] This approach, perhaps obviously, is analogous to Parfit's Valueless Level in calculating wellbeing (*Reasons and Persons*, 412). According to the Valueless Level approach, wellbeing only enters the calculus if it is above a certain quality threshold. Parfit's principle is introduced under similar philosophical circumstances, namely to avoid the (original, in this case) repugnant conclusion.

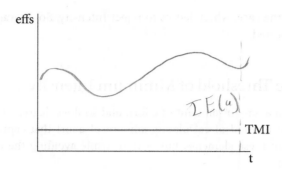

Figure 2.4

effort is determined by calculating the *total intense effort*—that is, the area between the curve of the graph of the intensity of effort over time and the TMI. We can now help ourselves to the Total method of calculating the amount of effort—intensity times duration—since the problem with Total has been avoided. The TMI, after all, has been introduced in order to avoid the ridiculous conclusion. Now, however, any area under the curve that is *below* the TMI line is *not* included in the calculation. This value, the amount of intense effort, IE(a), must be above the threshold of sufficient effort for difficulty.

I'll call this the view *Total Intense Effort*. The simplest way to capture this is with a *new* schema, where, rather than calculating amount of effort, we calculate the amount of *intense effort*. The new schema for Total Intense Effort, then, is this:

a is difficult just in case IE(a) ≥ d

where IE(a) is the total intense effort of activity a.

We can still calculate the overall total effort (including non-intense effort) that has been expended for the activity. But, according to Total Intense Effort, a high amount of effort does *not* entail that the activity is difficulty. Rather, a certain amount of *intense* effort qualifies an activity as difficult. So the method for calculating *total effort*, E(a), remains the same, namely, the Total view. But now the Total view is only good for calculating the amount of effort, *not* for determining difficulty. The schema for determining difficulty, on the other hand, only considers *intense* effort, IE(a), which is the effort above the TMI. The Total view is still good for calculating the amount of effort overall, which, as we will see shortly, is still useful. It's just not useful for determining whether or not something is difficult.

Recall that earlier I explained that degree of difficulty and comparisons of difficulty could be made by appealing to the difference between the effort expended for the activity and d (or by comparing total effort, if values for d are the same in both comparates). Now we can see that such a comparison will only succeed in showing difference in the amount of effort required, not degree of difficulty. The correct way to make comparisons of difficulty, as opposed to effort, is to compare the difference between total *intense* effort from d. So the new comparison schema for difficulty is:

a is more difficult than b just in case IE(a) – d > IE(b) – d

Again, for the time being, assuming d is constant, it can be dropped.

Sufficient Effort for Difficulty: The Percentage View

Now, of the total amount of effort that is expended above the TMI, how much need be expended in order for what the agent is doing to be difficult for him? That is, how much intense effort must an agent expend in order for what he is doing to be difficult? To clarify, an agent can expend eff-minutes above the TMI, but not expend *enough* of them to qualify as doing something difficult. According to the schema for determining difficulty, the amount of intense effort sufficient for difficulty is d. So what is d?

I will consider two different approaches. First, d might be a *percentage*. Alternatively, d might be some *absolute*. I will start by considering the *Percentage* view. According to this view, d is a percentage, which is taken from the maximum effort an agent is able to exert. This approach requires that we suppose that there is some maximum amount of eff-minutes that an agent can expend. Let's suppose for now that the maximum is the maximum amount of eff-minutes the agent could exert in the duration of the given activity, although there could be other ways to construe the maximum.[11] I will refer to this maximum amount of eff-minutes as "max."

---

[11] There are other options here. Another approach would take the maximum intensity of effort that an agent could exert (that is, the maximum value of effs exerted in a given time). But since the Percentage view is ultimately wrong, I won't take the time to develop other options here.

In order for an activity to count as difficult, an agent must expend effort at a rate that is at least some minimum percentage of max.

So according to the Percentage view, d is a *percent* of the maximum effort an agent can expend, such that

$$d = n\% \, max$$

where n is the requisite percent, and max is the maximum amount of eff-minutes an agent could exert in the duration of the activity. When the intense effort expended is at least n% of the agent's maximum, then, the activity is difficult. That is,

a is difficult just in case IE(a) ≥ n%max

Equivalently,

a is difficult just in case IE(a)/max ≥ n%

Now, it's possible that the maximum effort possible to expend is *uniform* for everyone. That is to say, it's possible that there is a universal maximum effort for all human beings—no one could ever exert more than this maximum, and everyone is capable of it. If this is the case, then the percentage required for difficulty would be the same *amount* of intense eff-minutes for everyone. As a result, the Percentage approach and the Absolute approach, which I consider shortly, are the *same*. That is, the amount of effs required to meet the percentage required for difficulty would be the same for everyone. In this case, there would be no reason to favor one method of determining d over the other.

But it seems far more likely that different people are capable of exerting different maximum levels of intense effort. It just seems to be true that some people can try harder than others. As a result the two methods of determining d diverge, and we need to determine which one is correct.

I believe the correct approach is the Absolute approach, and the Percentage method is mistaken. This can be seen by considering the following counterexample.

Running Buddies. Steph and Betty are running buddies. They are out for a run, and they're both working hard—they're both running fast and are really feeling the burn, as they say. Both, as it happens, are exerting the same amount of eff-minutes. Steph is at 80 percent of her maximum effort. Betty, however, is capable of exerting more effort overall than Steph is, so she is only at 60 percent of her maximum.

There is a strong intuition that what each runner is doing is equally difficult (or at least on a par). We can even imagine them agreeing with one another that they are both working similarly hard.

The Percentage approach will have us say, however, that what Steph is doing is *much more* difficult than what Betty is doing. Recall that according to the comparison schema, differences in difficulty are determined by measuring the distance of intense effort expended from d. The value for d for Betty will be *higher* than it will for Steph. According to the Percentage approach, d = n%max. Since Betty's max is a higher number than Steph's, the amount of intense eff-minutes needed in order to reach n% is a higher number than the amount required for Steph to reach n% of her max. That is to say, the value of d for Betty (d_{Betty}) is higher than the value of d for Steph (d_{Steph}). As a result, the difference between IE(Betty) and d_{Betty} is smaller than the difference between IE(Steph) and d_{Steph}. According to the comparison schema, what Steph is doing is *more difficult* than what Betty is doing.

But this seems very peculiar. It really does seem, to an observer, that Betty and Steph are exerting effort that's on a par with one another. We can even imagine that they agree with each other that they are working equally hard. That Betty could ultimately expend a greater effort than Steph just isn't *relevant* for whether or not what she is currently doing *is more difficult*. It just means that she is capable of doing *even more difficult* things—and more difficult things than Steph is. We count from the bottom up rather than the top down when it comes to effort.

This point can be seen even more clearly in the following example. Betty is now out running by herself, exerting x eff-minutes, which is y% of her max. She's working pretty hard, and definitely feeling the burn, so x is a significant amount of effort. Let's suppose that y% is greater than the requisite n% of max, so that her running is difficult for her, according to the Percentage account. Ten minutes into her run, unbeknownst to Betty, the Fairy Godmother of Abilities magically endows her with the capacity to exert far more effort than ever before—ten times her original max. The Fairy Godmother endows Betty with this ability for five minutes, and then reduces her max back to its original level. For the five minutes when Betty

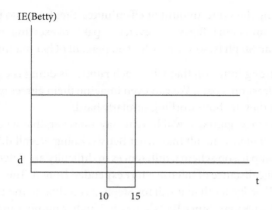

Figure 2.5

has the souped-up max, she continues to exert x intense eff-minutes, but with her increased max, x intense eff-minutes is only z% of 10max—which is a tenth the size of y. z% falls below the requisite n%, so Betty's running is *not* difficult for her during the five minute interlude (see Figure 2.5). But Betty continues to exert intense eff-minutes at the same rate even during this interlude. The increase in capacity is completely unperceived by her. Of course, it *would be* perceived by her if, during the interlude, she attempted to increase her effort to beyond her previous max. But the new capacity is imperceptible to her otherwise—we can even imagine asking her if she felt anything different during her run, and her reporting back that it was evenly effortful throughout.[12]

It seems absurd that this increase in capacity should affect the *difficulty* of her activity. Just because Betty is capable of exerting more effort than she currently is exerting does not detract from the significance of the effort that she exerts. Again it seems to be the case that we count effort from the bottom up, as it were, as opposed to from the top down, as we would be required to do according to the Percentage view. How difficult something

---

[12] We might think that when the increase in capacity for effort is increased Betty would "feel the burn" *less* than when it is lower. But this does not follow necessarily. Effort and the pain of exertion need not correlate. Effort need not bother somebody while they are exerting it. It is possible to exert a high amount of effort and not be bothered by it, and it is possible to exert a low amount of effort and find it very painful. So effort and the pain of exertion can move independently from one another.

is for you is a matter of how much effort you are exerting—not how much effort you *could be exerting*.

The Absolute View

A better approach is to hold that d is an absolute value. According to the *Absolute* view, d is an absolute amount of intense eff-minutes, regardless of how much effort in total an agent is capable of expending. To be precise, according to the Absolute view, the amount of intense eff-minutes required for a given activity is the *same* regardless of the agent, in contrast to the Percentage view, where the amount of intense eff-minutes required was *relativized* to particular agents depending on their maximum. In this respect, on the Absolute view d is an absolute amount, rather than a proportion relative to the particular agent. There is, of course, another sense in which something can be an "absolute" value: when something has the *same value* under various circumstances. The threshold for difficulty, d, it turns out, is *not* absolute in this second way.

In fact, d *varies* from activity to activity. Some activities seem to require a great deal of intense effort in order to count as difficult, while others require considerably less to count as difficult. If we're investigating the difficulty of marathons, for example, the threshold for what counts as difficult requires a great deal of intense effort, whereas if we're investigating the difficulty of a board game, the amount of intense effort required to be difficult seems to be fairly low. It could even be the case that, given the high threshold of difficulty required for marathons, a particular marathon is *not* difficult, whereas given the relatively low threshold of difficulty for board games, a particular board game *is* difficult, even though the marathon requires a greater amount of intense effort than the board game does.

My proposal is that difficulty is evaluated relative to a *background* level of intense effort expenditure. More precisely, there is a background average amount of intense effort expended—that is, an average, *unexceptional* level of intense effort for a given kind of activity. This average amount of intense effort is *not* difficult. Difficult things require some sufficient degree of intense effort *greater* than the average intense effort—or, for short, the average IE. When evaluating the difficulty of some particular activity, it is held up against this background, to determine the degree to which it contrasts against the background. When the activity pops out from the background, so to speak, as involving sufficiently more IE, it is difficult. So the background average determines the level of d, which is some degree higher than the background.

The background is the average amount of IE required for the relevant *kind* of activity. The IE required for each member of the kind is averaged, and this average amount of IE is the *background*. Merely attaining the average amount of IE is insufficient for difficult. When something requires sufficiently *more* IE than the average of its kind, it stands out from the background—it is difficult. But how much greater than the average need something be in order to be difficult?

It seems that something could require *a little* more intense effort than average, yet not be difficult, so the amount of IE that is required for an activity of the relevant kind to be difficult is somewhat *higher* than the average. As a result, d is *above* the background by some significant amount. Precisely how significantly higher d is above the background need not trouble us, but I will set d as 10 percent higher. So, pending further investigation that would secure the exact value of d, let's suppose that d is 10 percent greater than the background average (nondifficult) intense effort for the relevant kind of activity. We could wonder further as to whether there is a concrete value for d, or if d is set by context, but I'll leave these questions for another time.

Now, as straightforward as this may seem so far, we need to bear in mind that for any activity, there are numerous kinds to which it belongs. Obviously enough, one thing can belong to several *natural* kinds, and also to a huge multitude of *artificial* kinds. A game of backgammon, for example, belongs to the kind *board games*, along with chess and Parcheesi, but it also belongs to the kind *activities for a typical Sunday afternoon*, and *activities for this particular Sunday*, and a multitude of others. The number of kinds to which an activity belongs is virtually limitless.

Accordingly, since the kind determines the background average, there are numerous backgrounds of average IE with which we could potentially contrast the IE of a given activity. We might then wonder how the relevant kind is determined for an evaluation of difficulty. The relevant kind, and hence the relevant background, is determined by *what it is that we are interested in evaluating something as*. We might be interested in whether or not backgammon is difficult *as a board game*, or whether it is difficult as something to do on a typical Sunday, or for this particular Sunday. Whether or not backgammon *comes out as being difficult*, then, can depend on what *kind* we take it as belonging to. As a result, we might find ourselves saying such things as, "backgammon is difficult qua board game" or "the Hawaii marathon is not difficult as far as marathons go;" and yet also, "backgammon is *not* difficult as far as things to do this weekend" and "running the Hawaii marathon is difficult as far as things to do this weekend." So whether or not something counts as difficult will depend on what *kind* we are taking it to belong to.

So, then, according to the Absolute view of evaluations of difficulty, the schema for determining difficulty is:

a is difficult just in case IE(a) > d_a

where d_a is the threshold of IE required for difficulty according to the background which is relevant for this particular evaluation of a.

Recall the comparison schema that I introduced earlier to compare the degree of difficulty of two activities. It was:

a is more difficult than b just in case IE(a) – d > IE(b) – d

When the values for d are the same, then, they can be dropped from the schema. But we can now see that including the values for d on either side of the equation can be crucial, since the value for d can *differ* according to the activity being evaluated.

d will be the same for both comparates when we are comparing the difficulty of two activities against the *same background*. In other words, d will be the same for both comparates when the background is the same for both comparates. When we compare the relative difficulty of two *board games*, for example, against the background average of board games, this is exactly what we are doing—the relevant contrast background is that of playing board games.

But comparing two activities that are of the same *type* and the same *kind* is just one example of a comparison that we can make. *Type* and *kind*, in the senses I'm using them here, can come apart. A type, as I am using the term here, is what might be understood as a very obvious kind. Board games, marathons are examples of types. They need not be natural kinds, in the technical sense, but they are *more* natural categorizations of activities than other categorizations could be. Kinds, on the other hand, need not be obvious categorizations and can range from the natural to the most artificial. As we've already seen, board games and marathons are kinds, and so are activities to do on a typical Sunday, as well as activities to do on this particular Sunday. I take it that the distinction I'm drawing between more and less obvious categorizations is fairly intuitive, although these ways of understanding these terms need not be official or commonly used. So I will adopt these particular senses of the terms for this discussion.

Since it is *kinds* that determine backgrounds, rather than types, and types and kinds can differ, there are four in total type-kind combinations for comparisons. First, as I have just discussed, is the comparison between two activities of the same type and the same kind. Second, there are comparisons between the difficulty of two *different types* of activities against the *different* backgrounds. Third, there are comparisons between the difficulty of different types against the same background, and fourth, comparisons between the difficulty of the same type of activity against different backgrounds (although this last instance of comparison is less common).

In comparisons of the second category, we compare the difficulty of two different types against two *different* backgrounds. We do this when, for example, we compare how difficult this board game is *for a board game* with how difficult this marathon is *for a marathon.* So we evaluate how difficult the board game is against the background of board games, and we evaluate how difficult the marathon is against the background of marathons, and then compare the differences between the difficulty of the particular board game and marathon with their respective values of d. In this case, then, there are *different values* for d in the comparison schema—one value is determined by the contrast background for board games, the other for marathons. As a result, the comparison schema is as follows:

a is more difficult than b just in case $IE(a) - d_a > IE(b) - d_b$

But, to be clear, this schema is what we use when we want to compare the difficulty of two activities *relative to different contrast backgrounds* for each comparate—such as the following:

Backgammon is a more difficult board game than the Hawaii marathon is a difficult marathon.

Although this is one way that we can compare difficulty between two activities from two different *types* of activities, it is not the way that we *usually* compare difficulty between types. More often when we compare the difficulty across types of activities, we hold the activities against the same background, which is the first category of comparisons, or we use the simpler comparison schema, which I also discussed earlier.

Comparisons of the third category—different types against the same background—are quite common. Here we might be comparing the difficulty of board games with difficulty of marathons, for example. In this case, we are holding both types of activities against a background of, say, *activities to do on a weekend off*, or, more broadly, *activities*. Since the background is the same in both comparates, we can also drop the values for d from either side of the schema in cross-type comparisons of this nature.

Different-type, same-background comparisons alternatively can be made using the simpler comparison schema,

a is more difficult than b just in case IE(a) > IE(b)

On the simple schema, there is no need for d, since there is no contrast background against which we measure either of the comparates, but we just compare them to each other.

We might wonder, however, what entitles us to use this simpler schema in this case. The simpler schema is equivalent to the more complex comparison schema, where the two activities are being compared against the same background. As a result, the values for d are the same. But, we might wonder, how can we possibly be using the same background, since the simple schema is used here to compare different types? But the answer to this is clear: we know that every activity can belong to a virtually limitless number of different *kinds*. We have already seen that what appear to be different types of activities—say, board games and marathons—can be classified as belonging to the same kind, *activities to do on a Sunday afternoon*. We could even broaden a kind more liberally to the kind *activities*. So the simpler schema can be seen as an extension of the more complex schema in this way—d is dropped because both comparates are considered as belonging to the same kind, so the background is the same for both.

Just to exhaust the space of possible combinations of types and kinds, we should consider the fourth category of comparisons: comparisons between two activities of the same type but against two different backgrounds. Such a comparison might be uncommon, but not impossible given the schema I have developed here. For example, we could compare playing backgammon against the background of average board games with playing backgammon against the background of activities to do this weekend. Our comparison, then, is between backgammon *as a board game* and backgammon *as something to do this weekend*. Of course, part of what determines whether or not backgammon is difficult against the latter background depends on what else is in the offing for the weekend's activities. Supposing that there are many more difficult things to do this weekend than backgammon, backgammon *as a board game* is more difficult than backgammon *is*, as far as things to do this weekend goes. But such comparisons within one type against two different backgrounds aren't particularly common.

The Difficulty Condition for Achievements

Now that the nature of difficulty has been as thoroughly investigated as, I believe, it has ever been, let's return to the nature of achievements, and take a closer look at the role of difficulty. My account of achievements, as we saw in the first chapter, requires that things be difficult as a necessary condition for achievements. But it's clear that difficulty comes in *degrees*. This leads to wondering *how* difficult something needs to be in order to be an achievement. Is requiring even just the tiniest bit of intense effort sufficient for the difficulty condition of achievements to be fulfilled? My view is that this initially counterintuitive suggestion is indeed true: just being difficult *at all* suffices to fulfill the difficulty condition for achievements.

But surely, it might be objected, not just *any* difficult enterprise is an achievement, even when the other conditions of achievements obtain. Even some *very* difficult things just don't seem to be achievements. For example, consider the surgeon, Dr Bob.

> *Surgeon.* A typical day's work for Dr Bob is filled with difficult, albeit routine, surgeries (appendectomies, etc.). On even an average work day, Dr Bob is expending 75 intense eff-minutes, which, compared to many other jobs is quite a lot. As a result, an average work day for Dr Bob is *difficult*. One day, however, a very unusual case is presented to Dr Bob. Dr Bob is required to perform a rare and remarkable—and remarkably difficult—surgery, and he carries it out with success.

It seems that just getting through an ordinary day for Dr Bob is *not* an achievement, while completing the remarkable surgery *is* an achievement. After all, an ordinary day for Dr Bob is what he does *every day*. An average day for Dr Bob is routine surgeries, which he is required to perform all the time. It would be strange to say that getting through every ordinary day is an achievement for him. Yet my account seems to say that every day *is* an achievement for him.

Either my account of the difficulty condition for achievements is wrong, or the other condition, competent causation, doesn't obtain. But even though we haven't yet seen all the details of competent causation, it seems fairly plausible that Dr Bob competently causes the results of his ordinary day, and so the other condition for achievements is indeed fulfilled. So something must be wrong with my account of the difficulty condition.

Yet this is not the case. According to my account of difficulty, what counts as difficult varies according to the background of non-difficult things with which it is contrasted. In Surgeon, when we examine the difficulty of Dr Bob's routine surgeries, they *are* difficult when contrasted with a background of *an average day's work*, for surgeons and non-surgeons alike. On the other hand, when the background is an average day *for Dr Bob*, an average day for Dr Bob is not difficult—to be precise, it sets the standard for *not* being difficult. This is what explains why the remarkable surgery that Dr Bob performs stands out from the background as difficult and, accordingly, as an achievement. So my account is not committed to saying that an average day for Dr Bob is difficult, nor is it an achievement. An average day for Dr Bob is *not* difficult when it itself *is* the background of what is nondifficult.[13] As a result, my view is that just being difficult *at all* is enough to satisfy the difficulty condition for achievements.

But, as we've seen, what counts as being difficult can *vary*, according to the background. Because of this variation in backgrounds, my view has two implications that are worth noting about the *relativity* of achievements. First, because the background against which we contrast the difficulty of activities can affect what counts as difficult, whether or not the difficulty condition for achievements is fulfilled is *relative* to the particular

---

[13] Surgeon is like an inside-out version of the Virtuoso puzzle. In Virtuoso, Heifetz does something that is not difficult for him, yet seems to be an achievement. In Surgeon, Dr Bob does something that *is* difficult, yet is *not* an achievement. The solution to the Surgeon case is in some respects similar. All the machinery to explain why an ordinary day for Dr Bob is not an achievement is already present in the account. In Virtuoso, the solution is that difficulty is relativized to different classes of agents. In Surgeon, on the other hand, the solution lies also in relativization, but in relativizing to different kinds of activities.

background against which the activity is contrasted. Since whether or not something is difficult is relative to the background, this means that whether or not the difficulty condition for achievements is satisfied is relative to the background, and, as a result, what counts as an achievement is relative to the background as well. In other words, whether or not something is an achievement depends in part on the particular background against which we determine difficulty. Which background is relevant is a matter of the way in which we're interested in evaluating the particular activity: that is, the relevant background is a matter of the *kind* of thing of which a particular activity is a an instance.

Consequently, whether something is an achievement is (at least in part) a matter of the way in which we're interested in evaluating it—in particular, *as* a representative of some *kind*: we might be interested in things that are achievements over the course of someone's life, or on this particular day, or in the history of this particular sporting event. These determine which *kind* of activity is relevant, and, as we saw earlier, the members of this kind determine what the background average intense effort required is, which in turn determines d.

So something can be an achievement when considered one way, and not an achievement when considered in another. Held up against one background, an ordinary day for Dr Bob jumps out as difficult and therefore is an achievement, but, held up against another background—a background of Dr Bob's ordinary days—only the remarkable surgery is an achievement. What counts as an achievement, as a result, can be relative to a kind.

There is a second way in which achievements are relative. Recall Virtuoso, which shows that there can be things that are difficult, but not difficult *for* the agent who undertakes them. It follows that something can be an achievement, but not an achievement *for* the agent who accomplishes it. I think that this is perfectly reasonable, and I happily endorse it as a feature of my approach. Virtuoso is just such a case. It seems that Heifetz's accomplishment may indeed constitute *an achievement*, qua performance, but it doesn't seem to be an achievement *for him*, in the context of his own career. But nothing prevents us from saying that it is an *achievement* (*sans* "for") insofar as the difficulty condition *is* satisfied: relative to the comparison class of talented violinists, the performance is difficult, even though it is not difficult for Heifetz. Similarly, then, the performance is an achievement, even though it is not an achievement *for* Heifetz.

Later on, we will see the role that difficulty plays in the *value* of achievements, but before concluding this chapter, let me flag an issue about difficulty which is intriguing, but will have to be set aside for another time. Achievements, it seems, can vary in *size*, or greatness. By *size* of achievement, I mean something like *magnitude*—achievements, it seems, can vary in magnitude: some achievements are very great, and some are on a smaller scale. For example, baking a soufflé is an achievement, but it's a much *smaller* achievement than, say, summiting Mt Everest.[14] I would like to suggest that *difficulty* might play a role in determining the magnitude of achievements. It seems plausible that achievements that are very difficult are greater than those that, other things being equal, are less difficult. Baking a soufflé is difficult, but climbing Mt Everest is far more difficult. The extent to which magnitude of achievements is determined by difficulty, however, in conjunction with other elements, will be left for another time. While magnitude is an issue I will leave until another time, in what follows I will look at the role that difficulty plays in degree of *value* of achievements. But before we get to these value-theoretic issues, the descriptive part of the journey still needs to take us to the account of the remaining component of achievements, *competent causation*. I turn to this next.

---

[14] It seems possible that the magnitude of achievements be *independent* from their value. That is, it seems that a very great achievement need not be of very great value. But this question I will put aside until later.

3

Competent Causation

Now I turn to the second component of achievements, what I call *competent causation*. For something to be an achievement, as we have seen, it is necessary that there be a certain relation between the difficult process and the product in which it culminates. The process must not only cause the product, but it must be caused in a certain kind of way, to wit: competently.

Competent causation, as I understand it, is a *way* or *manner* of causing. That is, if C competently causes E, that means that not only does E result from C, but E results from C *in a particular manner*. That manner is competently. The focus here will be on what that manner amounts to, so I won't be addressing the nature of causation more generally. We start from the assumption that the relevant agent has indeed caused the product of the achievement. The interesting question for us is what distinguishes achievements from other processes that cause products. I'm going to propose one way of understanding this element. It may be the case that a different analysis might fare equally well, and I will turn to some alternatives toward the end of this chapter.

So here is one way that we might understand what it is for an agent to cause some outcome competently. Given that the agent's actions cause the outcome, the agent causes the outcome *competently* to the extent that he has justified, true beliefs about his actions causing the outcome. Or, to be pithy but slightly inaccurate, A knows what he's doing. So, to cause competently involves a relation among four elements: an agent, his action, an outcome, and the agent's beliefs about the action and the outcome.

For most kinds of manners, or ways, things can be done *more* or *less* in the manner. For example, speaking English with a French accent is speaking English in a certain way. A person can speak English in this particular way, with a French accent, to a greater or lesser degree. Similarly, you can cause an outcome more or less competently. The extent to which somebody causes something competently is a matter of the extent to which they have justified and true beliefs (JTBs) about what they are doing. Whether or not somebody is causing something *at all* competently is a matter of having some requisite measure of JTBs. So to cause something competently, you need to have enough JTBs, and the more JTBs you have, the more competently you cause it. To characterize the analysis in the slogan, how competently you cause something is a matter of how well you know what you're doing.

This slogan, of course, isn't quite accurate, since the analysis I've just given only appeals to justified and true beliefs, and it is widely held that knowledge requires a further, "anti-Gettier" component. So a more accurate characterization of the analysis is that an agent causes an outcome competently to the extent that he has justified, true, and anti-Gettiered beliefs about his action causing the outcome.[1] But for simplicity I will simply refer to the relevant epistemic entity as JTB, short for justified true belief.

To see the account in action, let's consider a successful case of competent causation. Imagine Rudy driving his Smart Car. Rudy is a good driver, and he is just driving along in the usual way. It seems fairly straightforward that Rudy is competently causing his car to take him from here to there. He believes that the various motions required for driving (foot on the gas, turning the wheel, checking for other cars, etc.) will make the car drive in the way that he expects, and his beliefs about these activities and their effects on the car are reasonable (he attended an excellent driving school), and true. In other words, Rudy knows what he's doing.

But there are a lot of effects that Rudy's activities have on the world that Rudy does *not* have any beliefs about. He may even have some false beliefs about some of the effects of his activities. As smart as Rudy is, he doesn't really have any idea how the engine of his Smart Car works. As it happens, he has some false beliefs about how it works. He thinks the car runs on Duracell AA batteries, and that the car is rear-wheel drive, when

---

[1] As it happens, it's actually quite difficult to make a case that competent causation requires anti-Gettiered JTBs, as opposed to simply JTBs without the extra condition. The way to show that the JTBs must be anti-Gettiered would be to devise a Gettier case in an instance of competent causation. As it happens, such cases are quite hard to find. Since there is nothing to be lost by including an anti-Gettier condition, I include one in this account just to be safe.

it's actually front-wheel drive. Rudy's activities of driving the car have effects on all the parts of the car. But Rudy doesn't have true beliefs about these effects. He doesn't have any beliefs about the engine, and his beliefs about the batteries and rear-wheel drive are false. But this doesn't seem to threaten the idea that Rudy is competently causing his driving. And this is indeed what the account entails: in spite of his false beliefs, Rudy has enough JTBs to be competently causing his driving.

The view, then, is that an agent competently causes the effects that ensue from his actions and about which enough of his beliefs are justified and true. If F and G are parts of the product, and the agent *fails* to have beliefs about F and G, or has many unjustified beliefs, or only false beliefs, then the agent does *not* competently cause F and G. Thus, insofar as Rudy's activities *cause* the engine of the Smart Car to perform thus and so, Rudy does not *competently* cause the activities of the engine in this way. He indeed causes the engine to behave this way—he is part of the causal chain—but he does not cause it competently. He fails to have the relevant beliefs. This does not mean that Rudy is an *incompetent* driver. After all, he has the relevant reasonable and true beliefs that seem to be required for driving competently.

Now, as far as *degrees* of competence of causation go, Rudy could be causing his driving more competently if he had more justified and true beliefs about how the car works. The greater the understanding that we have about how our activities influence the world, the more competently we are doing what we are doing. Thus the degree to which you cause something competently is a matter of the extent to which you have JTBs about it, and whether or not you cause something at all competently requires having *enough* JTBs.

We might wonder what it takes for a belief to be *about* something. No doubt there is a lot to be said about this question, but I will have to leave it aside here and hope that the commonsense notion is natural enough. I will instead turn my attention to this question: what makes for having *enough* beliefs?

The *number* of JTBs is a good initial candidate. It's plausible to suppose that in order to count causing something competently, you need to have some requisite minimal number of JTBs, and the more JTBs you have about what you are doing, the more competent you are at it. As we just saw, Rudy has a certain number of JTBs about his driving such that he is competently causing his driving, but had he more JTBs, he would be doing it even more competently. So number of JTBs is a factor. We will start with this as the basic view, but, as we will see, it's in need of some refinement.

Structural Beliefs

Starting with this basic view, we might think that it is a matter of having a sufficient number of JTBs, and that each JTB counts for the same amount. Thus, if two agents have the same number of JTBs about their activity and its effects, they are competently causing the effects to the same extent. This seems plausible. Yet it does not seem to be true in all cases. Some beliefs about an activity seem to count for more than others.

Consider agents A and B and an activity, φ-ing. Let's suppose that φ-ing requires of both A and B the same number of steps in order to culminate in the product. A and B both have the same number of JTBs about their respective instances of φ-ing. Let's say that they both have 25 JTBs. But the content of their beliefs differs. A has 25 beliefs about the steps he is undertaking. But although A has lots of beliefs, they are a jumble of discrete beliefs. A has no belief that connects his other beliefs to one another.

B, on the other hand, has JTBs with all the same content as A, except he lacks one and has a different belief in its place. Rather than yet another discrete belief about one of the steps of the process, B has instead a belief about the *relationship* that each of the discrete steps has to one another, and how they are connected in culminating in the outcome. In other words, he has one belief that we might say constitutes a global understanding of his activities. A's beliefs, however, are discrete and unconnected to one another in this global way.

It seems that B is causing the outcome more competently than A, yet they have the same number of JTBs. In these two cases, the number of beliefs is the same, but one of B's beliefs is about how all the discrete steps in the process *fit together*. So having a belief about the *structure* of the other beliefs that one has counts for more in determining the degree to which one is doing something competently. I will say more about these structural beliefs in Chapter 5, but I'll leave it at this for now: certain beliefs—specifically, beliefs about the structure of one's activities—count for more toward competent causation. So what we are measuring for competent causation is *weighted JTBs*. JTBs that are general and concern the overall structure of the activity are weightier than discrete individual beliefs. Certain kinds of beliefs thus count for more for competent causation: general, structural beliefs. This is a way in which content of beliefs is relevant. Beliefs that have a certain kind of content—that is, general, structural content—are weightier than beliefs that have a more local, discrete content.

So for A to cause E competently via his φ-ing, A must have a certain amount of JTBs about his φ-ing, and JTBs that are about the overall structure of his activities are worth more than discrete beliefs.

But just what is this amount? The natural thought is that the amount of weighted JTBs required is absolute—that is, the same for all cases. But contrast these two activities:

(1) Jennifer, an average adult, ties her shoes.
(2) Alec is a scientist with highly specialized knowledge about nanotechnology, working on building an incredible complicated nanomachine, using procedure P. But P is the wrong approach, although Alec doesn't know it. However, Alec sneezes part way through the procedure, causing one of the tiny pieces to jiggle in just the right way, and the nanomachine comes together, even though Alec continues to falsely believe that P is the correct way to build the nanomachine.

Jennifer, we will assume, competently causes her shoes to be tied. But Alec does not competently cause the nanomachine. However, even though Alec doesn't cause the nanomachine competently, he still has a *vast* amount of JTBs about the nature of his activities—although P isn't the right procedure, he knows an awful lot of other things about what he is doing. So Alec has many more JTBs about the nature of his activities than Jennifer does about her activities. If all that matters is having the right amount of weighted JTBs, where this amount is the same in all cases, then, since Jennifer has enough to cause competently, and Alec has *more* than Jennifer, he should be causing the nanomachine competently. But he is not.

This suggests that the amount of weighted JTBs at issue here isn't an absolute amount. Rather, a better way to understand it would be as a *percentage*. On a percentage approach, the amount of weighted JTBs required in any instance of competent causation is a percentage of the possible weighted beliefs that one might have about the activity. (Since we're clear that the JTBs in question are weighted in the way I described in the last section, I'll stop referring to them as "weighted JTBs" and simply refer to them as "JTBs.")

Given the activities in which you are engaged, depending on the details of the activity, there is a certain amount of things that you could have beliefs about. If an activity is a very complex activity, like making nanomachines, there are *a lot* of things about which you could have beliefs. If an activity is very simple, such as tying your shoes, then there are relatively fewer beliefs that you could have—there's only so much you can know about how to tie your shoes. So given some activity, there is some amount of beliefs about the activity that one could have—I'll call these *possible beliefs*.[2]

So the more complicated an activity is, the more things there are about which you could have beliefs. Thus, there is some amount of possible beliefs relative to the activity, given how sophisticated or simple it is. Competent causation requires having some *percentage* of those possible beliefs. Jennifer, tying her shoes, might have 100 percent of the possible beliefs about shoe-tying—there isn't much to know, after all, so this doesn't take much. Nanotechnology, on the other hand, is complicated. Alec may know a lot about what he is doing in the laboratory, but he still nonetheless has *less than* the requisite percentage of JTBs to count as competently causing the nanomachine.

To be clear, complex activities have a higher *base* amount of possible beliefs, and so it takes a high *number* of JTBs to meet the requisite percentage. Simpler activities have a *low* base number of possible beliefs, and so it takes a relatively smaller *number* of JTBs to meet the requisite percentage. Thus Jennifer may have a smaller number of JTBs, but a higher percentage than Alec—the base amount is lower for Jennifer because her activity is simpler.

One might think that a percentage is impossible—surely the amount of justified and true beliefs that one possibly could have about making a nanomachine, or any other activity, is infinite. Taking a percentage would then be impossible.

---

[2] There is certainly more to be said about possible beliefs. We might suppose that possible beliefs are a matter of beliefs that are possible *for this particular agent* to have, given her particular abilities, available evidence, and other considerations; alternatively, beliefs might be possible relative to an *ideal* agent. For now I set these details aside and assume that the notion of possible beliefs is sufficiently commonsensical.

In some sense, this might be true. If we have a very liberal notion of what it is for a belief to be *about* something, and tally up absolutely everything that is about X in even the most rarified sense—including beliefs about modal properties, relational properties, and even so-called Cambridge properties—then to be sure the amount of beliefs would be infinite.

But it seems that there is a sense in which a belief is *about* something where we mean to exclude many of these beliefs that are "about" it only in the most rarified of senses. Consider, for example, beliefs about very outré Cambridge properties. Suppose that a new species of jellyfish has just evolved this year. As a result, there is now one more thing you could possibly know about tying your shoes, since the activity of tying your shoes has just acquired a new feature—it is now the activity of tying your shoes in a world where there is one more species of jellyfish than there was last year. But clearly how many species of jellyfish there are is totally irrelevant for tying your shoes. Although there is some sense in which one might want to say that beliefs about Cambridge properties are beliefs "about" the thing in question, there are other ways in which we can understand these beliefs as *not* about it.

What we have in mind when we say that a belief is *about* an activity in our discussion of competent causation and achievement, it is in this sense. Whatever the details amount to, we can at least see that there is not an infinite number of possible beliefs that are relevant about tying your shoelaces. What it would be like to tie your shoes in zero gravity using a pair of chopsticks in a world where Socrates never existed is not relevantly about the task of tying your shoes here, now, on earth using your hands.

But there is also an alternative approach available. There is an option to forgo the Percentage approach altogether and instead take a cue from how we have been understanding difficulty. On this approach, we appeal to a *threshold*. The threshold for how much you need to know in order to cause competently is set by the sort of activity in which you are engaged on this alternative approach. Different standards are relevant for different activities.

Either way, the general notion is the same: there is more to know about some activities, and competent causation requires a certain portion of that understanding. I will proceed using the Percentage approach, but the threshold view is an alternative that one could hold.

Time

But here is a case we might worry about:

Retrospect. A ϕs at t_1, thus causing E at t_2. From t_1 to t_2, A has no beliefs whatsoever about ϕ-ing. Time passes, and at t_3 long after A has finished with his ϕ-ing, A comes to have a thorough understanding of his ϕ-ing, and now understands that his ϕ-ing, back at t_1 through t_2, resulted in E.

Let's assume that the beliefs that A later comes to have about the nature of his activities—that is, about his ϕ-ing and it causing E—are sufficient in amount to what's required for competent causation. This means that the conditions of my account as presented so far are fulfilled: I'm committed to saying that A competently caused E. This doesn't seem right, since A had no idea what he was doing when he was causing E, and only came to understand how it all works later. The way in which something was caused cannot become competent retrospectively.

The best way to refine the account is with time-indexed beliefs: if A's ϕ-ing causes E, A causes E competently when, *while* ϕ-ing, A has the requisite measure of justified true beliefs about his ϕ-ing causing E. This new detail to the view requires that A must have JTBs about the nature of his ϕ-ing causing E *during* A's ϕ-ing.

Just to be clear—the requirement here is *not* that A should be *consciously entertaining* his beliefs while ϕ-ing. After all, many things that we would agree are caused competently don't involve a great deal of consciously entertained beliefs.

In fact, for some activities, their success may *depend* on not consciously entertaining any beliefs. I have in mind here in particular athletic activities, or other physical activities such as music performance or dance. Consciously entertaining beliefs about what you are doing when engaging in these kinds of activities can actually hamper performance, as many athletes and musicians confirm.[3] These performers, of course, *have* JTBs about what they are doing—but these beliefs are not being consciously entertained at the time of the activity. Needless to say, not entertaining beliefs about their activities does not detract from the degree of competent causation—quite the opposite, in fact, since it seems that alleviating oneself of consciously entertaining beliefs about the activity is actually a

---

[3] Cf. Gallwey, *The Inner Game of Tennis.*

coveted skill and thus an indication of a high degree of competence. So consciously entertaining JTBs is not necessary for competent causation; rather, it is having the beliefs while engaged in the action.

So far, then, it looks like the time-indexing revision to my view that I have made is all that is needed to accommodate cases such as Retrospect. The view, to sum, is this: A competently causes E via φ-ing when A's φ-ing causes E, and while φ-ing, A has some requisite amount of JTBs about his φ-ing causing E.

We might then wonder *when* during φ-ing the agent needs to have the requisite JTBs. Need the agent have *all* the beliefs *the whole time* that he is φ-ing? This seems excessive. It's not unusual to begin an activity without a particularly strong grasp of just what it is that your product will be. In such instances, thus, you do not have *all* the JTBs relevant for competent causation over the entire course of φ-ing, since you have fewer at the beginning of the activity than at the end. It seems that you still cause the product competently, even if you don't have all the relevant beliefs about it at the beginning of the process. You might cause the product *more* competently if you have all the JTBs the whole time. But it doesn't seem to be required that you have *all* the JTBs the *whole* time.

So you need not have all the requisite JTBs at every moment of φ-ing. What's the alternative? Simply that you have the full measure of JTBs *at some point* during φ-ing. On this approach, we can account for the very common occurrence that I just described, in which you don't *initially* have a thorough understanding of our activity when you begin, but develop a better understanding as you go.

It's not apparent that this approach will do, however. Although it makes sense in the kind of case we just considered, in which you add more beliefs as you go, it seems less plausible in the opposite kind of case, in which you *lose* beliefs as you go. If it is required to have simply the requisite amount of JTBs at some point or other while φ-ing, it follows that someone could have all the required beliefs, but then forget them all, even before having completed φ-ing—even before causing E—and yet still count as having caused E competently. So long as he has the beliefs at some point during his φ-ing, E is caused competently. The view further entails that you could cease to hold the original beliefs, and instead come to have *different, false* beliefs about what you're doing, and yet still count as competently causing E. These are indeed implications of the view.

But are these implications so counterintuitive as to suggest revision is necessary? It's not clear that they are. Here's an example that would illustrate this putative puzzle:

Hypnotized. Derek is a highly skilled scientist, and he is building a robot. Starting at t_1—he makes the plans, commences building. Suppose that this is very difficult. Part way through the process, at t_2, Derek falls prey to the mischief of his colleague Harry, who has taken up hypnotism as a hobby. Derek is hypnotized by Harry into believing that it is not a robot that he is building, but a chocolate cake that he is baking. Derek continues to go through all the motions building the robot, exactly according to his plans, but his beliefs are such that he takes himself to be baking a cake. Either way, it's difficult for Derek. At t_3 the robot is complete. Derek is still under the spell of Harry and thinks it's a chocolate cake.

Does Derek competently cause the robot? Speaking for myself, my intuitions are a little hazy. But it does seem clear to me that the robot was an *achievement* for Derek, and so I'm inclined to say that he does cause the robot sufficiently competently. Admittedly, this is a bit peculiar. But we can alleviate hesitation here by bearing in mind that "competent causation" is a term of art that I have introduced. It is not exactly an account of *competence*, but an account of understanding the way in which an outcome is produced, that is, the name for the relation that links up a difficult process with a product that distinguishes achievements from merely lucky outcomes. So if we are resistant to the idea that Derek may be competent, this is beside the point. The question is whether he caused the outcome competently, sufficiently enough for it to be an achievement for him.

So competent causation, then, is just as I described it earlier: if, while ϕ-ing, an agent has a requisite measure of JTBs about his ϕ-ing causing E, he causes E competently.

The Basic Belief

Yet we might think the view requires a further revision. We might wonder whether or not certain *kinds* of beliefs also play a role in determining how competently something is done. We already know that the beliefs that matter for competent causation are the agent's beliefs about his activity and its effects. But beliefs *about specifically what* matter? Is there any requirement for more specific content of beliefs?

One possibility is that there is *no* further specification of content. This view would hold that all that matters for competent causation is simply having *enough* of the relevant beliefs. Yet, if *no* further content requirement is specified, and only amount matters, then the following situation could arise:

> A ϕs, causes E, has beliefs about his many complex sub-goals q, r, s (i.e. that they are the sort of thing one should do in order to E), but *does not believe* that his ϕ-ing causes E.

It would be strange to say that A *competently caused* E. After all, A *has no idea* that he is causing E at all! But, suppose that A has many beliefs about his subgoals—enough so that they make up the requisite amount of JTBs about the nature of his activities. If only amount of JTBs matters for competent causation, then A *does* cause E competently. In other words, when only amount matters, if you have enough beliefs about the nature of your activities, you competently cause E, even if *you do not believe that you were causing E*. This doesn't seem right. Surely you can't be said to be competently causing E if you don't even think that you are causing E at all. We might be inclined to say that A is causing *something* competently—to wit, that which he believes he is causing, namely q, r, and s—but it doesn't seem right to say that you are competently causing E if you do not believe that you are causing E.

This suggests that there is a further requirement for competent causation. In particular, in order to count as competently causing E, you must have the basic belief *that you are causing E*. This *Basic Belief*, then, is necessary for competent causation: you must believe *that you are causing E*. This belief is necessary for E to be a candidate for competent causation. Let's call this requirement the *Basic Belief Requirement*.

Although initially plausible, however, the Basic Belief Requirement causes problems for the view. In particular, it denies competent causation in what we might call *pessimist* cases. Consider Dr Downer:

> *Pessimist Chemist.* Dr Downer, the chemist, is exceedingly pessimistic about her efforts to create compound X. In fact, she genuinely does not believe that what she is doing is going to result in X. Nonetheless, the way in which she is proceeding is indeed the very way that one

ought to go about making X, and Dr Downer fully understands that if there *were* a way to successfully create X, this would be it. She just does not believe that she is going to succeed. Dr Downer indeed creates X, but right afterwards, she drops dead. She never realized that she created X, and never once believed that what she was doing was, in fact, causing X.

If there is a Basic Belief Requirement, then Dr Downer does *not* cause X competently. But it seems to me quite clear that she does. Pessimist Chemist suggests that there is no basic belief requirement. Now, of course Dr Downer would cause X *more* competently if she had the Basic Belief. But the question here is whether or not having the Basic Belief is required to count as competently causing *at all*. Pessimist Chemist seems to suggest that the answer to this question is *no*.

Subtler versions of pessimist cases, I think, are not too uncommon. It's not unusual for people who are engaged in doing something that is very difficult to be so exceedingly pessimistic about the success of their endeavor that they believe that what they are doing is futile, and is *not* going to cause the product they are trying to cause. Yet these pessimists do it anyway. Even if they never truly believe that what they are doing causes the final product, they still may nonetheless do so. But surely, being a pessimist does not preclude the success from being an achievement, and so shouldn't preclude the claim that the pessimist has caused the product competently.

Moreover, there are further kinds of cases where requiring the Basic Belief would be problematic. In some kinds of activities, we might not even be in a position to *ever* know anything about whether or not the outcome has or ever will come about. Philosophical activity might be just such a case. We may never really be in a position to know whether or not the philosophical answers that we defend are indeed the right answers to the questions we've been asking. Yet surely, if, say, Jaegwon Kim's theory of supervenience is indeed the correct answer to the mind–body problem, we would want to say that Jaegwon Kim competently produced the solution to the mind–body problem. Surely this would be an achievement— we just may never be in a position to know this for sure. So I suggest we reject the Basic Belief Requirement.

And yet, still other cases suggest that a Basic Belief *is* necessary. Without the Basic Belief, the view entails that you could cause something competently even in a case like this: you have a very high number of *discrete* beliefs about the various steps in the process, but have *no* beliefs about how these steps are related to each other, and no beliefs about this process culminating in its product (I'll call cases like this one *Discrete Belief* cases). So long as you have a sufficient amount of JTBs about the individual steps in the process, my view appears to entail that, in a Discrete Belief case, you would still count as causing competently. This sounds especially bizarre since you *have no beliefs at all* about your activities causing the outcome—you have no idea at any point in the process not only about what the product of your activity is, nor about how the various things that you are doing are related. In cases where those individual steps are difficult, it follows that Discrete Belief cases are achievements.

I admit this is very counterintuitive. However, the following point is not insignificant: Discrete Belief cases would be very *rare*, if not *almost impossible*. Recall that not all JTBs are created equal—some are worth more than others. To be specific, *general*, overarching JTBs that tie together discrete individual steps into one unified whole are worth a lot more than discrete, unrelated beliefs. So without any overarching, general beliefs, it's very unlikely that someone would indeed have the sufficient measure of JTBs to count as competently causing. The overarching belief, that is, is so very weighty that it is virtually impossible to pile up enough individual beliefs to make up for its absence.

And yet, of course, I have to admit that it nonetheless could be possible to do so. Discrete Belief cases are indeed possible. Yet in a Discrete Belief case, there would have to be a very great amount of individual beliefs—the beliefs would have to be extremely detailed and in-depth. Even with such a detailed understanding of each discrete step of the process, would we still say that you had not competently caused the outcome, given that you had no idea how all the things that you were doing were related to it? It's not entirely clear.

So I'm going to resist modifying the view in light of Discrete Belief cases. Rather, I'll suggest a way to understand Discrete Belief cases which I hope will lessen any worries. In a Discrete Belief case, we can say that its product *was an achievement for you, even though you didn't know it*. That means that *you competently caused it, even though you didn't know it*.

Initially, this might sound at odds with the view. After all, my catch phrase for competent causation is "you know what you're doing." But put it this way, and it's less bizarre: in a Discrete Belief case, you know what you're doing—you just don't know that what you are doing was *this*. So I'm comfortable saying that the view makes it possible for there to be cases where there is a large pile of very discrete beliefs, no overarching belief tying the discrete beliefs to the final product, yet the final product is competently caused.

Just to be clear, however, the issue here is whether or not you count as competently causing *at all* in Discrete Belief cases. I made a point similar to this one earlier. Of course, you would be *more* competent if you *had* the overarching beliefs and the Basic Belief. And, given the weightiness of the overarching beliefs, you would be causing the product *significantly* more competently. I am certainly not denying that the product would be caused more competently in the case where overarching beliefs are present. Rather, my position is this: in Discrete Belief cases, if the question is whether or not the product may be *at all* competently caused, my answer turns out to be yes—however, *just barely*, in the best of cases, which are very *rare*. This isn't a horribly counterintuitive point after all.

So I have resisted including a Basic Belief requirement for competent causation. Doing so is not without cost, since this means that Discrete Belief cases can be competently caused, and, as a result, can be achievements. Yet including a requirement for a Basic Belief would *exclude* pessimists from having achievements, and perhaps more worryingly, pose a problem for philosophy.

Moreover, by rejecting the Basic Belief requirement, my view does very well in accounting for posthumous achievements. Someone may begin a project that only comes to fruition after his death, and, of course, after you die, you don't have any beliefs (or at least it's natural to suppose you don't). So someone who has worked very hard toward something may never actually believe that he brought it about. But I think we generally want to attribute such difficult activities to their authors posthumously as achievements. We can do so on my view.

Another benefit of rejecting the Basic Belief requirement is that it allows the view to capture certain kinds of *group achievements*. It's plausible that Roman civilization was an achievement. But of course, no particular Roman needs to have believed that his particular activities were part of the cause of a great civilization. On my view, we can have achievements where a number of agents have a great deal of beliefs about their particular contribution to the final product, but no one has a belief that unites all the contributions of the agents in causing the final product.

The case is similar to a Discrete Belief case, where the members of a group can each have a high number of beliefs about all of their discrete activities, all of which cause a final product, but no agent in the group has any beliefs about the final product. So we have another reason not to worry too much about Discrete Belief cases being problematic, since they are helpful in the analogous group example. We will return to look at group achievements in Chapter 6.

Further Issues

You may have noticed a curious feature of my view. Since only true justified beliefs are relevant for competent causation, false beliefs play no role. You might think that false beliefs do indeed have a significant role to play—in particular, you might think that the more false beliefs you have, the *less* competently you are causing. Is this something that my view should be revised to capture? It is, after all, a very natural thought. False or unjustified beliefs ought to count against you—being *wrong* about what you are doing seems to be the very hallmark of incompetence. We can see this thought illustrated with some drivers.

Rudy and Judy are both good drivers, and they both get in their respective Smart Cars and drive to the grocery store. They are both good drivers, yet neither of them has a particularly strong grasp of how cars work, Smart or otherwise.

Rudy has a lot of beliefs about how cars work—but many of his beliefs are *false* beliefs. He thinks that under the hood there is a big Duracell, and inside the Duracell there are little demons running around, and this is what powers the Smart Car.

Surely these crazy ideas about what makes the car go make Rudy a less competent driver than Judy. Rudy's false beliefs about how the car works make it the case that he causes the car to drive *less competently* than Judy causes her car to drive.

Suppose that, being equally good drivers, Rudy and Judy have the *same* justified and true beliefs about driving the car. Since my account gives no discount for having false or unjustified beliefs, this entails that their levels of competent causation are *equal*. That seems funny. It seems like Rudy is *less* competent than Judy. In light of this unpalatable result, maybe my account is in need of further revision. Should I amend the view so that a discount of competence is taken off when we have false beliefs?

I do not think such a revision is necessary. In fact, when we take a closer look at our example of Rudy and Judy, we see that they are not actually causing their driving competently to the same degree.

It only seems at first pass that Rudy and Judy have the same amount of justified *true* beliefs, but they *don't*. Here is why: for every false belief about demons that Rudy has, Judy has a *true* belief that these things are *not* what is making the car go. She might not know what *does* makes it go, but she knows that things like demons and so on don't exist, so she also doesn't believe that these are what's making the car go. Judy, thus, has *more* JTBs about her activities than Rudy does about his; to wit, Judy justifiedly and truly believes that the car is *not* running on demon power.

On our first pass, we were confusing Judy's driving with a different sort of case, like the following one. Another driver, Julie, is *agnostic* about demons. This means that she does *not* have negative beliefs about whether or not the engine runs on demon power. She doesn't have any of the commonsense negative beliefs about her driving that Judy does. Yet Julie *does* have just as many and no more JTBs about driving than Rudy does.

Since Rudy and Julie have exactly the same amount and kind of JTBs about their activities, my view entails that Rudy and Julie are indeed competently causing their driving to just the same degree. Julie does *not* get the bonus of the additional JTBs with negative content about the demons that Judy has. And similarly Rudy does not get penalized for having false beliefs that Julie lacks, given her agnosticism.

But just how bad does this seem? Not really bad at all. Julie doesn't have the benefit of even having a basic negative understanding that would eliminate crackpot hypotheses from being true. So it doesn't seem quite so crazy to say that Julie and Rudy are on a par in terms of competently causing their driving, and Judy fares better, as far as competent causation goes. So I don't feel the need to refine the view to incorporate a discount for each false belief.

Here, then, is what competent causation amounts to. Given that A causes some outcome E, A competently causes E via his activity, ϕ, when A, while ϕ-ing, has the requisite amount of JTBs about his ϕ-ing causing E. The requisite amount is a percentage from the total possible beliefs about the activity, and JTBs that are about the overall structure of the activity are worth more than discrete beliefs.

But this is only one way that we might understand competent causation. There might be other approaches that characterize competent causation equally well. Let us now consider some other resources.

Alternatives

I have more or less taken *knowing what* you're doing to be the relevant ingredient, but an alternative might be *knowing how*. "Knowing how" might amount to having some set of propositional beliefs, or it might include more than this.[4] If the former, then it wouldn't be very different from what I have just proposed. Regardless, knowing how could be an alternative candidate for understanding what's at stake in competent causation.

Of course, knowing how isn't sufficient for competent causation, since one can know how to bring about some result yet fail to do so. Moreover, one can even engage in the very activity that one knows how to do, and bring about the relevant product, and yet fail to do so in the right sort of way, as the cases considered earlier show, such as Rewarding Benefactor. Don knows how to hunt for treasure, and does so in the way that he knows how, but doesn't competently cause his finding it.

We might say, then, that first, one must know how to cause the product, and be causing it in the way that one knows how, *and* one must also know that one is indeed causing the product *in the very way that one knows how*. So we might understand competent causation this way—one not only knows how to do the thing one is doing, but knows *de re* of one's activity that one is doing it in the way that one knows how. One might say the achievement must be brought about via the very activity that one knows how to do and one knows that this is what one is doing. So in this respect, we could understand knowledge-how to be at play in competent causation.

Nevertheless, doing so has curious results. Inventions and discoveries can constitute achievements, such as Alexander Graham Bell's invention of the telephone. But would we really want to say that Bell *knows how to invent the telephone*? This has an air of peculiarity about it. Inventing isn't really something that one can properly be said to know how to do. The same

---

[4] See John Bengson and Marc A. Moffet (eds), *Knowing How: Essays on Knowledge, Mind, and Action* (Oxford: OUP, 2011) for a collection of views on knowing how.

can be said about other one-offs, such as discoveries. Knowledge-how attributions appear to evoke the possibility of a repeat performance, but this of course is impossible in these cases.

The issue can be resolved if we alter the description of the achievement and that Bell's achievement was *making* the first telephone. Accordingly Bell *knows how to make* a telephone. Or at least he does after he has struggled and succeeded. So perhaps it's not so peculiar after all. On the other hand, we might be inclined to think that mischaracterizes something significant about the achievement. Bell *figured out how* to make the telephone, and this isn't captured by the know-how assessment. This reveals details concerning temporality once again. It's not necessary that one know how to do the thing that one achieves at the outset of the process. Rather, it seems that it's sufficient to know how at some point in the process. Just what this would amount to is a matter I'll leave open for exploration.

Another alternative is that, rather than knowledge, one might be inclined to take competent causation as involving *understanding*.[5] Indeed, in several passages I talk about competent causation as if it was a matter of *understanding* what you are doing. Of course, my use of this term earlier wasn't technical, yet there may be a deeper truth here. It is very natural to claim that more you *understand* about your activities and its product, the more competent you are. And understanding certainly admits of degrees, which is essential for competent causation. So perhaps competent causation could be analyzed as a matter of having an understanding about the nature of one's activities and their product.

If we construe competent causation in terms of understanding, we can relieve ourselves of some details of the account that I gave earlier that concern degrees. The account I proposed involves an amount of individual beliefs. Appealing to understanding instead would alleviate the need for the details considered earlier including the relevant requisite amount of beliefs, and so on. Instead, we can construe competent causation in terms of sufficient degree of understanding, whatever that might turn out to be.

For now, in what follows I will make use of the analysis in terms of JTBs since they provide an easy and appealing building block for degrees of

[5] Perhaps the most comprehensive discussion of understanding is Jonathan Kvanvig, *The Value of Knowledge and the Pursuit of Understanding* (Cambridge: CUP, 2003).

competence of causation. But the view is amenable to reconstrual with an alternative epistemic state. What I say here can be taken ecumenically concerning these issues. What's important is that achievement involves having a proper grasp of one's activities and their relationship to the product in which they culminate. This is essential for achievement.

4

The Value of Achievement

So far, we have seen what it is that achievements have in common. What characterizes climbing a mountain, developing a cure for cancer, performing a violin concerto, or baking a soufflé as achievements is that each of them is a *difficult* process that *competently causes* a product. In Chapter 2, I dug the surprising depths of what it is for something to be difficult, and in Chapter 3, I developed the notion of competent causation.

Now that we have a solid handle on what achievements are, we can turn to the question of what makes achievements *valuable as such*. To be clear, the aim is not simply to fill out yet another item on that objective list. Although it would be a worthwhile endeavor simply to do this, there are two more reasons why this is more significant than perhaps other objective list items. First, it's *neglected*. Pleasure, knowledge, and beauty are all objective A-listers—philosophical discussion abounds. But achievements have yet to even have 15 minutes of fame.

There is also a second reason why achievements are special. Achievements hit close to home for us as academics, or so we'd like to think. After all, no doubt a very large part of the reason why we do what we do is because we think that what we are doing is good and worth doing. But being an academic philosopher isn't good in all the ways that, say, being a pediatrician for Doctors Without Borders is good. We're not in this to save lives (although, for all we know, this may happen along the way). More puzzling still, many philosophers also aren't in this to produce the next great book of Western civilization—after all, there can only be so many Aristotles or Descarteses for each generation, and most of us are aware of this, and contentedly aware of the fact that this isn't us. Most of us will not be writing *the* great tome that survives for generations to come. But this fact (perhaps I speak for myself) does not diminish the value of our smaller, perhaps more ephemeral philosophical accomplishments. No doubt writing this book is difficult, and I hope very much that my own understanding of my work will be sufficient so that it will be competently caused. But what's so good about that? It's certainly not going to save any lives and, while no doubt I will feel a sense of personal satisfaction at my accomplishment, that feeling certainly doesn't account fully for its value.

This is the crucial question for not just philosophers, but for everyone who strives for achievements. *Why bother?* What's so great about this? At the risk of sounding dramatic, it's a sort of Camus-like moment we should be having here. The only truly worrisome philosophical question is, *what's so significant about what we do that makes it worth the effort?* If it's not, after all, why not just quit?

Getting down to business, the question here will be whether it is the *difficulty* that grounds the value of achievements, or *competency of causation* that grounds it, or whether both ground it, or neither do. Given my view, it's natural to think that difficulty and competent causation have something to do with the value of achievements. But I'll begin by considering a view that rejects difficulty and competent causation as relevant for the value of achievements. According to this view, neither of these essential features is the source of the value of achievements. Rather, on this view the source of the value of achievements is the value of their *product*.

The Simple Product View

Here's a very natural thought: if you're engaged in some activity that is aimed at some end, the activity is only as good as its end. If the end isn't valuable, it's just pointless, wasted effort. This thought leads people to believe that engaging in difficult activity is *worthless* by itself, and only of instrumental value, at best, insofar as it brings about some valuable product.

Wasted effort, in fact, seems to be not just of no intrinsic value, but worse. Difficulty that does not result in anything good may be of *negative value*. Difficult activities that come to nothing in the end are generally considered to be something *bad*. Just think of Sisyphus, rolling his rock up the mountain. This seems to be the very archetype of meaninglessness, according to virtually everyone except Camus. Difficulty appears to be of *negative* value. It is only instrumentally valuable at best, in those cases where it does indeed result in something of positive value. When it fails to result in anything of value, it is worthless, and maybe even worse. So what's valuable about achievements is the *product*—the bottom line, the output. What you get at the end of the day.

The Simple Product view captures these sentiments. According to the Simple Product view, achievements are valuable because of what they achieve. The value of an achievement on this view is entirely a matter of the value of the product. And, to be specific, the value of the product is entirely independently of its being difficultly produced and competently caused.

According to the Simple Product view, the difficulty and competent causation of the process of the achievement is irrelevant to determining the value of the achievement. Of course, difficulty and competent causation are necessary to guarantee the status of an activity as an achievement at all. But according to this view, the degree of difficulty and the degree of competence of causation are *irrelevant* for determining value. They guarantee achievement status, but do not contribute value. Rather, the value of the achievement is determined by the value of the product.[1]

The Simple Product view, I believe, captures the popular conception of the value of achievement I mentioned at the beginning of this section. Most people seem to think that what makes achievements valuable is the value of the thing that you get when you're done, regardless of how it came about. What really matters is the bottom line. Finding the cure for cancer, most people would say, isn't made more valuable by being so difficult to do—it's valuable because it is the cure for cancer. I may be wrong that this is the most commonly held folk conception of value of achievements. Nonetheless, the Simple Product view is a plausible view about the value of achievement.

According to the Simple Product view, then, what makes curing cancer a valuable achievement is that *it results in a cure for cancer*. A cure for cancer saves millions of lives, and this is valuable. The value of saving

[1] In what follows, I focus on the issue of *difficulty*, which the Simple Product view holds as irrelevant for the value of achievements. But the Simple Product view also holds that the degree of competent causation is irrelevant for value. Presumably, there could be a version of the Simple Product view that excludes difficulty as relevant for value, but includes degree of competent causation. But this view would be subject to the same objections as the Simple Product view as considered here, since its flaws result from its exclusion of difficulty. I take it as essential to any version of the Simple Product view that difficulty be excluded.

millions of lives, according to the Simple Product view, *just is* the value of the achievement of curing cancer, whether or not it was difficult to achieve or competently caused. Similarly, Picasso's *Guernica* is a valuable achievement because it is an incredible painting. The value of the painting includes its aesthetic value, cultural and historical significance, and so on, and its being difficult and competently caused are irrelevant. According to the Simple Product view, the value of the painting as such is what *constitutes* its value as an achievement. It is what makes *Guernica* an artistic achievement. This seems entirely plausible as an account of the value of this achievement.

But as plausible as the Simple Product view may seem initially, it is subject to serious objections. Most strikingly, there appears to be no good account for the value of achievements with *zero-value* products.

There are many particularly valuable and impressive achievements with products that have *no* value on their own. Climbing Mt Everest is a perfect example. Being on top of a mountain, just by itself, is intrinsically valueless. The value of being on top of a mountain is clearly zero. If being on top of a mountain had any particular value, then taking a helicopter to get to the top would be just as valuable as climbing by your own efforts.[2] This clearly seems false. The value of climbing a mountain is in the *climbing*, not in *being* at the top.[3] The Simple Product view seems to tell us that the value of summiting Mt Everest is zero, which is clearly wrong.

But the view can offer this reply: the goal of climbing Mt Everest isn't simply to *be* on the top of the mountain. It's to *get* to the top of the mountain in a particular way, namely by climbing. The climbing *is* the product— the process by which the product is attained is itself *part* of the product. So the view can account for the value of climbing Mt Everest by appealing to the value of the process of climbing, which is itself also part of the product. Presumably, climbing a mountain has value. There is value in displaying the virtues of courage, tenacity, physical skill, and endurance, and so on. Since climbing a mountain has value, and the climbing is the product, or

---

[2] Contrary to my own example here, however, taking a helicopter to the top of Mt Everest would, as a matter of fact, be incredibly difficult, and take days of logistical planning, not to mention expert piloting skills. I credit my classmate the mountaineer and philosopher Heidi Lockwood with pointing this out.

[3] A similar example plays a prominent role in possibly the most underappreciated philosophy book of all time, Bernard Suits, *The Grasshopper* (Toronto: Broadview Press, 2005).

is an element of the product, the achievement of climbing the mountain appears to have a value greater than zero.

I certainly agree that there are achievements whose product is part of the process. Typical examples of process-as-product achievements are performances, such as musical or dance performances, where the very product of the performance is that the performing be carried out. What I called "zero-value product achievements" are (in most cases) actually process-as-product achievements. The product of climbing a mountain isn't *only* being at the top of the mountain, but *climbing* the mountain and subsequently arriving at the top. The climbing is a sort of performance and, let's grant, is valuable. Thus, it seems that the Simple Product approach *can* account for the value of these achievements. So-called zero-value product achievements, then, don't really have zero-value products. Their product *includes* their process, and so they have value insofar as the process has value. Admittedly, it's not clear that *all* zero-value product achievements will have valuable processes, and whether or not they do will depend on what it is that *grounds* the value of the process (product in this case). But in those cases where the process-performance does have value, the Simple Product view *can* account for the value of these achievements.

And yet this response is not enough to save the Simple Product view from the objection, for we need to ask *why* would the climbing of the mountain have greater than zero value? The Simple Product view, after all, can only account for the value of mountain climbing if the value of climbing is *independent* of its being difficult or competently caused. Yet the most plausible account of why climbing a mountain has a value greater than zero is, perhaps, because it is a great display of virtue, involving courage, tenacity, physical skill, endurance, and so on. Exercising these virtues, the story could go, is of intrinsic value. Insofar as climbing a mountain displays these virtues it's of greater than zero value. But to say this is just to give an account of *why engaging in difficult activity is valuable.* So in claiming that climbing has value, the Simple Product view *is* appealing to the difficulty after all. And this is precisely what the Simple Product view wants to *deny*. This view holds that difficulty is *irrelevant* for the value of achievements. So the Simple Product view cannot account for the value of zero-product achievements by appealing to the value of the virtues displayed in difficult activity.

Moreover, this view suffers from a further flaw. There is a very strong intuition that hard work, perseverance, and effort matter for the value of an achievement. Even if it is not obvious at first how much effort matters, it is clear that it does indeed play a role in determining the value of an achievement. Yet the Simple Product view isn't able to distinguish between the difference in value between achievements with a product of similar value caused in the usual way, on the one hand, and as a result of overcoming exceptional obstacles and adversity on the other.

In the following example, Smith and Jones, over the course of a year, each write a very good novel, each novel as good as the other.

A Tale of Two Novels

I. Smith. Smith's experience working on his novel was typical for a novelist (if there is such a thing as a typical novel-writing experience). There were ups and downs, periods of writer's block, months of carefully finessed work that ended up not being useful for the book, pressure from the editor, but also enjoyable and productive days, and so on.

II. Jones. Jones endured hardships similar to Smith's, and, in addition, suffered major obstacles. Jones' house burned down, along with everything he owned (not to mention several months worth of work on the novel), his dog died, and his wife left him. In addition, Jones suffers greatly from depression, which can make an ordinary day—let alone a productive one—utterly agonizing. In spite of all this, Jones has struggled and fought, and in spite of these obstacles, he has produced his novel, equally as good as Smith's.

Assuming that both Smith and Jones exert sufficient effort and competently cause their novels, writing both their novels are achievements for Smith and Jones respectively. While both novels are equally good (assuming it's possible for two different novels to be equally good), I think it seems quite clear that there is a significant way in which Jones' achievement is *a better achievement*. Thus it seems that effort matters for the value of achievements.

This element, however, is just not captured by the Simple Product view. According to the Simple Product view, the only source of value in Smith's and Jones' achievements is in the value of their novels—that is, the value of the products of their achievements. The difficulty and competent causation are irrelevant to the value of their achievements. This does not capture the relevance of Jones' remarkable struggle. According to the Simple Product view, the value of an achievement is equal to the value of its product. It's clear that Jones' triumphs over these obstacles matter, so we should reject the Simple Product view.

In order to save itself, the Simple Product view needs deny one of these:

1. The value in Jones' achievement is greater than the value of Smith's achievement.
2. The value of the product of Smith's achievement and the value of the product of Jones' achievement is the same.

To deny 1 is to say that there is just *no value* in Jones' overcoming adversity. My reply to this is that I simply do not have that intuition. Like most people, I have a strong and clear intuition that triumphing over extraordinary obstacles is valuable. Succeeding in the face of incredible difficulty is appropriately met with respect, awe, admiration, and approval, all of which are pro-attitudes that we think are appropriate responses to things that have intrinsic value. If you don't share this intuition, I'm not sure that there is anything that I could say here that would convince you—it's just among the things that most people have a very strong intuition about being valuable. Clearly people who are unmoved by such intuitions won't feel the pressure of this argument. But for most of us, I think that we'll want to say that there is more value to Jones' achievement than there is to Smith's. Fans of the Simple Product approach who agree with me will have to move on to try to deny claim 2.

Yet one might first object that 1 begs the question. The claim in 1 is that the values of the two achievements are different, but this is precisely what's at issue; namely, what it is that determines the value of an achievement. Thus, a proponent of the Simple Product view would accuse me of pulling the famous "one man's counterexample is another man's question-beg" move. Now, it seems quite clear to me that the intuition that the values differ is strong enough for this to be a genuine counterexample. Nevertheless, there is another claim to consider:

3. The total value in I is equal to the value of Smith's achievement, and the total value in II is equal to the value of Jones' achievement.

That is, the achievements in both scenarios account fully for the total value of each scenario. The intuition remains that there is more value in II than in I.

Of course, the proponent of the Simple Product view could try to deny that the total value in I and in II is sourced entirely in the value of the achievements. One could try to say that Jones' triumph is indeed additionally valuable, but that this value *is not part of the value of Jones' achievement*. Indeed, says the response, displaying perseverance and courage are valuable—they are virtues, and it is valuable to exercise virtue. This value is what accounts for the additional value in II. It's not the case that Jones' achievement is more valuable, it's that he has displayed his virtues of courage and perseverance, and it is his exercising these virtues that is valuable. The total value in II *is* greater than I, but the difference in value isn't a difference in the value of achievements, but is accounted for by the additional value of Jones' display of virtue.

Yet this response falls into the same trap as similar moves made by the Simple Product view earlier. This response acknowledges that difficulty is valuable, and so ultimately agrees with my position, since displaying perseverance just is to exert effort and do something difficult.

But to acknowledge that doing something difficult is valuable isn't quite the same as the position that it is the difficulty *that makes the achievement valuable*. One could coherently have a view where difficulty is valuable (due to the exercise of virtue, or perhaps something else), but it contributes nothing to the value of achievements. But why would anyone want to have such a position? Difficulty, after all, is an *essential* feature of all achievements. To say that difficulty is (either itself or derivatively) valuable, and that it always is present when an achievement is present, and yet insist that its value has no role to play in the value of achievements would be a strange position to have. It's true that it's a coherent position, but unless there is some strong theoretical pressure to accept it that we haven't uncovered yet, it's not a very appealing position at all. A Simple Product fan might cling to it, but only out of sheer dogmatism.[4]

---

[4] Yet there is a plausible approach that denies that the total value in I and II is entirely sourced in the value of achievements, even when difficulty *is* captured on the value of achievements view. Such a position would double-count the value of difficulty: the difficulty makes the achievement valuable, and Jones' exercising virtue is itself of further intrinsic value. So in II, according to this double-counting approach, the net value is *not* entirely a matter of the achievement-value, but also includes Jones' exercising virtue. If double-counting is right, I will concede denying that there is the same amount of value in I as there is in II. But to deny this on these grounds is not the same as denying it for the reasons that Simple Product would like to deny it—Jones' achievement is still more valuable in virtue of its additional difficulty on this approach, which Simple Product denies. As a result, denying 3 in this way would not lend support to the Simple Product view (quite the contrary, since this position embraces the role of difficulty in the value of achievements).

Denying 1, then, is clearly implausible for the Simple Product. But what about 2? Claim 2 is that the value of the product of Smith's achievement is the same as the value of the product of Jones' achievement. *Ex hypothesi* the value of the two novels is the same. But, as a clever fan of Simple Product can point out, the *products* of the achievements might not in fact be the same. If the *process can be included in the product* of achievements, and the *processes* of the achievements in I and II are different, then the *products* in I and II are different from what we originally thought they were. If the products are different, then it might be the case that the values of these products are different. The fan of Simple Product who shares the intuition that 1 is correct will indeed want to make this claim in order to preserve the truth of his view.

However, this move is unsuccessful. Although, as we saw earlier, there are many achievements where the process is part of the achievement, writing a novel just doesn't seem to be such an achievement. The *novel* is the product of the achievement, and the writing process is not properly speaking part of the product in the same way that the climbing is part of the product of climbing a mountain. The novel is quite distinctly the product of the achievement, and the writing process is the process. Claiming that the writing process is actually part of the product of writing a novel is a bit of a stretch.

Even if we pretend to be flexible enough to accommodate a stretch as implausible as this one, Simple Product still cannot account for the difference in the values of the achievements on its own terms. To agree that the values of the (stretched out, process included) products in I and II are different is simply to *agree with me* that difficulty plays a role in determining the value of achievements. The only difference between I and II, according to my examples, is that Jones has struggled to overcome many more obstacles than Smith. Once again, the Simple Product view falls into the trap. If we think that there is more value in II, that's just to say that difficulty plays a role in shaping the value of achievement, and this is precisely my point.

Ultimately, then, the Simple Product account can't capture the difference in value between Jones' achievement and Smith's. It's clear that difficulty matters for the value of achievements, and Simple Product denies this. So we should reject it.

All this, however, is not meant to say that the products of achievements have no value that contributes to the overall value of achievements. I think that they *can*. I address this in the next chapter.

Difficulty: Worth the Effort

Difficulty may at first seem like an unlikely candidate for a source of value, yet we have already seen very good evidence that difficulty does indeed matter for the value of achievements. Most clearly, achievements that have inherently valueless products gain value in virtue of their difficulty. In mountain climbing, the state of affairs that one aims at—being on top of a mountain—is valuable *only* in the instance when it is attained in a difficult manner, keeping the other features the same. If we get to the top of the mountain by taking a helicopter or an escalator, it's not especially valuable. So it seems that at least in these cases—achievements with zero-value products—difficulty is responsible for the value of the achievement. More vividly, we also saw in *A Tale of Two Novels* that difficulty matters for the value of achievements that also have products of value greater than zero.

Further, the value of achievements increases as difficulty increases. The *more* difficult getting to the top of the mountain is, the more valuable it seems to be. Holding the other features of the achievement constant, it seems to be the case that the *more* hardships that are overcome, and struggles that are endured, the greater the value of summiting a mountain. The value of the achievement of reaching the top of the mountain increases with difficulty, other things being equal. Similarly, it was difficult for Smith to write his novel, but it was more difficult for Jones to write his, and accordingly, Jones' achievement is more valuable.

There are real-life examples that illustrate this point as well. Consider, for example, winning a medal at the Olympic Games. This, I take it, is an impressive and valuable achievement, and no doubt (at least in part) because it's very difficult to do. It takes courage and perseverance to endure a lifetime of training, not to mention focus, presence of mind, and strategy on the day of the event. All of these elements require a high degree of effort. So clearly winning an Olympic medal is a valuable achievement. The winner of the 1992 bronze medal in women's single sculls rowing, Silken Laumann, however, not only persevered through all the usual trials of a lifetime of training, but, just 10 weeks before the Olympic Games, she was in a collision with another boat on a training day, and suffered a horrifying leg injury. Incredibly, she managed to continue her training and triumphantly won the bronze medal.[5] The added

[5] <http://sportsillustrated.cnn.com/events/1996/olympics/daily/july21/laum.html>, retrieved June 2009.

difficulty of her achievement, it seems to me, makes her bronze medal an even more impressive and valuable achievement than winning a gold medal would be for an athlete who had not endured such additional difficulties. So increasing difficulty of an achievement increases its value.

But surely there is an air of absurdity to this idea. It can't be right that making all our accomplishments *more difficult* makes them better. If it were, then it would appear to follow that we should make every task that we undertake as difficult for ourselves as we can! If difficulty is valuable, we ought to want to have as much of it in our lives as possible. My position about the value of difficulty seems to advocate an absurd lifestyle, replete with needless difficulty.[6]

This objection both gets it right and gets it wrong. The objection misses the mark, however, in that it concerns how we should act—and I've made no claims about that here. I have only been talking about what is *good*, and not about what we ought to do. Of course, it is perfectly reasonable to hold, as many people do, that we ought to pursue what's good. Supposing that is true, this objection points out that because I have said that difficulty is good, it follows that we should pursue difficulty at every opportunity, and so I advocate an absurd life of needlessly difficult tasks.

But I haven't claimed that achievements are the only valuable thing, so of course, when we are deciding how to spend our time, achievements will need to be weighed against the other valuable elements in life. It need not follow that we ought to take every opportunity to engage in difficulty that presents itself to us. It seems perfectly plausible that there are *other* things that are also worth pursuing, such as knowledge, or pleasure.

Moreover, even if the value of achievements were the *only* thing that were valuable, it does not follow that we should take every opportunity to make absolutely every activity we engage in as difficult for ourselves as possible. We're mortal, after all, and our time is limited. It's plausible that it's good to achieve as much as we can in the time that we're given, and it seems that we might be able to achieve *more* if we ration our time and efforts in certain ways. Further, we've seen some indication that some achievements are *more valuable* than others. If we make every mundane task absurdly difficult for ourselves, then it seems likely we won't have time and energy left to pursue the best achievements we can devote

---

[6] Douglas Portmore advances an objection like this in "Welfare, Achievement, and Self-Sacrifice," *Journal of Ethics and Social Philosophy,* 2 (2007): 1–28.

ourselves to. All this, of course, assumes that we should go for quality over quantity, when it comes to achievements. This may turn out to be false, but it seems plausible to assume for now. So my position that difficulty is a source of value does not, in the end, entail a life of pointlessly absurd difficult tasks.

Yet I hinted that there is something that this objection gets right, as well. My view is that difficulty is of positive value. But is this really so absurd? As we have just considered, there are often other values that compete for our time and energy. The value of difficulty is often eclipsed by other, more pressing necessities of daily life. But we can see the value of difficulty for what it is if we dim the brightness of the competing values for a moment. If we truly want to consider the intrinsic value of difficulty, we need to imagine ourselves unhampered by the necessities of daily life.

Almost all of our time is spent in activities that are instrumentally necessary for attaining important and vital ends that are themselves necessary for—well, for whatever it is that is of the highest good. We work to make money to pay for food and shelter to take care of ourselves and our families, so that ultimately we can do those things that we think are of intrinsic value, whatever they might be. There are only so many hours in a day, and it takes a lot of work to get all these things that we need, just so that we can live a reasonable life. So it's hard to imagine that difficulty is valuable when there are so many things competing for our time and energy—it seems we value efficiency and expediency, if anything. But once we peel away the instrumentally necessary activities, we see the value of difficulty for what it is, shining, perhaps even jewel-like.

Let's imagine what it would be like if we didn't *have to* do anything. Let's imagine, then, a Utopia, where everything we could possibly need is at arms' reach, or at the touch of a button. This is the Utopia we find in *The Grasshopper*—there is no poverty to alleviate, there is world peace, not only does fruit grow on trees, but so do sandwiches and five-course meals. [7] All the problems of science and philosophy are available in the Universal Book of Answers, which we may consult at anytime, as if it were the fully complete and authoritative Wikipedia. Moreover, we can instantly attain any mental state we want, just by popping a pill—tranquility, pleasure, total bliss, whatever we wish, instantly. In this Utopia, all the necessities of life and everything we could possibly want is available at the touch of a

---

[7] Suits, *The Grasshopper*, 149 ff.

button, and, as Schopenhauer imagines it, everything grows of itself, and pigeons fly around roasted.[8]

Schopenhauer, being Schopenhauer, thinks that we would all go bananas with boredom, but the less pessimistic among us think just the opposite. If we didn't *have* to do anything, wouldn't it seem that we could enrich any daily task by increasing its difficulty—by making it a game? Indeed, just picking off a cheese soufflé from the soufflé tree *would* be boring (or it would be boring after the fifteenth time), but what would be lots of fun is attempting to make this difficult dish, and successfully perfecting these gourmet cooking skills. In our Utopia, your dream house can appear with the wave of a wand, but *building* your dream house with your own two hands would be far more satisfying and exciting. And so, in our land of Cockaigne, we would make our lives abundant with achievements, were we so unconstrained.

What we would be doing in Utopia is significant. In Utopia, since everything that we could possibly need or want is available at the touch of a button, there isn't anything that is *necessary* for us to do in order to get something that we want. Our every wish simply appears before us, as we command it. In Utopia it's always possible to skip steps in any activity—no activity is necessary. Don't want to climb the mountain to get to the top? Take the escalator! Don't want to mix the batter to bake a cake? Pick a cake growing on the cake tree! Don't want to drive the car to get to the beach? Teletransport! In our Utopia, every activity that is merely instrumental is eliminated—simply by the sheer existence of these alternatives. Everything we want, we can instantly have: so it's always possible *not* to engage in an activity.

It seems that among the things that we might do in Utopia—Schopenhauer aside—are many of the things that outside of Utopia are necessary. We would, it seems, undertake a great many difficult projects—such as building houses and baking cakes. Even if these products were available for us, instantly and ready made, as well as everything else we could possibly need or want, we would still value undertaking the process that results in them. Even though we *could* just pick a cake off the cake tree, it seems that we *would*—at least sometimes—choose to bake a cake by ourselves. And even though we could instantly have the house of our dreams,

---

[8] Arthur Schopenhauer, *Parerga and Paralipomena*, tr. E. F. J. Payne, ii II (Oxford: Clarendon Press, 1974), 293, section 152.

many of us would choose to undertake building our house with our own two hands. Even though we could instantly beam to the top of Mt Everest, many of us would choose to climb to the summit by way of our own efforts.

Since all these activities are entirely unnecessary in Utopia, that is, unnecessary for acquiring the products in which they culminate, there must be something about the *processes themselves* that is choiceworthy for its own sake. We do not, it turns out, just value the activities of cake-baking and house-building and mountain climbing because they result in cakes, houses, and being on top of mountains. We value these activities *themselves*. And it seems that we are right in valuing these activities. Insofar as any activity is worth doing, it is worth doing at least in part for its own sake, and so plausibly intrinsically valuable.

What is it that these activities have in common? They are all *needless*—we don't have to do them. But we have made the case such that these activities are unnecessary in order to see if they have intrinsic value. The needlessness, remember, was brought in by the thought experiment to isolate the activities to see if they are valuable in themselves or only because they lead to further valuable ends. And it turns out that these activities are not valuable only because they lead to further valuable ends. Still, it's not the needlessness that's doing any of the work in making these activities valuable—it's just what allows us to see that these activities are valuable themselves.

A further thing that all these needless activities have in common is that they are all—to one degree or another—*difficult*. They may share some other features too, but at least we can say this much: these activities all require some effort. Now, I haven't yet shown anything from which we can conclude that these activities are valuable in virtue of being difficult or needlessly difficult, but at the very least we now can see that all these intrinsically valuable activities are also all difficult.

Yet some people might find themselves thinking that this doesn't mean that it is *intrinsically* valuable to do things that are difficult. Maybe what we are responding to in this thought experiment is that we would do *anything* in order to stave off the incredible boredom that might set in while in Utopia. So difficult activity is of necessary instrumental value in this respect—it's necessary for our sanity.

But in our Utopia, as you will remember, there is no worry that we would ever become bored. There are pills that we can take give us whatever mental state we want, so feelings of boredom can be eliminated instantly. There are no activities that we would *have* to engage in to alleviate boredom.

Fair enough, then, difficult activities are indeed intrinsically valuable—in Utopia. But skeptics can object: it's not yet clear that difficulty is valuable *in the real world*. After all, this Utopia is highly contrived and entirely unlike the real world.

What exactly is this objection getting at? On the dominant view, if something has intrinsic value, *then it has intrinsic value*—meaning that if something ever has intrinsic value, then it always has intrinsic value. Our reflections on Utopia indicate that difficulty has intrinsic value—if it's valuable over here in Utopia, then it's valuable anywhere, and that's just what it means to have intrinsic value. So it doesn't really make sense to object that something could have intrinsic value over there, in Utopia, but fail to have intrinsic value over there, in the real world.

However, intrinsic value may be *conditional*. Something is of conditional intrinsic value when it is of value *as an end*, but it *only* has that value providing that certain conditions obtain. Kant, for example, thinks that happiness is of intrinsic value, but that it is only of intrinsic value when it is the happiness of someone who is virtuous. The condition for happiness being of intrinsic value for Kant is virtue. Happiness in the absence of virtue is not valuable.[9]

Philosophers who hold that intrinsic value can be conditional, then, can object to my conclusions about difficulty by pointing out that the Utopia thought experiment doesn't show that difficulty is of *unconditional* intrinsic value. It could be the case that the conditions in Utopia are the conditions for difficulty being of intrinsic value, and since these conditions fail to obtain in the real world, difficulty does not have value outside Utopia.

That's a reasonable objection, at least, in principle. But what are the conditions that obtain in Utopia that are different from the real world? There is only one: there is nothing of necessary instrumental value. Why should *this* condition be the condition for difficulty having intrinsic value? It's a strange sort of condition that we would think would be responsible

<hr>

[9] Although in the minority, several important philosophers today also hold that intrinsic value can be conditional. Cf. Shelly Kagan, "Rethinking Intrinsic Value," *Ethics* 2 (1998): 277–97; Christine Korsgaard, "Two Distinctions in Goodness," *Philosophical Review*, 2 (1983): 169–95.

for changing the valence of value for difficulty, of all things. Generally, if something is the condition for some potentially valuable thing's having value, there is some at least vaguely plausible story that we could tell about why the condition for value is the condition, or at least there is some overall intuitive plausibility about it's being the condition. There just doesn't seem to be any such relationship here. So if the objection here is that the absence of necessary instrumental value is the condition for difficulty's being valuable, then it's not a very compelling objection.

A better objection concedes that difficulty is intrinsically valuable, but it takes issue with the *comparative* value of difficulty. In the real world, says this objection, there are *always* more important (and perhaps also necessary) things for us to attend to—there is always more value at stake, there is always a better way for us to spend our time to produce more value. The world is indeed filled with incomprehensible amounts of horrible suffering that most of us just ignore or pretend to forget about, and surely alleviating this and attending to all sorts of other important things is much more valuable than baking a cake, or anything else.

I am, of course, willing to concede this. It would be ridiculous for me to insist that baking a cake is of greater value than saving human lives. Such a position would be the philosophical equivalent of fiddling while Rome burns, to be clichéd about it. In the real world, there are quite often more pressing things to engage in than difficulty. Our lives are indeed spent largely engaging in activities that are primarily of instrumental value.

But really, even though it's true that a lot of the time there are more valuable things than difficulty, this is a contingent matter. It just so happens that the world that we live in is riddled with important things that need our urgent attention. It doesn't take away from my position, which is simply that difficulty has intrinsic value. I haven't yet said anything about *how* valuable it is. So how valuable is it? It's grossly implausible that difficulty is of such small intrinsic value that there is or would be *never* anything that's less significant than it. Surely alleviating the pain equivalent to a hangnail couldn't be *more* valuable than the difficulty of winning a game of chess. In fact, there is excellent evidence that difficulty is *very* valuable. Many people are willing to endure a great deal of pain and other bad things in order to engage in difficult activity—just think of the incredible grueling exertion involved in running a marathon!

Difficulty only *seems* disvaluable when there are more valuable or pressing things to do. When there are other values competing for our time and energy, difficulty is a burden. But when our time and resources are limit-less, the very best activities are the difficult ones. When we have nothing else getting in the way, we can see the true value of difficult activity for what it is: intrinsic.[10] └→ *atelic* 🖊 🖊

Yet for all this, we still wonder about the slight air of absurdity that my position about the value of difficulty seems to have. What sort of a theory of value is going to endorse and explain the value of difficulty? Difficulty doesn't jump to mind as a prime candidate for intrinsic value. Difficulty, after all, is typically painful and unpleasant—characteristics of things that are bad, not good. So it's surprising to think of it as some-thing that is valuable. And if it is valuable, is it valued directly, intrinsic-ally, or because it is a sign of something else, where that further thing is the source of value? But I will leave these questions aside for now, and I'll turn to particular theories of value that can explain the value of diffi-culty later. For now, it suffices to say that difficulty is either intrinsically valuable itself, or that difficulty is a constant companion to some further source of value. Either way, it's clear that difficulty is a source or sign of value of achievements.

But does difficulty account for *all* the value of achievements? I have already mentioned that the value of the product and the process also can contribute to the value of achievements. But are achievements valuable *only* because of the value of the product and process and the value of dif-ficulty, or are there further sources of value in achievements? As we will see shortly, these elements do *not* account for all there is to the value of achievements.

Hunting for Treasure: Competent Causation

The other feature common to all achievements is competent causation. Does competent causation shape the value of achievements? I think that it does. To see that this is the case, all that need considering are some exam-ples that we first saw in Chapter 1.

---

[10] This, I believe, is the very point of *The Grasshopper*. I argue more extensively for this point, and for the intrinsic value of difficulty in a paper published by the University of Toronto undergraduate journal of philosophy, "Kudos for *Ludus*: Games and Value Theory," *Noesis*, 6 (2003): 15–28.

Buried Treasure. Lucky Lon comes to believe that there is treasure buried somewhere in the area, and embarks on a vigorous but hare-brained research plan involving magic 8-balls, ouiji boards, séances, and dowsing wands. Suppose that Lon's research program is, in spite of its questionable reliability, quite difficult for Lon to carry out and requires a great deal of effort. He eventually settles on what he believes is the precise location of the treasure, digs for days, and lo and behold! there just happens to be treasure buried in this exact spot.

Lucky Lon does not competently cause the product of his activities, and so it fails to be an achievement. Moreover, not only does Lon's "discovery" fail to be an achievement, but I think we can agree that there isn't much of *value* in Lon's activities.

I'm sure we all remember what happens when we add in the proper dose of competent causation to the same amount of efforts.

Deserving Discovery. Diligent Don has been conducting a research project and has good reason to believe that there is treasure buried in the area. He systematically scrutinizes various historical documents and maps, and conducts land surveys, and once he has pinpointed the location of the treasure, uses a metal detector to find it. He digs and, lo, the treasure! just where it was expected.

Diligent Don's discovery, in contrast to Lucky Lon's, is an achievement. They both exert the same amount of effort, but Don causes the discovery competently, whereas Lon does not. I think we will also all agree that not only is Don's discovery an achievement, it also has *value* as such. Now we can also see that not only does competent causation guarantee the status of a sufficiently difficult activity as an achievement, it also plays a part in shaping its value. If difficulty were the *only* source of value in achievements, then Lon's and Don's discoveries would have the *same value.* But this is clearly false. Lon's activity is practically worthless, but Don's is clearly of positive value.[11]

---

[11]   Now I should point out that there are some obstacles in our way when it comes to comparing activities with lesser degrees of competent causation. Competent causation, after all, is necessary for an activity to be an achievement. So if we are going to lower the amount of competent causation below the threshold required for achievements, we won't be able to compare two *achievements* with greater and lower degrees of competent causation. But instead we are comparing two *activities*, one of which is an achievement and the other is not, strictly speaking. Since, typically, only the process component of achievements is an activity, I am in fact comparing here an achievement (which is an activity and

So competent causation is clearly relevant for the value of achieve-ments. Without it, not only does an activity fail to have the special status of an achievement, but the activity also fails to have the special value that achievements have.

Now, it might improve the case for competent causation being a source of value if I paused here to consider an objection. Does competent causation seem like a good candidate for being a source of value? Unlike difficulty, competent causation has intuition on its side. It is, after all, just a matter of having justified true beliefs about the nature of one's activities. There is a long philosophical tradition of thinking that having justified true beliefs, or knowledge, or being a good epistemic subject, or something like it, is of positive value. So the burden is on potential objectors here to motivate their case. I'll take this as an indication that competent causation is indeed a plausible source of value of achievements.

Putting It All Together

Here is something curious about competent causation. When difficulty is *not* in the picture, competent causation is of minimal value, if any. We competently cause virtually everything we do, and it certainly doesn't seem to be the case that every little mundane thing we do is more valuable for it. Brushing your teeth is not particularly valuable just because you have justified true beliefs about how you are brushing your teeth. And this seems to be true about most things we do—we generally have a very high number of justified true beliefs about the nature of our activities. In other words, we competently cause lots and lots of things that are not difficult, and we do this all the time, every day. But it's hardly the case that most of what we do every day is of any particular value.

And yet for all that, competent causation by itself isn't *entirely* devoid of value. Sometimes, it seems, activities—even ordinary ones—can become

a product) with an activity *plus* a product. In this case, I sometimes refer to the composite of Lon's non-achievement activity *and* its product (namely the "treasure") as his "activity." This is because we don't have a term that categorizes non-achievement activities that have products.

enriched with value when we have a deeper understanding of what it is that we are doing. If, say, we have a truly deep understanding of coffee brewing techniques—the explanations behind the various stages of grinding the beans, the temperature of the water, the kinds of various oils and antioxidants released in the brewing of coffee—there seems to be value in having this richer understanding of what is happening as the coffee is brewing. This value seems to go beyond just the mere instrumental value of having a possibly superior cup of coffee at the end of the procedure; rather, it's the value of having a richer understanding of the activity in which one is engaging.

Similarly, it seems reasonable that there is some minimal value in perfectly competently causing your shoes to be tied. Further, it seems reasonable that the *more* justified true beliefs we have about the nature of our activities, the more valuable they might be. The more justified true beliefs we have about tying our shoelaces, the more competently we cause them to be tied—and this seems *better* than causing them to be tied less competently.

But on this small scale, the value that an increased level of competent causation brings is still not especially great—although there is more value when shoelaces are tied more competently, it's not an overwhelmingly huge amount of value. *upper limit*

So the more competently you cause your activities, the better: the more we understand about the nature of our activities, and the effects they produce on the world, the more value our activities have. So competent causation is a source of *some* value. But by itself, absent any difficulty, it's not a source of very much value at all.

Attentive readers may notice, then, just why this is so curious. If competent causation on its own is of such little value, then why is it that there is so *great a disparity* in value between Lucky Lon's incompetent so-called discovery, and Deserving Don's achievement? Don's achievement is significantly valuable, and Lon's activities seem to be of virtually *no* value. Yet both activities are equally difficult, and the value of the product and the value of the process are the same in both cases. Any difference in value between the two activities must be made by the difference in competent causation. This difference in value between the two discoveries is *significant*. Yet the value of competent causation is *not* significant. Clearly, the difference between these two activities can't possibly be made up by the small amount of value that competent causation appears to have on its own.

Now let's think back carefully to the adventures of Lucky Lon. What Lon does, according to our example, is equally as difficult for Lon as Don's activity is for Don. Yet what Lon does has virtually *no* value.

To be sure, we find Lon's activities to be valueless not *merely* because he ought to be doing something better with his time than following along his cock-eyed schemes, but his activities seem to be *intrinsically* valueless. Even if Lon were in Utopia his hare-brained schemes would be worthless.

Lucky Lon in Utopia. In Utopia, of course, all the treasure that could be acquired can be plucked instantly from the treasure tree. But, if you wish to try to find your own buried treasure—you can arrange to have treasure buried at a location unknown to you, and various documents, clues, and equipment made available so that you can search for it. Lucky Lon wants to hunt for buried treasure, so he makes these arrangements. But, as we all know about Lucky Lon, his idea of how to hunt for treasure is to use all kinds of crazy methods—magic 8-balls, ouiji boards, séances, and so on. He uses his usual hare-brained methods in Utopia. He's lucky here too, and miraculously finds his "hidden" treasure.

So even if Lon had nothing more important to do with his time and energy, his incompetent difficult activity would be worthless. Difficulty, then, *without some sufficient degree of competent causation is not intrinsically valuable.*

So neither difficulty nor competent causation on its own have significant value. What this means is that the value of the overall achievement can't just be a matter of the value of the difficulty on its own *plus* the value of the competent causation on its own. Zero plus zero, after all, is just zero; and little plus little will still fall short of a lot. And, as we already know, the value of the process and the product apart from difficulty and competent causation are unnecessary for an achievement to have value as such. So even if they *do* contribute to the value of achievements in some cases, they can't be what makes achievements valuable in all cases.

Yet, somehow, when difficulty and competent causation come together in the same activity, there is value. Great value, in many cases. So both difficulty and competent causation are sources of value for achievements—not so much individually, it seems, but *jointly*. The value of the achievement, then, is not the sum of the value of the difficulty of the activity, the value of the competent causation of the activity, the value of the product, and the value of the process (apart from the value of difficulty and competent causation). That is, the value of the achievement is *different from the sum of its parts*. In value theory, of course, we have a term for such entities: *organic unities*.[12]

But to say *that* achievements are organic unities doesn't yet explain *why* they have the value that they do. After all, an organic unity is just something that is such that its value is different from the sum of its parts. I haven't yet said anything about why the various parts, or features, of achievements are valuable to begin with. *Explaining* why the features of achievements are sources of value will be the next task. We've just seen that competent causation, considered just by itself, isn't a promising candidate for a source of any great value. And difficulty is a funny sort of thing to think of as valuable at all, since difficult activity is generally unpleasant and painful. Why are these things valuable? And why, when you put them together, are they so remarkably valuable?

Now, I should point out that you could disagree with the story that I give here about the value of difficulty and competent causation, but still agree with me that achievements are valuable in the way that I've argued in this chapter up until now—they are valuable insofar as they are organic unities. It's also possible to disagree with my accounts of the nature of difficulty and competent causation and still find my arguments about the value of achievements as organic unities compelling (and I hope that everyone will). If I have been convincing in showing that achievements are valuable in this way—as organic unities—and that they are comprised of the essential components of difficulty and competent causation—I will be happily satisfied. But, of course, there is more to be said.

I'm going to present what I take to be the most plausible explanation of why the components of achievements are valuable and why they are valuable as organic unities. But I won't be defending this account against all possible attacks. Rather, what follows here will be my description of the

---

[12] There is considerable debate about precisely what characterizes organic unities. Moore appears to characterize organic wholes as such that the value of the whole "bears no regular proportion to the sum of the values of its parts," *Principia Ethica* (Cambridge: CUP, 1971), 27, but Fred Feldman shows that this is problematic, *Utilitarianism, Hedonism and Desert* (Cambridge: CUP, 1997), 112–24. Chisholm offers a different analysis (*Brentano and Intrinsic Value* (Cambridge: CUP, 1986), 75), with which Lemos takes issue (*Intrinsic Value: Concept and Warrant* (CUP, 1994), 196–200; and also "Organic Unities," *Journal of Ethics*, 2 (1998): 323–4).

account and its merits presented in the best possible light in hopes that its inherent plausibility shines through.

Essentialist or Nonessentialist Approach?

My contention is that the best accounts of what makes achievements valuable will have the essential features of achievements—difficulty and competent causation—playing a *central explanatory role* in the account of why they are valuable. To see that this *essentialist* approach is the most plausible, I'll start by first entertaining some *nonessentialist* approaches to the value of achievements. Nonessentialist approaches hold that the essential components of achievements—difficulty and competent causation—do not themselves play a central role in the explanation of value. Rather, on these approaches, the essential components of achievements are instead merely *signs* of the presence of further features that are of central significance in the account of value. In other words, nonessentialist views account for the value of achievements without appealing to the essential features of achievements, and when they do incorporate the essential features, they do not play a central role in the account.

Nonessentialist approach #1: effort-requiring features as valuable

One initially very plausible nonessentialist approach explains the value of achievements by appealing to the value of the *effort-requiring* features of the achievement. All achievements, we now know, are difficult, and difficulty arises as a result of having *effort-requiring features*. These features can include complexity, precision, requiring physical endurance, exercising skills at a high level, having multiple steps, and many others.

According to what I'll call the *Feature* view, the value of achievements is a matter of the value of these effort-requiring features. The Feature view holds that at least *some* effort-requiring features are also valuable. Achievements, therefore, are valuable in virtue of having these valuable effort-requiring features.

Since there are no effort-requiring features common to all achievements, as I contend in Chapter 2, the Feature view maintains that there is an *assortment* of features that are valuable. According to the Feature view, then, there is no single feature in virtue of which all achievements are valuable. All achievements are valuable, but in each case, the value of the achievement is sourced in one or more of an assortment of different features, not all of which are shared with other achievements. What the Feature view holds is that all achievements have at least one feature such that this feature has these two properties: (1) it is effort-requiring, and (2) it is valuable. In other words, common to all achievements would be having properties of requiring effort and of being valuable. So the Feature view holds that these two properties often coincide. There is no deep connection between the value of achievements and their difficulty apart from this, according to this view. The same features that make achievements difficult in many cases also just happen to be the same features in virtue of which they are valuable. But there is nothing essentially relating these two aspects of the features, it is just coincidence.

This last point, I think, should count against the Feature view. There is something theoretically unsatisfying about holding that the value of achievements is explained by the same features that, entirely by coincidence, also happen to ground one of the features that is essential to achievements. It makes it seem almost coincidental that achievements are valuable. A more philosophically satisfying explanation would have something to say about why the ground of the value of achievements and the essence of achievements are located in the very same features.

Admittedly, this theoretical unattractiveness is only a mild drawback. But there is a further flaw with the view: it's messy. The Feature view appeals to the value of a diverse array of otherwise unrelated features. A nicer explanation of the value of achievements would be more unified, appealing to a single element that achievements have in common, rather than value a myriad assortment of things. This too is by no means a fatal blow to the Feature view, but it is less plausible and messier than a direct view would be, which are certainly considerations against it.

But the assortment of value-bearing features that the Feature view advocates leads to a worse problem. Many very common effort-requiring features don't seem to be plausibly held to be intrinsically valuable. Having many complicated steps is an effort-requiring feature of many achievements, and it doesn't seem especially valuable. Worse still, being painful and being dangerous are also common effort-requiring features of achievements. But far from being intrinsically valuable, these features are of negative value, if anything. Such negatively valuable characteristics are the *only* effort-requiring features of many achievements. Counterexamples to the Feature view, then, abound, such as the following.

Pain Contest. Contestants in the Pain Contest compete to see who can hold their hand in a bucket of ice for the longest duration. (No one is allowed to keep their hand in the ice long enough to incur any lasting damage.)

I think it's quite clear that winning the Pain Contest is an achievement. What makes winning the Pain Contest difficult, of course, is enduring the pain. Enduring pain is the *only* effort-requiring feature of the achievement. According to the Feature view, the achievement is valuable only in virtue of its effort-requiring feature. But that seems ridiculous: it's not valuable *in virtue of being painful.* We would have to have a really exotic theory of value to say that something is of positive value in virtue of being painful. So the Feature view doesn't quite work out.

A fan of the Feature view might try to respond by denying that there are difficult things that only have non-valuable or negatively valuable effort-requiring features. The Feature view might then seek to establish that anything that has non-valuable or negatively valuable effort-requiring features will *also* have some *other* valuable effort-requiring feature. The argument could go something like this: if a central effort-requiring feature of an activity is that it is painful, then the activity will *also* have at least a second effort-requiring feature, in that it will require the *capacity to persevere while enduring pain.* The Feature view would then attempt to establish that requiring the capacity to endure pain is itself an effort-requiring feature.

Now, it's quite plausible to hold that having the capacity to endure pain and persevere while suffering is valuable. To put it in more familiar terms, we could say that the ability to persevere while suffering is a *virtue.* Virtues are certainly among the things that it is very reasonable to hold are intrinsically valuable.

But even if we grant that all difficult activities include such further effort-requiring features, this move still won't save the Feature view in its original form. It is true that having the capacity to persevere while suffering could be a virtue, and so valuable. But the Feature view, on its own terms, holds that it is the effort-requiring *features of the activity* that are valuable. The effort-requiring feature of the activity here is the feature of *requiring* the capacity to persevere. But we don't think that it's the *requiring* of the capacity that is valuable. We think that it is the *having* of the capacity to endure while suffering that's valuable. So the Feature view gets close, but not close enough.[13]

But this new move opens up a different nonessentialist approach to valuing achievements: a *virtue* view, which I will turn to in the next section.

One proposal for a species of the Feature view grounds the value of achievement in *self-sacrifice*. Douglas Portmore proposes an account of the value of achievements according to which the more one has *sacrificed* for or invested in a goal, the more valuable it is.[14] Self-sacrifice is here understood as when you undertake a course of action knowing that it will make you worse off than an alternative, and do so for the sake of some further end. There is a general principle underlying this notion, which Portmore calls the *Not-for-Naught* view, which he characterizes in the following way:

> The redemption of one's self-sacrifices in itself contributes to one's welfare—the closer that one's self-sacrifices come to being fully redeemed, the greater the contribution their redemption makes to one's welfare.[15]

This is an appealing principle to be sure. It captures so many of the thoughts that we have about how the shape of a life can shape its value, apart from and beyond the value of the discrete parts of the life. We might be inclined to think, as Portmore does, that this principle covers the value of achievements. Many achievements typically involve a great deal of personal sacrifice and investment. Perhaps this is what makes them valuable. Here is an example from Portmore to highlight this possibility.

> Fred and Greg are training for the Olympics. The both exert themselves equally in their workouts. Greg, however, is a father and husband, and hates being away from his family. Fred, on the other hand, is a bit of a loner and likes being away. Moreover, Greg hates training, whereas Fred likes it more than anything.

---

[13] Exercising the virtue, in a sense, is also a feature of the activity that is effort-requiring. The line between features of the activity that are effort-requiring and virtues, then, bleeds. There is a sense in which the exercising of the virtue is itself a feature of the activity. However, it's not the case that it always requires effort to exercise this, or any, virtue. We can imagine someone who has the virtue of perseverance but effortlessly perseveres.

[14] Portmore, "Welfare, Achievement, and Self-Sacrifice," *Journal of Ethics and Social Philosophy*, 2 (2007): 1–28. Portmore's discussion is about the relevance of achievement to welfare, to be precise, but I'll discuss in terms of straightforward intrinsic value.

[15] Portmore, "Welfare, Achievement, and Self-Sacrifice," 13.

From this, Portmore concludes that Greg has had to sacrifice more to achieve his goals, and as a result, Greg gains more from succeeding—or stands to lose more from failing—than Fred does.[16]

But Portmore assumes that Greg and Fred have put the same amount of effort into their goals. This seems false. Greg has done much more that was difficult than Fred—he has exerted effort in sticking to his training schedule when he really dislikes it and wants nothing more than to go see his family, and no doubt has endured countless difficult phone conversations with his children whom he misses very much. We could then consider a version of the example where the effort is indeed equal. Suppose Fred has an injury during training, causing him all sorts of problems which make his time in training now just as difficult as Greg's. Is Greg's achievement still more valuable? It doesn't seem to be.

Making sacrifices *is* difficult. It takes effort—great effort in some cases—to make a sacrifice, and to endure the consequences of the loss of what has been sacrificed. If it weren't difficult to make a sacrifice, it probably wouldn't be much of a sacrifice. For this reason, self-sacrifice can contribute to the value of achievements.

Yet sacrifice can't account for all the value of all achievements. Some achievements do not involve sacrifice, and are nonetheless very valuable. It's perfectly possible to relish every moment of the difficult process of an achievement and not see it as a sacrifice at all. There might be nothing in the world you would rather be doing. (This is, perhaps, the ideal attitude for students to have in graduate school in philosophy—or any other discipline, for that matter.)

I agree that Portmore's principle has real appeal as a general principle. If it does indeed capture something about value, then in cases where self-sacrifice occurs in an achievement, this might shape its value. But it can't account for all the value of all achievements on its own.

This is true of other effort-requiring features as well, which also can contribute to the value of achievements in this way. It's very plausible to hold that an activity is valuable in virtue of its complexity, for example. Being complex, then, could add value to an achievement, perhaps in addition to the value that it has from other grounds. This would be an instance of the process having some independent value, which will make its own contribution to the overall value of the achievement. So I'm open to some

---

[16] Portmore, "Welfare, Achievement, and Self-Sacrifice," 20.

of the effort-requiring features of achievements contributing to their over-all value. But it's clear that effort-requiring features are not the ultimate source of value for all achievements.

Nonessentialist approach #2: virtues

As I just suggested, another way of accounting for the value of achievements is to appeal to virtues. A *Virtue* view holds that the value of achievements is a matter of the value of exercising virtues. According to this view, achievements are valuable insofar as they are instances of achievers exercising various virtues. The Virtue view is a nonessentialist view because the value of achievements is not grounded in either of the essential features of achievements. That is, the Virtue view is nonessentialist insofar as it does not give difficulty or competent causation a central role in the explanation of the value of achievements. Instead, it values exercising virtues that are associated with exerting effort or competently causing things. That is, on the Virtue view, what's valuable is exercising virtues. When virtues are exercised in an achievement, exercising these virtues is valuable. Insofar as the achievement is an instance of exercising virtue, it is valuable.

It seems highly plausible that achievements display virtues in many, if not all cases. Climbing a mountain, for example, can exhibit courage and tenacity, and so can advocating for social change, or competing in a tri-athlon. Writing a book, creating a vaccine, or winning a game of chess all may display theoretical virtues. Even virtues such as generosity, just-ice, or compassion can be exercised in a variety of achievements, such as rescuing a drowning child, or fundraising for a charitable organization. So as long as all achievements involve exercising some virtue or other, it's possible—plausible, even—that exercising virtues makes achievements valuable.

But as plausible as it may seem, the Virtue view has drawbacks. First, the Virtue view does not account for the special value of achievements *as such*. The Virtue view only values *virtues*. Achievements are only valuable inso-far as they are instances of virtue being exercised, and achievements, on this view, are just one among many different instances of virtuous activity. There is nothing, on this view, that is specially valuable about achievements per se. But this "special value" point isn't really an *objection* for the Virtue view. It just is, after all, what the Virtue view says: it values virtues primarily, rather than anything else. This point is only a disappointment if,

like me, you have the sense that there is something special about achievements as such.

The Virtue view is further subject to an objection similar to the one
I raised for the Features view: it's messy. Clearly, not all achievements
require, say, courage, nor do they all require theoretical virtues. The Virtue
view, then, won't provide a unified account of the special value of achievements. This means it will be a messy view. It will be messy, unless, of course,
there is one virtue that is exercised in common in all achievements.

Yet there may indeed be one such virtue. There may be two, in fact. It
may be the case that there are particular virtues that are exercised every
time we do something difficult, and every time we cause something
competently.

And there does indeed seem to be a virtue that is exercised whenever
exerting a certain amount of intensive effort over a time. It's similar, I think,
to the virtue that is displayed in Pain Contest. We might say that engaging in difficult activity always requires a certain degree of *perseverance*.
Since difficulty just is a matter of exerting significant effort, the virtue of
perseverance, then, will always be exercised whenever there is an achievement. We might wonder whether it is possible to exert intense effort without persevering. However, although you can persevere more or less, it
seems that even just exerting whatever the sufficient effort required for
being an achievement is going to be persevering to some degree. Insofar,
then, as all achievements are difficult, all achievements will require some
perseverance.

Similarly, there seems to be something virtuous about competently
causing things. Prudence, or good practical reasoning is a plausible candidate virtue to capture this, but competent causation isn't simply a matter of
practical reasoning, it's also a matter of causally efficacious practical reasoning. Perhaps this isn't among the stock cast of characters of virtues, but
there certainly seems to be something good about this trait—it's clearly
better to be disposed to display causally efficacious practical reasoning
than it is *not* to be. So this seems like it might be a virtue, or maybe at least
a species of one. Since all achievements involve competent causation, then
all achievements also involve this virtue of *causally efficacious practical
reasoning*.

So the virtue view *can* account for the value of achievements in terms
of the exercising of the virtues that are common to all achievements: there

is the virtue of *perseverance*, and the virtue of what I am calling *causally efficacious practical reasoning*.

Yet with these new developments, the Virtue view is now no longer a nonessentialist view. The Virtue view's best account of the value of achievements values the essential components of achievements directly. After all, what it is to do something difficult *just is* to exert a certain amount of intense effort—that is to say, to *persevere* in exerting effort. What it is to cause something competently *just is* to exercise causally efficacious practical reasoning. The Virtue view, then, at its best, values the essential components of achievements, and should be more properly classified as an essentialist view.

Furthermore, the Virtue view's explanation of the value of achievements is incomplete until we also have an account of why exercising the virtues is valuable. This, it turns out, is very similar to the view that I advocate. So to a certain extent, the best version of the Virtue view isn't that far away from what I think is the best view.

And yet, the Virtue view on its own isn't enough to fully account for the value of achievements. We've already seen that just engaging in difficult activity with no competent causation isn't especially valuable, nor is causing competently in the absence of difficulty. So exercising the corresponding virtues on their own won't be enough to account for the value of achievements. So if the Virtue view is going to be able to successfully account for the value of achievements, it's got some further explaining to do as to why there is further value when these two virtues are exercised in tandem.

It's possible that the Virtue view could just hold this as a basic principle—namely, that when these two virtues are exercised together, there is greater virtue-value than there is just in either of them by themselves. But a more satisfying account is available, which I will turn to in a moment.

Now, before I move on, I should acknowledge there are *other* ways of valuing achievements, albeit indirectly—hedonism, for example. But such views would value achievements *instrumentally* rather than intrinsically. This is fine, I think, if you subscribe to such a view already. I don't think I'm going to succeed in convincing any card-carrying hedonists that they're wrong, so I won't be spending time on this issue. Many people, however, disagree with hedonism largely on the grounds that they object to this very feature of hedonism—because they have the sense that achievements are not just instrumentally valuable, but intrinsically.

But other so-called subjective accounts might offer plausible accounts of the value of achievements, and we shouldn't overlook these. We might suppose that the value of achievements is a matter of attaining *what you want*. A desire satisfaction approach gives a very natural account of the value of achievements along the following lines: achievements are valuable just because you attain a goal that you desire. Getting what you want is good for you, and achievements are a paradigmatic example of this.

This is a very natural thought. But it's not too hard to see that such an approach cannot account for all the value of all achievements—the value of achievements *as such*. Consider *A Tale of Two Novels* from earlier in this chapter. How would a desire satisfaction account distinguish the value of these two achievements? We cannot appeal to the usual apparatuses that a desire satisfaction approach ordinarily does. The first thought is that Jones' achievement is more valuable on this approach because, say, he *wanted it more*. But this need not be the case since we can suppose that Smith and Jones both wanted to write these novels with equal intensity. Nor can we appeal to the structural significance of the desire to write the novel, since it plays a similar global structuring role in the lives of both Smith and Jones.

Perhaps the desire satisfaction theorist might have a more sophisticated approach that says that desires that are attained as a result of more *effort* have more value in virtue of this effort. I wouldn't disagree with this, as we will see in what develops next. The distinguishing feature of their view, then, would have to be something like this—these views *exclude* achievements that the achiever doesn't particularly *want* from being valuable. This seems plausible. Let's return to this later. As we will see in what follows, I do not think that this desire condition is necessary for the value of achievement.

Essentialist Approaches

We have just seen that nonessentialist approaches to the value of achievements are unsatisfying. The upshot, then, is that the best account of the value of achievements will hold that the essential features of achievements—difficulty and competent causation—play a central role in the explanation of their value.

There are (at least) two different ways in which difficulty and competent causation could play a central role in the explanation of the value of achievements. First, difficulty and competent causation may play central roles in the explanation of the value of achievements because they are *indicators* of the features that ground the value of achievements. On this kind of essentialist approach, difficulty and competent causation play a central role in the explanation of the value of achievements, but they are not themselves the *source* of the value of achievements. On such views, the value of achievements is not *located* in the essential features of achievements. Rather, these essential features are, for example, *signs* of the source of value of achievements, and only figure into the explanation of their value in this way. So these views value difficulty and competent causation *indirectly*.

Alternatively, essentialist approaches can give difficulty and competent causation a central role in the explanation of the value of achievements by holding that difficulty and competent causation are themselves the source of value. On a view like this, a *direct* view, difficulty and competent causation are valued directly. That is to say, the value of achievements is *located* in the difficulty and competent causation.

The view that I defend is a direct essentialist view. I think that the best way to account for the value of achievements makes use of difficulty and competent causation in a central way, and does so because achievements are valuable in virtue of their being difficult and competently caused.

The story that accounts for the value of difficulty and competent causation is, as I will present now, a *perfectionist* story. This, perhaps, will not be a surprise. Perfectionism has a long history of valuing achievements. It's worth mentioning, however, that there could be other (non-perfectionist) accounts of the value of achievements that also are direct essentialist. The perfectionist account that I propose, then, may be only one among several good accounts of the value of achievements. Regardless, it's the one that I am developing and defending here.

Perfectionism

Perfectionism is the view that explains the value of the traditional "objective list" of values by appealing to their relationship with certain special human features.[17] Knowledge, pleasure, achievement, loving

[17] This section draws from my paper, "The Value of Achievements," *Pacific Philosophical Quarterly*, 94 (2013): 204–24.

THE VALUE OF ACHIEVEMENT   115

relationships, and so on are valuable according to perfectionism because they are manifestations of special human features. Having these special features, and manifesting them, according to perfectionism, is having a good life. According to most perfectionist views, these features are certain *capacities that are special to human beings*. Developing these capacities to the most excellent degree possible is what perfectionism values. To be precise, on the version of perfectionism that I will be taking up here, the *excellent exercise* of these special perfectionist capacities is intrinsically valuable. Just what the perfectionist capacities are, and what it takes to *be* a perfectionist capacity, will vary according to the details of a perfectionist account. But on most views, to put it roughly, the capacities that are significant for perfectionism are those that *characterize us* as human beings. That is to say, they are the features that make us who we are.

Delineating exactly what these characteristics are and what makes them perfectionist capacities, and doing so successfully without being circular are the most difficult tasks for any perfectionist. The question of what constitutes being a perfectionist capacity—we could call this the *metaphysical* question—could be answered by holding that the perfectionist capacities are those that are *unique* to us as human beings, or those that are *essential* to human nature. Another approach is to say that the special capacities are those that are *fundamental*, meaning that their exercise is "near-inevitable" for almost all human beings. None of these approaches is without its flaws.

Here, however, I'm going to stop short of providing an answer to the metaphysical question. Instead, I will give a rough guide as to how the perfectionist capacities are to be identified. We might say that what I am giving here is an answer to the *epistemic* question—how do we tentatively identify which capacities are the perfectionist capacities? Whether or not this guide accurately identifies perfectionist capacities can be answered only once the complete metaphsycial account of perfectionism has been determined. To be clear, then, the epistemic identifying criteria are thus defeasible. Once the full metaphysical account is determined, it may turn out to be the case that there are *surprises*—that is, it might turn out that some capacity that we hadn't identified by the epistemic criteria is indeed relevant for perfectionism. So satisfying my two epistemic criteria is sufficient for inclusion in the presumptive account of perfectionist capacities, but it is neither necessary nor sufficient for *being* a perfectionist capacity.

The epistemic guide I propose is this: the relevant capacities are those capacities that are (I) *characteristic* of human beings and (II) *worth developing*. If a capacity has both parts of these criteria, this is sufficient for its inclusion in the presumptive account of perfectionist capacities.

First, the relevant capacities are those that are *characteristic* of human activity. By this I mean that they are special and important to humans and central in human activity. To be precise, they are special to human activity (although not necessarily unique to humans), and they are typical to human activity (although they may not be necessary). They are *essential*, we might say, in an evaluative sense, even if not in a metaphysical sense. One way of elaborating on characteristic features is to identify them as *fundamental*.

According to George Sher's account, fundamental features are those that are *near-universal* and *near-inevitable*.[18] As he puts it, "to be fundamental, a capacity must be one that virtually all humans possess, and, second, that it must be one whose exercise its possessors either cannot avoid at all, or else can avoid only intermittently."[19] Drawing from this account, let us say that capacities of human beings are characteristic when they are fundamental in Sher's sense; namely, their exercise is near-universal and near-inevitable. To elaborate, near-universal capacities are those that virtually all human beings have. There can be exceptions, but these would be rare.[20] Near-inevitable capacities are prevalent insofar as they are central to the life of any particular human being; their exercise permeates human activity. I will incorporate this notion of fundamentality in the epistemological guide, holding that near-universal and near-inevitable traits are fundamental to humans, or, in my terminology, *characteristic*. Hence the

---

[18] *Beyond Neutrality: Perfectionism and Politics* (Cambridge: CUP, 1997), 199 ff. On Sher's perfectionist account, fundamentality is not merely an identifying criterion for the perfectionist capacities, but it is part of his metaphysical account of what constitutes the perfectionist traits.

[19] Sher, *Beyond Neutrality*, 202 ff. To be precise, on Sher's account, the fundamental capacities are characterized by an inherent teleology. Many of the capacities have built-in goals, the pursuit of which is inevitable. What is of intrinsic value according to Sher is success in the goals that are integral to our characteristic capacities.

[20] Why not just go whole-hog and say that the traits are indeed universal? First, this would require a full-blown account of what it is to be a human being, and this, I think is too involved a task for this project. Second, it seems perfectly plausible that there may be people that we would want to say are indeed human beings, but are completely devoid of the capacities relevant for perfectionism. This may turn out to be false, once a full-blown account of human beings is established, but for now I take the modest route and hold that these characteristics are at least *near* universal.

first identifying criterion of putative perfectionist capacities: their exercise is characteristic of human beings.

In addition to being characteristic, there is a second identifying criterion for the perfectionist capacities: they are intuitively worth developing. Because we are trying to identify the features that make us good as human beings, we should expect them to be intuitively worth developing.[21] In other words, the prima facie case for something's being a perfectionist capacity is generated by its being intuitively good to develop. I will refer to this as the *value criterion*.

It is important to recognize that this criterion—the value criterion—is *only* a criterion for the epistemic guide. It cannot, of course, be an element of a metaphysical account of the perfections; that is, it cannot be part of the account of what *constitutes* being a perfectionist capacity. The reason for this, of course, is that such a criterion would be circular: perfectionism is the view of what capacities it is intrinsically valuable to develop. It would be entirely unhelpful to define them as those that are good to develop. So the value criterion cannot be an element of the account of what constitutes being a perfection, but it can, of course, be appealed to as an epistemic criterion useful for identifying them, particularly in the absence of a metaphysical account.

As I acknowledged earlier, the metaphysical account may generate surprises: it may turn out that there are perfectionist capacities that are intrinsically valuable that do not pass the epistemic criteria. There may even be perfectionist capacities that are intuitively *not* good to develop. But the epistemic account is defeasible, and so long as we are indeed committed to the truth of perfectionism, and this fully developed theory is the correct account and all around theoretically very attractive, we should then be good philosophers and hold that the exercise of these capacities is indeed valuable, even though we may lack the intuition, pre-reflectively, that they are. [22]

---

[21] Cf. Thomas Hurka, *Perfectionism* (Oxford: OUP, 1993), 9.

[22] Dale Dorsey argues that if perfectionism yielded some surprising features as relevant, then we would feel *no* theoretical pull to include them in our account of what is intrinsically valuable. But I think no perfectionist would accept this: if the perfectionist account of what constitutes the relevant capacities is sufficiently theoretically compelling, then a good perfectionist *would* incorporate the surprising feature. Merely failing the epistemic identifying guide is not sufficient for rejection from the metaphysical perfectionist account, and a committed perfectionist would indeed include nonstandard capacities if the metaphysical account entailed them. See Dale Dorsey, "Three Arguments for Perfectionism," *Noûs*, 44 (2010): 59–79.

With the epistemic guide in place, we can identify some capacities as belonging on our presumptive list of perfectionist capacities. Let's begin with the classic accounts of perfectionism. Traditionally, the most basic and general capacities in perfectionism include our *rationality*, both theoretical and practical. Some perfectionist views also include our *physical capacities*.

It's clear that our rational capacity is characteristic in the way that I have just outlined. Rationality has long been considered as a near-universal— if not universal—feature of human beings. We are, after all, by some accounts, essentially rational animals. Although, of course, we often fail to use our rationality as best as we can or should, our rational capacity is exercised virtually inevitably in virtually everything that we do so long as we are conscious. Being near-universal and near-inevitable, then, is clearly true of rationality, and so it passes my first identifying test as being characteristic of human beings. As for the second criterion, the value criterion, it's relatively uncontroversial that it is good to develop the rational capacity as best we can, and so it passes my second identifying criterion. Naturally, then, I agree with all other perfectionists that the rational capacity belongs on the presumptive list of perfectionist capacities.

Turning to consider our physical capacities, although it's unclear that we *essentially* have bodies, it certainly seems to be the case that all humans as we know them have physical bodies, meaning that our physical capacities, at least some minimal capacities, are at least near-universal to all humans. Further, it seems that we make use of our body in a wide range of things that we do, if not everything that we do. So it's quite clear that our physical capacities, then, are characteristic of human beings.

Whether or not the value criterion is met by our physical capacities is less obvious. Although it seems that there is a philosophical tradition going back to Plato of pooh-poohing our physical aspect as not only less valuable than our rational capacities, but also as bad and distracting, I think these views are mistaken and fly in the face of widespread general valuing of physical excellence. Excellence of physical appearance may be neither here nor there, but it seems quite clear that excellent exercise of various athletic capacities is something that is indeed intuitively worth developing. So I agree with those perfectionists who include physical capacities as relevant for perfection.

Overall, then, among perfectionist capacities are at least these two: our rational capacity and our physical capacity. But are they the only capacities identified by the epistemic guide? I believe that there is also a further capacity that perfectionism should acknowledge. This capacity has yet to be acknowledged by perfectionism as widely as it deserves. It is the capacity to exercise our will.

The will has been unacknowledged by typical accounts of human capacities relevant for the perfections. Yet the will is paradigmatically characteristic. It seems quite clear that every human being has a will, and its exercise is entirely inevitable in every activity in which we engage. Indeed, it seems that we can't even engage in activity of any kind without exerting the will. It's so fundamental that it underwrites our abilities to deploy all our other capacities. Thus the will clearly fulfills the criterion of fundamentality on the epistemic guide. Moreover, the will passes the value criterion. Indeed, it seems worth having and developing. So it is my contention that the will should be included in an account of the relevant capacities for perfectionism. It clearly passes the epistemic guide of being a characteristic human capacity, and it is intuitively good to develop.

For these reasons, the will belongs on our list of perfectionist capacities. This, then, is the innovation I propose for perfectionism: to acknowledge the will as a characteristic human capacity.[23]

Although including the will on the list of perfectionist capacities is an innovation among current perfectionist views, there is another perfectionist account that acknowledges the significance of the will as a characteristic feature—as *the* characteristic feature. This is Nietzsche's perfectionism. Needless to say, it's contentious to pin any particular view to Nietzsche, but nonetheless there is a plausible interpretation of Nietzsche that casts him in a perfectionist light.[24]

---

[23] Now you might think that there are philosophers who would immediately reject the will as a fundamental capacity because they think that the will does not exist. These would be any incompatibilist determinists—i.e. those who hold that free will is incompatible with causal determinism, which they also take to be true. But the compatibilism–incompatibilism debate is not about on whether we *have* a will; rather, this debate is focused on a particular aspect of its nature—namely, whether or not the correct account of the nature of the will would be compatible with causal determinism (and then, of course, whether or not causal determinism is true or even relevant is an entirely different question). That is, the focus in metaphysical debates on freedom of the will is not whether or not we *have* a will, but whether or not *what we have is free*. Even perhaps the will's greatest fan, Nietzsche, does not see the possibility of determinism as a threat to its significance (e.g. *Beyond Good and Evil*, tr. Walter Kaufmann (New York: Random House, 1989), section 21).

[24] See Thomas Hurka, "Nietzsche: Perfectionist," in Brian Leiter and Neil Sinhababu (eds), *Nietzsche and Morality* (Oxford: Clarendon Press, 2007). To be clear, I'm hardly a Nietzsche scholar; here I simply intended to draw some interesting parallels to the extent that they are illuminating for my discussion of the value of achievements.

On Nietzsche's view, our preeminently characteristic feature is the will to power. In numerous passages throughout his works, Nietzsche identifies our "essence" with the will to power, calling it "the innermost essence of being."[25] More broadly, Nietzsche appears to hold that the will to power is the essence of *all* being and all existence, saying, for example, that this is "a world whose essence is will to power"—a fortiori, it's our essence too.[26]

The precise nature of the will to power, of course, is a matter of some discussion. It is not precisely the same thing as the will (at least not in Nietzsche's own terminology), but is rather the inner drive to overcome resistance, we might say. Some scholars have characterized it as a kind of second-order desire, in particular the desire to satisfy our other desires,[27] while others have characterized it as the drive to develop mastery over other drives.[28] A further intriguing account is from Bernard Reginster, who characterizes the will to power as "the will to the overcoming of resistance."[29] The will to power, on this view, is the drive to be *in the process* of overcoming resistance. To be clear, Reginster's view differs from the first account mentioned, which was the drive to *satisfy* one's further drives. On Reginster's account, the will to power is the drive to *continually have drives*, such that there is always something that one is in the process of pursuing, and so that there is always resistance to be in the process of overcoming.[30] What's distinctive about this is that the will to power, then, to put it in my terminology, is the drive to *be engaged in difficult activity.*

Having identified our characteristic, special human feature, Nietzsche also holds that the *development* of our essence, namely, the will to power, is valuable (as much as Nietzsche thinks anything is valuable, of course). That is, the flourishing of those who best express the will to power is

---

[25] Nietzsche, *The Will to Power*, tr. Walter Kaufmann and R. J. Hollingdale (New York: Random House, 1968), 398, section 963.

[26] *Beyond Good and Evil*, section 186.

[27] Maudemarie Clarke, *Nietzsche on Truth and Philosophy* (New York: CUP, 1990).

[28] John Richardson, *Nietzsche's System* (New York: OUP, 1996), 18 ff.

[29] Bernard Reginster, *The Affirmation of Life* (Cambridge, MA: Harvard University Press, 2006), 132–3. Cf. 133 ff.

[30] Reginster, *Affirmation of Life.* Also see Reginster's wonderful article "Happiness as a Faustian Bargain," *Daedalus* (2004): 52–9, for more elaboration on this very interesting view.

valuable. Those who are capable of such high expression of the will to power Nietzsche calls the "higher men."[31]

Moreover, Nietzsche can be said to hold that *achievements* are valuable as a result of his valuing of the will to power, and, moreover, he can be said to hold that the difficulty of achievements is a source of their value. According to Reginster's account of Nietzsche, achievements are valuable insofar as they are expressions of the will to power. To be more precise, achievements are valuable because they are *difficult*, and difficulty—which is to say, overcoming resistance—is the expression of the will to power.[32] This account is, as we will see in what follows, remarkably similar to the one that I am developing here.

The Value of Achievements

Now let's put my perfectionism together with my account of achievements. An achievement, you will recall from my discussion in the preceding chapters, is a process and product such that the process is difficult and competently causes the product. Here, then, is the heart of my account of what makes achievements valuable. First, engaging in difficult activity *just is* the excellent exercise of the will. On the perfectionist view that I am endorsing, what is valuable is the excellent exercise of the perfectionist capacities. Engaging in difficult activity requires the exercise of the will, which, as we have just seen, is among the perfectionist capacities. It follows that difficult activity, according to perfectionism, is intrinsically valuable. Second, competent causation requires the excellent exercise of the *rational* capacity. According to perfectionism, then, competent causation is intrinsically valuable. Achievements, as a result, are intrinsically valuable in virtue of the very things that they are.

This account is thus a *direct essentialist* account. Essentialist accounts are those that give the essential features of achievements a central role in

---

[31] Granting that there is anything that can be properly said to be valuable on Nietzsche's view, it's controversial what it is that Nietzsche values: there is discussion over whether it's the expression of the will to power, the achievements as expressions of will to power, or the people—the "higher men" who have the wills to power that are expressed in achievements. See Brian Leiter, *Nietzsche on Morality* (New York: Routledge, 2002), 113 ff.

[32] Reginster, "The Will to Power and the Ethics of Creativity," in Leiter and Sinhababu, *Nietzsche and Morality*, 44 ff.

the explanation of the value of achievements. Direct accounts are those that locate the value of achievements in their essential features. My account does precisely this. Engaging in difficult activity *is* intrinsically valuable, on my account, because it is the excellent exercise of the will. Similarly, the exercise of rationality involved in competent causation is also intrinsically valuable. The value, then, is located in the competent causation itself; more precisely, it's located in the competence of the competent causation. The value of achievements is thus located in their essential features.

To be sure, the process and product of the achievement may themselves have value in addition to, and independently of, the value of the difficulty and competent causation, as I have acknowledged earlier, and that value can indeed contribute to the overall value of an achievement. However, since the process and product have value only contingently, meaning that not all achievements will accrue this sort of value from their process or product, this value is not part of the essential story of what makes achievement valuable. So the account of the value of achievements is that achievements are *essentially* valuable insofar as their essential features are valuable. For this reason, I will call the value that is grounded in the essential features of achievements the *Essential Value* of achievements.

Before moving on, let us return to an important question. One thing that we can see from the view so far is that it isn't necessary to *want* the achievement or its goal in order for it to be a valuable achievement. On the perfectionist account, it appears that it is possible for an achievement to be valuable even if the achiever *hates* the achievement, or feels completely alienated from it. This is particularly significant when we think about the notion that achievements are adding value *to our lives* when they are our achievements. To be fair, I haven't directly addressed the question concerning how our achievements can shape the value of our lives, but it's reasonable to think that insofar as your achievements are part of your life, they shape its value. Now, on the perfectionist view I have just put forward, it appears that an achievement adds value to your life, even if you hate that achievement.

Nevertheless, I do not see this as an objection. While I acknowledge that some people are of a different sensibility, there are certain cases that provide compelling examples that we need not identify with or endorse our achievements in order for them to be valuable. Consider Piano Prodigy, a case that may sound familiar to readers who endured a musical childhood.

Piano Prodigy. Young Prodigy is a remarkable pianist. His performances are dazzling and impressive. He practices for many hours every
day, and maintains a grueling performance schedule. But Prodigy
hates it, hates all the pieces he plays, and gets no pleasure from the
applause and so forth. He is being forced to do all this by his pushy
parents. He can't wait until he can shake off his repressive parents do
something else.

One might be inclined to think that his achievements are not valuable.
They make his life miserable. I agree that Prodigy's achievements make
his life miserable. For this reason that are at the very least instrumentally
bad, insofar as they interfere in a negative way with other dimensions of
how well his life goes. But they are nonetheless achievements, and it is very
difficult to suppose that just because Prodigy doesn't want to perform that
his performance isn't an achievement. His achievements are still valuable,
even though he doesn't want them.

Moreover, there is a further substantive question as to whether having
one's desires fulfilled has intrinsic value, or the converse, getting what you
don't want has disvalue. If these notions are compatible with the perfectionist account that I have put forward, then we can still account for the
potential ways these factors might shape the value of achievement. As we
have just acknowledged, the process of an achievement may have additional value or disvalue beyond the Essential Value of an achievement.
Accordingly, if an achievement involves something that you don't want,
such as an Olympic silver medal rather than a gold, or getting what you *do*
want, then this can be incorporated into the overall value of the achievement. But it is not my view that one *must want* the goal of an achievement
in order for it to be valuable, as we see in cases such as Piano Prodigy.

Organic Unity

Ultimately, then, there are *two* fundamental human capacities that are
necessarily exercised in achievements: the will and rationality. The excellent exercise of each of these capacities, according to the account of perfectionism that I have been developing, is intrinsically valuable. But we have
seen earlier that neither competent causation nor difficulty alone seem
to be especially valuable. It's only when taken together, in the instance of

achievements, that they seem to have great value. That is, as we know from earlier in my discussion, achievements are organic unities.

So what we now need to explain is *why* achievements are organic unities. Why is the value of an achievement greater than the sum of the value of its component parts?

The answer is that achievements are paradigmatic instances of *unity in diversity*, which is one way of accounting for organic unity. When diverse elements are united together, there can be greater value in the unity of the diverse elements than there is in the diverse elements themselves when they are in a mere aggregate. The more diverse the elements, or the greater the unity, the better: increases either along the diversity dimension, or along the unity dimension, result in increases in value.[33] A non-unified aggregate of parts can have less value in total than the very same parts unified.

Indeed, achievements exemplify unity in diversity. First, all achievements involve the exercise of two capacities, rationality and the will; thus, there is diversity. Second, in achievements these two diverse capacities are exercised together, in unity.

Unity, in the case of achievements, is the will and rationality being exercised *together in a single process* that culminates in the same product. Their exercise is harmonious and unified—the very same process is both difficult and competently causes its product. This co-location, as it were, of exercise of rationality and the will within the same process is what unifies achievements. In contrast, in a nonunified aggregate, the exercise of will and the exercise of rationality would *not* be located in the same process.

As it turns out, however, there are no examples of entirely nonunified aggregates like this. The reason is that exercising the will is always accompanied by a certain amount of exercise of rationality. So there will never be an entirely nonunified exercise of will and rationality. Even the most rudimentary seemingly mindless exercise of the will—say, Sisyphus rolling a rock up a hill—is at least somewhat competently caused, meaning that there is a certain amount of exercise of rationality. As a result, finding an example of a largely nonunified aggregate of exercise of will and exercise of rationality is peculiarly challenging. We will need to envision an

---

[33] Cf. Robert Nozick, *Philosophical Explanations* (Cambridge, MA: Harvard University Press, 1981), 415 ff.

exercise of the will that is *virtually* free of exercise of rationality—meaning here that there is a very small number of justified true beliefs.

Happily, there is a familiar philosophical example that can help us imagine just such an instance: the Experience Machine.[34] In the Experience Machine, on the particular model that I will make use of here, let us suppose that we can indeed exert effort, which is to say we genuinely exercise our will. But as is the case with any model, our understanding of what it is that we are doing is false. We believe that we are indeed engaged in the activity that we are experiencing, when we are in fact only inside the machine, which is simulating the experience. So the Experience Machine allows us to envision a case in which we are exerting our will to a very high degree, but have only a minimal amount of justified true beliefs about our activity.

The nonunified aggregate will consist of two processes: a noncompetent exercise of the will and a noneffortful exercise of rationality. Let's make our noncompetent exercise of the will "running" a five-mile race in the Experience Machine. Jane is in the Experience Machine, and believes that she is running a five-mile race, and is exerting all the effort that this would require, yet she has virtually no true beliefs about the nature of her activities (she believes justifiedly that her legs are moving, and that she is outside, but of course she is inside the experience machine, not moving at all). So here we have the exercise of the will *not* united harmoniously with (any significant degree of) competence. This comprises one piece of our disunified aggregate.

To compose the nonunified aggregate, we add to the exercise of the will largely *sans* competence an instance of exercise of rationality largely *sans* will. Here we simply need to consider an example of exercise of rationality that would be competent to the same extent as in a typical achievement—say, in running a five-mile race (in real life, to be clear, rather than the experience machine). Let us suppose that in running a five-mile race, rationality is exercised to the same degree as it is for Jane to drive her car to the grocery store. So the second element of the nonunified aggregate will

---

[34] I take it that most readers are familiar with the Experience Machine, which originated in Nozick's *Anarchy, State, and Utopia* (New York: Basic Books, 1974), 42. When in the Experience Machine, a program simulates any experience, entirely vivid and indistinguishable from how it would seem in real life. A key element for the Experience Machine is that when you are in the machine, running the simulated experience, you do not know that what you are experiencing is not in fact real.

be this: Jane driving her car to the grocery store. Jane causes this competently, but it is not difficult.

The aggregate, then, of difficult and noncompetent activity and competent but nondifficult activity is made up of Jane "running" a five-mile race
in the Experience Machine, and then getting into her (real-life) car and
driving to the grocery store. Here we have both will and rationality, but at
work in distinct processes.

Contrast that with a genuine achievement: Jane running a *real* five-mile
race, which involves exercise of the will and rationality in a unified way. In
the real, bona fide achievement, the very same process is both difficult and
competent at the same time, whereas in the aggregate, there are two processes, one which is difficult and one which is competently caused. In the
achievement, the exercise of will and the exercise of rationality are united
by being co-located; that is, they are exercised *at the same time in the same
process*. In a mere aggregate of exercise of will and exercise of rationality, the will and rationality are *not* exercised at the same time in the same
process.

So achievements involve *diversity*, insofar as they make use of two of our
characteristic capacities, and they are also *unified*, insofar as these characteristic capacities are exercised in the same process. So achievements do
indeed exemplify unity in diversity. This, then, is what accounts for the
value of achievements beyond the individual value located in excellent
exercise of rationality and the will: they exemplify unity in diversity and
are thus organic unities.

 So in sum, my basic account of the value of achievements is this: according to perfectionism, the will and rationality are fundamental human
capacities, the exercise of which is intrinsically valuable, and when they
are exercised together, there is more value in this harmonious exercise
because it is an organic unity.

Before I move on, a perfectionist account can elaborate on this explanation of the value of achievements as organic unities. As we have seen,
there is unity in achievements, and the feature of achievements that is
responsible for this unity is *sameness of process*. Now we can ask, *what
causes this feature to obtain?* That is, what causes rationality and the will to
be exercised in the same process?

Here is one putative answer that perfectionism can give. It could be that
additional exercising of our rational capacity and will are what enable us to
unite their own use together in the same process. There is, in other words,

second-order exercise of our will and rationality, and this second-order rationality, we might suppose, is what unifies the diverse elements into a single whole, thus unifying achievements.

However, if this is the case, then the following objection is in order: achievements do not need to have their value explained by unity in diversity. On this approach, what is unifying achievements is *additional* exercise of the will and rationality. As a result, there may be no less value in the sum of the parts than there is in the whole. On the first-pass assessment of the value of the parts, as it were, we did not include the second-order exercise of rationality and will that was directed toward unifying the achievement. But once this second-order exercise is included, and its value is added to the sum of the value of the other elements, it is quite possible that the sum of the value of the elements of achievements is indeed no less than the value of the whole. In other words, there is an extra *part* that has value that was not tallied up with our original first pass calculation of the value of achievements. We counted the value of the exercise of the will in difficulty, and we counted the value of the exercise of rationality in competent causation, but we did *not* count the value of exercise of the additional exercise of will and rationality that is responsible for the unifying. Now that this extra exercise of capacities is tabulated into our calculations, the objection continues, we can see that this is why there *appears* to be more value in achievements than the sum of their parts—there is in fact an *extra, valuable part*. The value of achievements is *not* greater than the sum. Rather, the sum is greater than we thought it was. If this is the case, then achievements are *not* ultimately bona fide organic unities. Their value would be accounted for fully by the excellent exercise of rationality and the will.

This is indeed an interesting thought. It's plausible to think that the unifying of the process and product is indeed the result of additional exercise of the will and rationality. But even if this is so, on close reflection we can see that the value of achievements cannot be accounted for entirely by the additional exercise of these capacities as this objection suggests it can.

For if the additional exercise did fully account for this value, then there could be a *nonunified* activity that is difficult and competent *to the same extent as an achievement*, that is just as valuable. But this doesn't seem to be the case. Compare on the one hand an *achievement*: Jane running a five-mile race. Let's suppose that this is difficult, such that it manifests excellent exercise of the will in the amount of a, and the competent causation manifests rationality in the amount of b. Additionally, there is the unifying second-order exercise of the will, which in this case is amount c, and the second-order exercise of rationality is amount d. So there is total manifestation of will equal to a + c, and total manifestation of rationality equal to b + d.

Contrast this to a nonunified aggregate of processes that involve rationality and the will. Let's consider my earlier example of a nonunified aggregate: Jane running a five-mile race on the Experience Machine, then getting out of the Experience Machine and into her (real) car and driving to the grocery store.

To clarify, to make the comparison fair, in the aggregate we need *additional* first-order rationality and exertion of will in the aggregated bits. This is to match the total amount of rationality (b + d) and will (a + c) that are being expended at the second order in the achievement, which unify it. Let's imagine that the effort exerted in running one extra mile in the experience machine is equal to the additional effort (second order) in the five-mile *real-life* achievement, and likewise the extra rationality spent in competently causing oneself to drive the car around the block is equal to the additional rationality (second order) in the real achievement. So we'll need to add an extra mile to the Experience Machine route, so Jane is having the experience of running *six* miles. Suppose, then, that the overall effort and rationality expended in the aggregate is equal to the total in the real achievement, even though the former isn't unified in a single process.

Which of these activities seem more valuable? It seems quite clear to me that the nonunified activity is simply less valuable. If all the value of achievements were accounted for fully by the exercise of rationality and the will, in the case of achievements, the mere fact that the exercise of the two capacities is unified *adds nothing* to the value. The value is entirely a matter of the extent to which the will and rationality are exercised excellently. But it seems (to me at any rate) that a nonunified aggregate of noncompetent difficult activity and nondifficult competently causing activity would have *less* value than an activity that made use of the same capacities to the same degrees but was unified.

I acknowledge it may not seem as clear to others, and if it doesn't, then what I'm saying here will no doubt seem to question-beg. If my intuitions are leading me in the wrong direction here, then so be it, and achievements are not in fact bona fide organic unities, and the excellent exercise of rationality and the will are all there is to the value of achievements. This means that achievements lose their special value as such. After all, we would have just acknowledged a nonunified aggregate activity that is not an achievement but has just as much value and the very same explanation of value. But this might not be so bad, in the end. After all, my theory of the value of achievements would itself gain the unification that achievements have lost: if this is the case, then perfectionism entirely explains the value of achievements. Appealing to unity in diversity is not necessary to augment my account.

Regardless, I feel confident enough in my intuition that the nonunified aggregate of equal difficulty and competent causation is less valuable than its unified counterpart to move on. There is more value in the unified activity than can be fully accounted for by the additional value of the second-order exercise of rationality and the will.

As it happens, perfectionism also has an alternative explanation for the unification. There could be some *third* capacity—a *unifying* capacity—that is responsible for our ability to unite our utilization of our diverse capacities. Such an idea might seem especially plausible since there is a philosophical tradition of acknowledging such a unifying master capacity, which centrally controls and manages the exercise of all the other capacities. It's a plausible thought that there is indeed such a capacity, which at the second-order level controls and guides the exercise of our other capacities.

However, even on this alternative approach, the earlier objection can be levied. If there is a capacity being exercised in achievements that is not the rationality or will, then its exercise was not included in the initial first-pass tally of value. Once we accurately include its exercise in the calculation of value, then we can see that the value of the whole is not in fact greater than the sum of its parts. Again, there was a part that was missing in the initial calculation. If true, once again, it could be the case that achievements are not instances of bona fide organic unities.

The response that I gave to the earlier version of this objection was that a nonunified aggregate of the same amounts of excellent exercise of capacities would not have as much value as the same exercise of capacities when unified. We saw that this was the case by considering examples of nonunified aggregates. However, in this case, there can be no similarly nonunified aggregates. The reason for this is because, of course, the unifying capacity, if there is such a thing, is only exercised *when there is unification*! The unifying capacity can *never* be exercised in a mere aggregate: it is, after all,

130 THE VALUE OF ACHIEVEMENT

the capacity to *unify* the exercise of other capacities, and so is exercised only in (and in all) instances of unification. So we can't isolate it to test our thoughts about its value in isolation.

Consequently, then, if there is a unifying capacity, there isn't much that can be said to deny that its excellent exercise is responsible for the value of achievements that I earlier attributed to their being organic unities. And indeed in some moods I am persuaded by this suggestion. It comes with the further appeal that my account of achievements would be even more theoretically unified: perfectionism would be accounting *fully* for the value of achievements.

In other moods of reflection, however, I do not find myself persuaded by the thought that the exercise of the unifying capacity can account for the value of achievements I was earlier attributing to their being organic unities. After all, the gap in value between the nonunified aggregate and the unity is quite a big gap. Is our unifying capacity really so special that its excellent exercise is going to be able to make up for that great a differ-ence in value? Ultimately, I find the explanation of organic unities a more appealing route to account for the value of achievements. But I acknow-ledge that the alternative is a plausible approach as well.

Affirming that achievements are organic unities and valuable for this reason may make my overall account less unified than it could be if per-fectionism fully accounted for all the value of achievements. However, it's possible that my account might be ultimately more unified than it cur-rently appears. After all, I have not given any sort of response to what we might call the axiological question of perfectionism—that is, I have not given any explanations for *why the excellent exercise* of our fundamental capacities is valuable. It just might be the case, as I suspect it is, that the ultimate explanation for this axiological position is the very same explan-ation as that for the principle of unity in diversity. Such a view isn't entirely unheard of, and its theoretical virtue, of course, as far as achievements are concerned, is that it would unify the diverse elements of my explanation, thus succeeding at least by its own lights.

We might wonder if my view of the value of achievements is still, as I claimed, a direct essentialist view. In order to be an essentialist account of the value of achievements, the essential features of achievements must play a central role in the explanation of value, and on direct accounts, the value of achievements is located in the essential features. But appealing to achievements as organic unities is compatible with the direct essentialist nature of my account: after all, it is *essential* to achievements that the difficulty and competent causation are related centrally in the same process—that is to say, that they are *unified* is indeed essential to achievements. So my account is indeed direct essentialist.

So this is the account of the value of achievements, according to the perfectionist theory that I am developing here: achievements are valuable because they are the excellent exercise of two fundamental human capacities, united together.

Now, there is still more to say about the value of achievements. I have already mentioned elsewhere that the process and product of an achievement can have value independently of the role they play as components of the achievement. The value of both the process and the product, I earlier remarked, can also contribute to the value of an achievement, either by augmenting or diminishing it. I discuss this question in the next chapter.

5

The Relative Value of Achievement

In the last chapter, we saw that one very plausible account of the value of achievements is *perfectionism*, according to which the excellent exercise of our characteristic human capacities is intrinsically valuable. Achievements *essentially* make use of two of our characteristic capacities, the will and rationality. Since it is also essential to achievements that these two capacities be exercised in harmony, this unity means that achievements are instances of unity in diversity, and are as a result *organic unities*, and so additionally valuable. There are thus three sources of value that is essential to achievements, or, using the terminology I have introduced, there are three sources of the Essential Value of achievements. These three sources are the excellent exercise of the will, the excellent exercise of rationality, and unity in diversity. All achievements require excellent exercise of the will and rationality and display unity in diversity, and so all achievements are valuable in these ways.

Now, so far this is only the story of what makes any particular achievement have value at all, and we have yet to see to what *degree* any particular achievement is of value—that is, what it is that makes one achievement more valuable than another. Clearly, achievements vary in value. Running a marathon is a better achievement than winning the sack race at the church bazaar, winning the Nobel prize is a more valuable achievement than winning at tic-tac-toe, and getting a PhD is a more valuable achievement than learning how to parallel park.[1]

---

[1] Of course, we can imagine scenarios where these things are perhaps not the case—it might be very easy for someone to run a marathon, but the church bazaar sack race might have been an incredible feat of prowess, or involved a huge donation of money to charity

Recall in the last chapter the Tale of Two Novels, where Smith and Jones both write novels of equal value, but Jones does so while overcoming extraordinary adversity. Jones' achievement, we noted, is a more valuable achievement than Smith's. So we have an indicator of one source of the relative value of achievements: difficulty. Achievements that are more difficult than others are more valuable.

We shouldn't be surprised, then, if it's also the case that the *other* sources of Essential Value in achievements generate differences in relative value as well. It seems reasonable that the more competently something is caused, the better it would be—the more you know about what you're doing, the better. While beginner's luck might be the source of many impressive feats, it is a more valuable achievement for a seasoned pro to accomplish a big win than it is for a beginner to attain the same results with a lot of help from luck. So a greater degree of competence might also appear to be a source of increased value in achievements in addition to difficulty.

Similarly, it is also reasonable to imagine that, with regard to our third source of Essential Value, unity in diversity, the value of an achievement would increase as degree of unity in diversity increases. Admittedly, it isn't clear that achievements *can* vary in degree of unity in diversity. Supposing they could, however, this would be a reasonable source of changes in value for achievements, and we will look at this closely in what follows.

Beyond the Essential Value of achievements, I have also already acknowledged that the value of achievements can be shaped by factors that are not essential to achievements. The value of the process or product can shape the value of the achievement. As valuable as running a marathon might be, if running the marathon somehow also resulted in a cure for cancer, this would clearly be even more valuable an achievement, and to deny this would be absurd. If an achievement has an especially valuable product, this seems to make the achievement all the more valuable. Moreover, if the process has additional value—say, if it is especially pleasurable—then it also seems reasonable to say that this value augments the value of the achievement.

In what follows, I will first show how the various elements of Essential Value shape the relative value of achievements, then turn to the value of the process and product. Let's start with difficulty.

which is extremely valuable. Nonetheless, the point remains that some achievements are more valuable than others.

Excellent Exercise of the Will

As we have just seen, it's quite plausible that the value of achievements increases as difficulty increases, other things being equal. After all, an ordinary, non-difficult activity can turn into a valuable achievement if it becomes difficult to do. Tying my shoes might not be an achievement for me, but it is a valuable achievement for an amputee who has recently lost an arm. This seems to extend more generally. Typically, the most valuable achievements are those that are the most difficult. Winning an Olympic medal, climbing Mt Everest, writing a doctoral dissertation—all are more valuable than winning the sack race, hiking up a hill, or writing a term paper. All are achievements, and difficult, but the better achievements are the more difficult ones.

In Chapter 2, we saw that difficulty is a matter of exerting a certain amount of intense effort (in units of intense eff-minutes). Exerting effort, we have seen now, is a matter of exercising the will, which is one of our characteristic human capacities. Exercising these capacities is intrinsically valuable, and thus doing difficult things—to wit, achievements—is intrinsically valuable. Moreover, according to perfectionism, the more excellently we exercise our perfectionist capacities, the more valuable it is.

So now we turn to how achievements can vary in their value where the variation in value is sourced in difficulty. We might think that if difficulty is a source of value, then the more difficult something is, the better it will be, other things being equal. And roughly speaking, this turns out to be true—*the harder the better.*[2]

Yet it's not entirely accurate to say that the value of exercise of the will tracks difficulty. After all, as we saw in Chapter 2, there is such a thing as *non-difficult effort*. If effort is exercise of the will, and exercise of the will is valuable according to perfectionism, then perfectionism tells us that this non-difficult exercise of the will has value as well. This would mean that an

---

[2] If at this point we are tempted once again by the thought that what I have just said implies that we ought to go about making everything we do needlessly difficult, since doing so will increase the value of our lives. Surely this is absurd. But let us recall the response to this objection in the previous chapter. While the view is that difficulty is valuable, the claim is not that it is the *only* thing of value. Other things may be more valuable and more pressing. Yet recall also the example of Utopia, in which we saw that in the absence of any other source of value, additional difficulty does in fact seem plausibly valuable.

exercise of the will that is of minimal effort but long duration would be of considerable value.

Admittedly, a version of perfectionism could reject this position, and hold instead that minimal exercise of perfectionist capacities is not valuable. On such a view, only the exercise of perfectionist capacities beyond a certain point of excellence is valuable, and so a minimal exertion of will would not be valuable.

But this approach is ad hoc. Why not instead simply maintain that minimal exercise of the will is, accordingly, *minimally* valuable? After all, what makes exertion of intense effort valuable is that it is the excellent exercise of one of our fundamental human capacities, the will. Presumably even nonintense effort is itself an exercise of the will, and so for this reason it too ought to be valuable. But of course insofar as nonintense effort is the minimal exercise of will, it's only minimally valuable.

So just how valuable is it? We already are on board with the view that *the harder the better*, so the general idea we begin with is *the more effort, the better*. We have resources from Chapter 2 for calculating amount of effort. Should we suppose, then, that the greater the amount of effort, the better? Such a view would be a Total view, where the total effort maps onto a value—the greater the total effort, the greater the value.

You might worry, however, that given that nonintense effort is valuable, a scenario reminiscent of the ridiculous conclusion from Chapter 2 could arise. If the value of exercise of the will is entirely a matter of the total effort, there could be some maximally long but minimally intense exertion of the will that outweighed in value some shorter burst of intense effort. In other words, there could be some activity that required a tiny exertion of will that was *more valuable* than some shorter, but excellent exercise of the will. More strongly, for *any* excellent exercise of the will—that is, for any *achievement*—there could be a minimally effortful activity of long duration that was *more valuable* than the achievement. This of course is a cousin to the ridiculous conclusion we saw earlier in the discussion of difficulty, and it seems just as wrong. As a result, we should draw the analogous lesson: the Total approach to valuing effort is wrong, just as it was for calculating the amount of effort relevant for difficulty.

In this context, the analogous response to the ridiculous conclusion would be to say that nonintense effort is simply *not relevant for value*, just as nonintense effort is not relevant for difficulty. But I have just argued that perfectionism should not adopt such a position. It's a better version of perfectionism to say that even minimal exercise of the will is of some value. Yet we need to avoid the ridiculous conclusion redux.

Here is what I propose. Nonintense effort is indeed valuable, but only to a certain point. The value of exerting nonintense effort does not increase beyond a certain amount. There is, we might say, a *value ceiling*.

Effort can, we might suppose, be exerted in limitless amount. But when nonintense, the value of effort is not limitless. Quite the contrary, there is a limit of value for nonintense effort. So value increases as nonintense effort increases, but it will never exceed the value set by the value ceiling. In other words, the value of nonintense effort in any activity hits a plateau—once a certain amount of nonintense effort has been exerted, no additional nonintense effort will add value. Furthermore, the ceiling is low since the value of nonintense effort maxes out at a fairly low level. The most value that an exercise of nonintense effort can be worth is very low—it doesn't take very much to reach the maximum amount of value you can generate by minimal exercise of the will, that is, nonintense effort.

This pattern is illustrated in the graph in Figure 5.1. Value increases proportionately with exertion of nonintense effort, but only up to a certain point, at which the value of the nonintense effort remains constant, even while the amount of nonintense effort increases.

Lest this notion of a value ceiling seem unusual or ad hoc, I should point out that this pattern of value is not unique. A similar pattern of value is found in other instances as well. Parfit describes a view of population value according to which lives of a certain level of wellbeing may contribute value to the overall population only up to a certain point beyond which an additional life does not add value.[3]

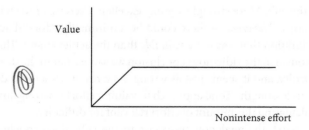

Figure 5.1

[3] Derek Parfit, *Reasons and Persons* (Oxford; Clarendon Press, 1984), 412.

So I will return to focus on the value of intense effort (IE), which seems to be much more valuable, and, of course, is what characterizes achievements. We already are comfortable with the position that value increases with IE, namely, the *more intense effort* something requires, the more valuable it is. But just what does this amount to? How much *more* valuable is more intense effort?

A basic approach would be something like this—a higher total IE means a higher value for the activity. On this basic view, value increases at the same rate as the increase of IE. But variations of the view are also possible. It might be the case that the value increases at a different rate from total IE—so it could be that doubling the total IE, say, is worth more than twice the value.

Alternatively, we might be inclined to think that achievements that are of a long duration but involve relatively low intensity of intense effort are *less* valuable than achievements that make use of a very high intensity of intense effort, albeit for a shorter duration—even if the total intense effort is greater in the former.

If we are inclined to think that this is the case, then we might instead favor a view that *weights* intensity of effort in a certain way, so that increasing the intensity of effort increases the value disproportionately to level of intensity. It seems to me that such a view has some intuitive appeal—it really does seem to be the case that increases of greater intensity of effort are even more impressive than they are at lower levels.

So just what is the rate at which value increases? In other words, how much more does intensity matter? Much, it turns out, hangs on this. We might be deciding about a way to apportion our time: should we take a long-term project that uses a moderate level of intense effort over a long period of time, such as writing a book, or is it better to embark on a series of relatively shorter projects that require a slightly higher intensity of effort? If intensity is weighted more greatly, then we might be able to have a greater number of more valuable achievements if we take on the series of short-term, high-intensity projects than if we take on a long-term, lower-intensity project.

Weighted Intensity

Let's consider a weighted view according to which both duration and intensity shape the value of effort, but intensity generates a greater increase in value than a similar increase in duration. Let's suppose that intensity is twice as significant for value as duration is. This relationship is captured as follows:

$$V = t + 2i$$

Value (v) is a matter of duration (t) plus twice the intensity (i). This formula captures the relevance of duration—increases of duration (holding intensity constant) yield an increase in value—and it captures the relevance of intensity, which is here weighted. As a result, increases in intensity result in *greater* increases in value than increases in duration alone, other things equal. (I choose 2 here as our weighting factor, but there are other possibilities. Intensity might have an exponential relationship to value—such that $v = t + i^2$.)

Let's now consider the implications of this *weighted intensity* view. It turns out that assessing whether or not a weighted intensity view is the way to go doesn't have an obvious solution. Although the practical implications are serious, in the end there doesn't seem to be much to tell either for or against weighting.

First, note that on the weighted intensity view, value no longer tracks *amount* of effort, therefore it does not track degree of difficulty. This might seem like an undesirable complication, but quite the contrary, since it turns out that this adds a nice symmetry to the view. As we will see later, where competent causation is concerned, value doesn't track degree of competent causation, but instead value tracks excellence of exercise of rationality. Accordingly, supposing that excellence of exercise of will is captured by weighted intensity, and the value of achievements is a matter of the value of the exercise of characteristic capacities. So the value of achievements doesn't track the degrees of the essential features of achievements. Rather, it tracks those features of the essential features of achievements that make them valuable.

Should we accept the weighted view?

If intensity is weighted as more valuable than duration, then there can be cases where an achievement of very long duration but low intensity is more valuable than an achievement of higher intensity and short duration.[4]

---

[4] How we weight intensity will determine the precise details of this case. If intensity is as proposed in the initial formula, $v = d + 2i$, it will take a certain (very long!) duration of low intensity activity to outweigh a short duration high-intensity achievement. In contrast, if we opt for an alternative weighting approach, such as $v = d + i^2$, it will take an even longer duration activity to outweigh in value an activity of high intensity but short duration.

Although on the surface this point may resemble the ridiculous conclusion, it is not an objection. At this point, we are considering *only* intense effort. So the long-duration, relatively low intensity achievement we are contrasting involves *intense* effort, albeit *less* intense than that in the more valuable, more intense shorter-duration achievement. As a result there is none of the ridiculousness that we considered earlier—it is not the case that an activity of such minimal intensity of effort as merely lifting a single finger could outweigh a high-intensity achievement. Rather the contrast here is more like running at a moderate pace for long enough outweighing sprinting for a short time. This, I think, is not implausible, but it's not particularly clear either way.

Let's consider a case. Suppose two people are taking a math test. Both answer the same number of questions correctly, but one finishes sooner through greater intensity of effort, while the other exerts less intense effort but for a greater duration. Which achievement is better? We might think at first that it's more impressive to complete the test quickly, that is, we might be impressed with their ability to deploy their skills rapidly, which is something we generally prize as a sign of intelligence. But supposing this skill itself has value, it's not relevant for determining the value of the intensity of effort. Besides, it's not obvious that he has a more adept ability for math than the other test-taker since he has to exert more intense effort to get it done faster. So which achievement is better? Myself, I don't have a strong inclination either way.

I think it is ultimately unclear whether or not intensity should be weighted. Moreover, there is considerable intuitive noise in considering cases since the instrumental effects of exertion and the value-theoretic possibilities pertaining to products as a result make it very difficult to isolate the relevant factors to test our intuitions. So there isn't much in favor or against weighting intensity, and so I conclude that is not an important refinement for the view.

Our initial concern arose when we wondered how we ought to apportion our time—is it better to take on a short-term, high-effort project or a long-term, lower effort project? Assuming the amount of intense effort in both options is the same, the intrinsic value of the effort itself, other things being equal, is not going to make a difference in this decision. However, there are certainly instrumental considerations that weigh in. It's possible that the high-intensity project will be very tiring, and prevent subsequent projects from taking flight. Alternatively, the high-intensity project requires less time, and so it might be possible, in the absence of fatigue, to achieve more than one achievement in the same time frame. Moreover, there is another important question which concerns the relative value of achievements compared to *other* things that may be valuable.[5] But none of these issues relates to the intrinsic value of achievements themselves, which is our concern here. These and other instrumental considerations are relevant for how we ought to apportion our time. But they do not concern the intrinsic value of the achievements themselves.

Infinite Effort

We might further wonder how difficult can something get. Assuming intense effort increases limitlessly, should we also think that there is some ceiling beyond which its value fails to increase? Should we think, that is, that there is a limit to the value of intense effort, as there is for nonintense effort?

If it is indeed the case that the value of intense effort could increase *limitlessly*, the issue here is really whether or not there could be *anything*—that is, in the universe—that could be more valuable than a limitlessly excellent exercise of will. Considering an absolutely limitless exercise of the will, it actually does not seem wholly unreasonable that the value of such magnificent exercise of will just might be the most supremely valuable thing in the universe. Something like God's act of creation could be the closest thing to this. And if anything is of supreme, limitless value, an act of God's will seems like a good candidate.

Yet it's unclear that this is what perfectionism would in fact entail. After all, perfectionism values the exercise of those capacities that are characteristically *human*, and *infinite* acts of will are not, I think, characteristically human. Yet it isn't an implausible extension of perfectionism to think that this is what it would have to say about this question. After all, the limits of our capacities as humans are merely contingent—so

---

[5] The relative value of achievement compared to other values such as pleasure is discussed nicely by Dale Dorsey, "First Steps in an Axiology of Goals," *International Journal of Wellbeing*, 1 (2011): 167–85.

were the characteristically human will limitless, then perfectionism would say that such exercise is valuable. How exactly this all should play out, however, is, I suppose, yet another area of perfectionism I will save for another time.

This, then, is the view: as the amount of intense effort increases, the value of the exercise of the will increases, and so too the value of the achievement, other things being equal. This, it seems, matches our intuitions. Running a marathon is a more valuable achievement than running two miles, cooking an elaborate gourmet meal is a more valuable achievement than cooking a simple meal; performing a more difficult violin concerto is a more valuable achievement than performing a less difficult one. In other words, other things being equal, the more intense effort is involved, the more valuable an achievement is; which is to say, *the more excellently the will is exercised, the more valuable is the achievement, without limit.*

This is assuming that these activities are indeed more difficult for the achiever in the way that I have sketched. Of course, it's quite possible that running two miles could be far more difficult than running a marathon, depending on the case. And I think, other things being equal, in that case it would be a greater achievement. Moreover, in the cases I've just mentioned, it's possible that *other* factors make the less difficult achievements more valuable—for example, the less difficult violin concerto might have more aesthetic value than the more difficult one; or the less elaborate meal might be prepared for a starving family whereas the more elaborate meal is only sampled delicately by overfed food critics.

In addition, without a doubt, difficult things are often painful. If an achievement is very difficult, shouldn't the *pain* caused by the effort detract from the value of the achievement? It's possible, but so far we're imagining cases that hold the other factors *constant*, including also the nonessential features such as how pleasant (or not) the achievement is. If my discussion of the value of the will has been convincing, then even if exerting the will is unpleasant, its value could even outweigh the disvalue of the pain of exertion.

So it seems quite clear that there are indeed other factors beyond excellent exercise of the will that contribute to the value of achievements. I will examine some of them in what follows. But first I will turn to the other essential feature of achievements: competent causation.

Competent Causation and Rationality

Now having just seen that the value of achievements increases when one of the sources of Essential Value increases, we shouldn't be surprised to see that the same thing happens when the *other* sources of Essential Value increase. And this indeed seems to be the case as far as competent causation is concerned.

Imagine two players at billiards. One is a beginner, who roughly knows what he is doing, and the other is a professional, who practices for hours, daily. Suppose that there is a shot to be made that's exceptionally tricky—the cue ball must ricochet just *so* in order to have the right velocity to knock the ball into the pocket. The professional knows exactly the right way to tap the cue ball just so, and exactly how to line up the shot. Let's suppose he makes the shot perfectly and sinks the ball, and it takes a certain amount of effort—an impressive achievement!

Now imagine the novice lining up the same shot—he knows enough about how to play to know roughly what he needs to do—namely, hit the cue ball so it knocks the other ball into the pocket. But, being a novice, he doesn't really have the knowledge about the exact angle the cue ball must take and the kind of velocity it must have in order to get the shot. He exerts some effort (suppose it's the same amount as the professional), and happens to makes the shot.

The novice, of course, understands what he is doing much less well than the professional. The professional knows exactly all the details of the nature of his skill—just what angle and speed and so on. The novice had the right general idea, but luck did a lot of the work in helping him sink the shot.

Which is the better achievement? It seems quite clear to me that the professional has exhibited a far more impressive achievement. The novice may have performed an impressive *feat*, but as far as valuable achievements go, the more valuable accomplishment seems to be the professional's.

We could also imagine a similar case with chefs: an amateur home cook and a professional gourmet chef both put the same amount of effort into preparing a five-course meal. The amateur follows the recipe, but doesn't exactly know what he's doing and sort of blunders through, more or less haphazardly, guessing on measuring ingredients and cooking temperatures. He understands what he is doing well enough to be causing it competently, but certainly doesn't have much understanding beyond this. The

professional, on the other hand, deploys her vast knowledge of every precise detail, slicing with perfect technique, drawing from not only practical
knowledge of how to cook, but also historical and cultural knowledge of
the origins of the various dishes. We can even imagine that the outputs
of both cooks are equally valuable—suppose that luck helped the amateur get the meal just so. It seems to me that, although both may indeed
be impressive achievements, the more valuable one belongs to the professional chef. An achievement just seems to be more valuable when you
really know what you're doing.

The general point seems true: achievements that have a higher degree
of competent causation do indeed seem to be more valuable. It just seems
to be better the more you know what you are doing. So it seems plausible
to propose that, other things being equal, *the more competently caused, the
better the achievement.*

In the previous chapter, we saw that the reason why competent causation is valuable is because it involves the exercise of one of the perfectionist capacities, the rational capacity. As such, then, it is of intrinsic value.
Unsurprisingly, then, the *more* excellently the rational capacity is exercised, the better. And so, it seems to follow here too, *the more competently
caused, the better the achievement.*

But it's not quite that straightforward. According to the view that
I described in Chapter 3, rationality plays its role in competent causation
in the following way: competent causation is a matter of having a certain
amount of justified true beliefs about the nature of one's activities. The
requisite amount of JTBs is a *percentage* of the *possible* relevant beliefs.
Whatever the nature of one's activities, there is a certain amount of things
that *one could know* about them. If the activity is very complex, that means
there are a lot of possible beliefs. If it's less complex, then there are fewer
possible beliefs. The degree to which the product of the achievement
is competently caused is a matter of *how much* of those possible beliefs
you actually have. The greater the percentage, the greater the degree of
competent causation. Having JTBs is, of course, exercising the rational
capacity, and this is why competent causation is valuable according to
perfectionism.

Now, since the degree to which something is caused competently
is a *percentage* of the relevant possible beliefs, it's possible to exercise
one's rational capacity very *limitedly* and yet cause something perfectly
competently. If we cause something very simple, when there is a small

number of possible relevant beliefs, we could have 100% of these beliefs, but only be exercising our rational capacity to a very small extent. Since the value of competent causation is a matter of the degree of excellence of exercise of rationality, this would mean that this particular exercise of rationality would *not* be particularly excellent, nor, then, particularly valuable.

The value in achievements that comes from the competence of causation doesn't come from the competent causation per se, but from the exercise of rationality that is manifested in competent causation. So, contrary to the first-pass slogan, even though the initial idea was that the more competently something is caused, the more valuable it is, this is not *exactly* what the view is. Rather, causing something competently is valuable *to the extent that it exercises the rational capacity*, and this is *not* always the same as the extent to which something is caused competently. So it isn't entirely accurate to say that the value of achievements increases as the degree of competent causation increases. (This *can* be true, but only if base amount of effects caused is also held constant.) What really determines the value of achievements, as far as the value sourced in competent causation goes, is this: other things being equal, the more JTBs, the better.

But even this is slightly misleading. After all, some JTBs are weightier than others. We need to get really clear about what it is to exercise the rational capacity excellently. As we saw in Chapter 3, not all JTBs count equally. To understand this, we need an account of what it is to exercise rationality excellently, and I draw from Hurka's account to elaborate. The view is, roughly, that excellence of exercise of rationality is a matter of having a certain measure of the relevant states—in this case, justified true beliefs.[6] The measure of JTBs is determined first, by *quantity* of individual JTBs. But we can quickly see that quantity isn't all that matters—it seems more valuable to have JTBs about some things than it is about others. To use Hurka's example, it would be more valuable to know a fundamental

---

[6] For the rational capacity, beliefs, justified beliefs, justified and true beliefs, and knowledge are all possible contenders for the relevant states. Presumably, all of these are manifestations of our rational capacity, and so a thorough account would count all of these. One plausible approach would be weighting the units assigned to each, where knowledge would be worth the most, and mere beliefs the least, as Hurka suggests, *Perfectionism* (Oxford: OUP, 1993), 112. Ultimately Hurka adopts the simple view that I use here, where justified true beliefs are the relevant states (*Perfectionism*, 113).

law of the universe than it would be to know the number of redheads in Beiseker, Alberta.[7] The relevant quality that makes some JTBs better than others, following Hurka, is determined *formally*.

To put it roughly, what matters for quality of JTBs can be accounted for in terms of their *generality*, or *explanatory power*.[8] JTBs that explain or entail other JTBs are of high quality. What makes for a high measure of JTBs, then, is having not only a large number of individual beliefs, but also having JTBs of high *quality*, which is to say of great explanatory power. So to exercise the rational capacity excellently is to score highly in terms of JTBs, which means having a high number and a high quality of JTBs. Thus, achievements in which competent causation makes use of such high-scoring JTBs will be *more* valuable than achievements in which competent causation is comprised of discrete, less explanatorily powerful JTBs.

An interesting implication of my view is this: we could exercise our rational capacity relatively well, and yet fail to cause something competently. So there could be some activity that is *not* competently caused, and therefore not an achievement, and yet is valuable in just the very same way that an achievement is valuable—more strongly, it could be *more* valuable than an achievement.

At first this might seem peculiar, but on closer investigation the peculiarity goes away. It seems reasonable that even something that is ultimately a failure of competent causation could involve a great deal of rational activity. For example,

Chemist. Dr Menhaji, a well-trained and intelligent organic chemist, is hard at work on synthesizing compound X, using a particular method, a. a requires Dr Menhaji to exercise her rational capacity to a very high degree. Unfortunately, even though a was a good approach, it ultimately doesn't produce X, meaning that Dr Menhaji fails to competently cause X.

Dr Menhaji has clearly exercised her rational capacity to a very high degree, even though she failed to competently cause X. This seems perfectly reasonable: one can exercise the rational capacity excellently, and yet fail to competently cause the product of the activity.

[7] *Perfectionism*, 100.   [8] *Perfectionism*, 114 ff.

Now consider Betty:

Omelet. Betty studies several recipes and watches a few YouTube clips on the technique used to prepare a French omelet. She tries it out, and voila! Omelet success.

Making an omelet the French way is moderately difficult, and requires a specific technique which Betty knows and follows—so she has a very high percentage of the possible relevant beliefs, meaning she competently caused the omelet, and it is an achievement.

Thus Dr Menhaji has not achieved compound X, and Betty has achieved her omelet. But let's be honest, Dr Menhaji's scientific work requires a far greater exercise of rationality than Betty's omelet. And it seem that even though Dr Menhaji was unsuccessful in this particular case, her activity is a more valuable activity than Betty making her omelet. So my view entails that you can do something that exercises the rational capacity more excellently than it would be in an achievement, and that this activity is *more valuable, for this reason,* than the achievement.[9]

But should we think that this is a problem with my view? I don't think that it is—it seems like a perfectly reasonably implication that excellent exercise of rationality is intrinsically valuable—no matter whether or not it's in an achievement.

So far I've been arguing that the greater the exercise of rationality, the greater the value. But one might object that my view seems a bit lop-sided. There are, after all, *two* components to competent causation—the competence *and* the causation—and I have located the value of achievements in only one of them, competence. But why should this be the case? After all, so far it looks to be the case that each of the essential features of achievements is a source of value—so it's a natural thought that the *causation* side of competent causation, essential feature of achievement that it is, would also be a source of value.

We might further think that this could even fit in quite nicely with the perfectionist story about the value of achievements that I have been telling. Presumably this line of thought would be that our ability to *cause* things is a characteristic human capacity, and hence its exercise is valuable. This

---

[9] Just to be clear, although Dr Menhaji does not achieve compound X, there is another sense in which her activities do constitute an achievement. I discuss this in the next chapter.

wouldn't be an implausible idea, since it certainly seems to be an inevitable feature of us—indeed we can't do anything at all without causing something.

But I reject the idea that there is a need to acknowledge such a capacity as a perfectionist one—after all, although it may indeed be an inevitable feature of human beings, it hardly seems *characteristic* of us, or special to us in any way. Virtually *everything in the universe* has the capacity to cause effects. More importantly, it doesn't seem like it passes my other perfectionist heuristic test, namely that it is intuitively worth developing. So it's hard to see why this would be something worth capturing by perfectionism.

Yet it's not a wild thought insofar as it seems that there is an intuition here: the *more* we *cause*, the more impressive our competent causation. According to what I have proposed so far, the value of competent causation is in the *competence*, and so a greater amount of effects other things being equal shouldn't have an impact on the value of the activity. So is the approach as I have described it so far inadequate? Does it need to be expanded to capture the intrinsic value, if any, of causing?

It's difficult to see what it really means to cause "more." The analysis of competent causation starts with the assumption that an agent causes a product, via his action, and is a relation between the agent, the action, the product, and the agent's beliefs. So there isn't an obvious way in which one can cause "more" on this analysis.

But what we might mean is that the achievement has *multiple products*. Is producing more products a further source of value for achievements? Even if there was no initial case for a perfectionist capacity to cause, if we have a strong intuition that causing is indeed valuable then perhaps there is such a perfectionist capacity after all. So let us consider holding constant the degree of difficulty and the degree of rationality as well as the value of the products: would producing *more* add to the value of the achievement?

It is hard to see why one would be tempted to think so, but let's consider an example. Suppose that tiny log cabins made of popsicle sticks have virtually no value. Alice makes twelve popsicle stick log cabins exerting the same amount of effort and exercising the same amount of rationality as Bob does to make just one. Assuming that both activities fulfill the criteria for achievements, is Alice's achievement more valuable than Bob's? At first one might be inclined to think that Alice causes her log cabins less competently because with the greater number of products, there is a greater number of base beliefs, so the percentage that she has of these beliefs must be lower than Bob's because both Bob and Alice exercise the same amount of rationality. But really there must be very *few* additional beliefs since the nature of the activity is so repetitive. So Alice is still causing her log cabins just about as competently as Bob.

It seems there is a very slight intuitive pull in favour of Alice's achievement having more value. But this hardly seems to be sheerly from the multiplicity of the products. Rather, it seems that the additional source of value is the ability to produce a greater number of these things by exerting the same amount of effort as it takes someone else to produce only one, you probably have a special talent for these things, or for crafts in general. It's plausible that such a crafty talent would have intrinsic value (Martha Stewart, case in point). So it's not the causing of many products that's valuable, but a special ability. (I discuss the way in which additional, non-essential elements such as talents can add value to achievements in what follows.)

So the value of the achievement increases as the exercise of rationality increases, other things being equal, but an increase in amount of products caused does not result in a similar increase in value.

Unity in Diversity

Now that we've seen that the value of an achievement, holding the other factors constant, increases when the exercise of the will increases, and increases when the exercise of rationality increases, we might expect to see that the value of achievements also increases as degree of unity in diversity increases.

Unity in diversity, as I briefly discussed earlier, can increase with an increase along either of its two dimensions, unity and diversity. If an organic unity becomes more unified, holding diversity constant, it becomes more valuable. Similarly, if it gains additional diversity, holding unity constant, it also gains value.

As far as achievements go, it seems at first glance that neither of these dimensions can increase. Unity, as we saw earlier, is a matter of exercise of the will and rationality being located in the same process, and *sameness* of process doesn't admit of degrees—it's either the same, or it isn't. As far as diversity is concerned, there are only two necessary features of achievement, difficulty and competent causation, and these features require the exercise of two of our characteristic capacities. There are only two essential features of achievements that require the exercise of perfectionist capacities, and so the exercise of the will and the exercise of rationality exhaust the opportunities for the exercise of perfectionist capacities that could be unified within achievements. So there is no opportunity for increases in diversity.

Diversity

Now it's true that there is no room for increase in diversity as far as the Essential Value of achievements is concerned. There are only two essential features of achievements, which involve perfectionist capacities to be unified—difficulty and competent causation. But in some achievements, there can be additional diversity. This can happen if other perfectionist capacities are exercised as well. There is, after all, at least one more perfectionist capacity that I have noted, namely, our physical capacity. And there may be others as well. (To keep things simple, I will focus here only on the physical capacity.)

Of course, according to perfectionism, the exercise of *any* of our characteristic capacities is of intrinsic value, so we already know that if an achievement involves the exercise of any additional perfectionist capacity, such as the physical capacity, this is indeed additionally valuable. Presumably, if the physical capacity is exercised in an achievement it would be exercised in the *process* of the achievement. I will return to the issue later on in this chapter, but we can for now note that the auxiliary exercise of perfectionist capacities can augment the value of an achievement by contributing additional value to the process. But here my interest is in the additional *diversity* that an achievement would gain with the additional exercise of a further perfectionist capacity.

What makes achievements diverse is that they involve, necessarily, the exercise of *different* perfectionist capacities. So the *more* perfectionist capacities are exercised, the more diverse the achievement will be, and, accordingly, the more valuable. It follows, then, that when the physical capacity is exercised in an achievement, this achievement will exhibit more diversity than one in which it is not and, accordingly, it will be *more valuable*.

Needless to say, this is the case so long as the other features of achievements are held constant while the diversity is increased, and, moreover, this is assuming that the additional diversity is also *unified*. As I discussed earlier, the unifying relation relevant for the unity in diversity of achievements is *co-location* of process. That is, the exercises of the diverse perfectionist capacities are unified in achievements by being exercised in the *same process*. So, if an achievement makes use of the physical capacity, and the physical capacity is exercised in the very same process in which the will and rationality are, there is an increase in diversity of the sort relevant for value, and the achievement is, accordingly, more valuable. What this means, then, is that Baryshnikov's magnificent performances, Wayne Gretzky's epic career, and Paula Radcliffe's world-record marathon are all the more valuable as achievements because of the excellent exercise of the physical capacities that they involve.

Now, I've just said that an achievement that makes use of the exercise of our physical capacity could be *more* valuable than an achievement that does not. Here is a notable implication: this means that playing some very challenging sport such as hockey could be more valuable than doing some moderately decent philosophy.[10]

This is indeed an implication of my view that I am willing to embrace. If the degree of excellence of exercise of the will and rationality is the same in both hockey and the philosophy, and hockey has the additional exercise of the physical capacity, then indeed hockey will be a more valuable achievement. Some people might balk at this. Surely, one might think that this view is going against the grain of intuition, and that holding the position that hockey is more valuable than philosophy is to some degree anti-philosophical of me. But lest we languish in our *ressentiment*, I think we should be more open-minded to excellence that we ourselves may not find within our own reach.

Nonetheless, the bottom line of my position still sides with the nerds rather than the jocks. Doing philosophy, in the majority of cases, is better than playing hockey. Typically, in philosophy, we are exercising the

---

[10] As a matter of fact, according to an analysis by ESPN, hockey is indeed among the most demanding sports, second only to boxing. <http://sports.espn.go.com/espn/page2/story?page=degree/index>, retrieved May 2010. ESPN's analysis of difficulty differs from the one that I give in Chapter 2, but is interesting nonetheless. What the analysis captures is perhaps more accurately described as how skillfully demanding the sport is.

rational capacity *far more* excellently than we typically would when playing hockey. The number and quality of the JTBs that we entertain in philosophy are both very high, meaning that the structure of the kinds of things that we aim to figure out in philosophy have a very high level of explanatory power, and so it is very valuable to think about them. Really, then, it's only going to be mediocre philosophy that runs the risk of being outweighed in value by very good hockey—philosophy in which, relative to good philosophy, the rational capacity is exercised very poorly. To outshine the value of the rational capacity exercised in philosophy would take a much greater good, it seems, than can typically be generated by the exercise of physical excellence.

Besides, there is more to be said to explain why doing philosophy is typically more valuable than sports. The explanation for this has to do with the *limits* of our capacities, which I will turn to in greater depth shortly. For now, the explanation has to do with this: the rational capacity has a *higher limit* than both the will and the physical capacity. It's possible to exercise the rational capacity *more excellently* than it is to exercise the will or physical capacities. The will and physical capacity hit their limits, as it were, sooner than rationality does. This, of course, varies for different people, but the idea is that the very best of these capacities hit their limits in the way I've just described.

To sum, then, diversity can account for changes in value in achievements, by way of increased degree of organic unity, as well as adding value to the process.

Unity

A natural thought might be that unity, too, can come in degrees, and then accordingly value would vary with degree of unity.

But it isn't clear that unity in achievements *can* come in degrees. My view, as we saw earlier, is that the unifying relation of achievements is *sameness of process*. The diverse elements of achievements, namely exercise of two different characteristic human capacities, are united in achievements because the exercise of both these capacities is located in the same process. Co-location of process doesn't admit of degrees: either the two capacities are being exercised in the same process, or they are not. So there is no variation in degree of unity in achievements that could result in variation in value.

To be clear, the sort of unifying relation that's at issue here is the relation that obtains in achievements which is responsible for establishing their status as organic unities—that is, it is the relation that unites the diverse elements of achievements, and thereby generates value. So the particular unifying principle at stake here is a *value-theoretic* principle. This opposed to, say, a *metaphysical* principle. Achievements, as we know, are organic unities as a result of their being comprised of diverse elements that are unified together, and they are valuable as a result of this structure. No doubt there are myriad ways in which things, including achievements, can be unified. But the issue here is just to look into the specific relation that unifies achievements in a particular way crucial to their value, namely, the relation that is at stake in making achievements instances of unity in diversity.

Yet it seems that there is another, highly plausible way in which we could conceive of the unifying principle of achievements. After all, the same process can be more or less difficult or competent *at different times*—part of the process might not be difficult, or part of it might not be quite so competent. So perhaps this is a way to understand achievements as being unified. The difficulty and competent causation *overlap* in the same process. Overlapping admits of degrees—difficulty and competent causation can overlap to a greater or lesser extent. So here's an alternative view of the unifying principle for achievements: *overlap*.

We need to decide which account of unity is relevant for the unity in diversity of achievements—is it co-location, or is it overlap? We can investigate this question by looking at a pair of achievements where both achievements have co-location of difficulty and competent causation, but one has complete overlap of difficulty and competent causation, while the other one has only partial overlap. Then we should compare our intuitions about the value of these two cases. Since co-location is the same in both cases, if there is any difference in value, it won't be explained by co-location. But if there *is* a variation in value, and it tracks variation in overlap, then this will give us a reason to endorse overlap as the unifying principle of achievements, rather than co-location.

Suppose that achievement A competently causes its product, and is difficult to the same consistent degree throughout the duration of the process. Achievement B also competently causes its product, but, in contrast to A, it is *intermittently* difficult. For some portions of the process, it's difficult, but it's not difficult in other portions of the process (yet B is still difficult *overall*).

I will represent A and B in Figures 5.2 and 5.3. Competent causation is consistent throughout the duration of the process. This is represented by the solid line—competent causation extending over the course of the activity. A is consistently difficult throughout, and the solid line stretching over the course of the activity represents this. The difficulty, that is, overlaps entirely with the competent causation in A.

(A)

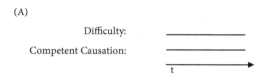

Difficulty:

Competent Causation:

t

Figure 5.2

In B, on the other hand, there are difficult and non-difficult portions of the process, meaning that some parts of the process that are competently causing the product are not overlapped by difficulty.

(B)

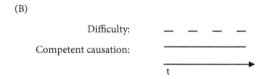

Difficulty:

Competent causation:

t

Figure 5.3

So which seems to be the better achievement? The natural sense is that A is better. B is only partly difficult, after all, and it just seems more impressive that something be difficult all the way through. So perhaps overlap does indeed generate value.

But this is too hasty—B, in this example is *less difficult* than A. It's not overlap that's responsible for the difference in value, but the difference in difficulty.

So to really see if overlap is responsible for a difference in value, we need to be careful to consider two cases where the amount of difficulty is the same. This is easily accomplished by adjusting the original B case to make the difficult intervals slightly more difficult so that there is the same amount of difficulty overall in B as there is in A (Figure 5.4).

(B')

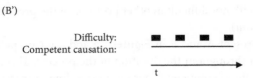

Difficulty:
Competent causation:

t

Figure 5.4

In B' the difficult intervals are each *more* difficult than any particular moment of A, but overall the total degree to which A is difficult is the same as B—that is, they both have the same amount of total intense effort.

Now which seems to be more valuable? I don't think that either does. Many achievements, in fact, are not uniformly difficult, and even have stretches that aren't that difficult at all. Just consider building a canoe. It's an achievement, and overall very difficult. But it also involves stretches of non-difficult activity—taking measurements, sanding the wood, and painting the canoe, and so on. These non-difficult interludes are indeed parts of the process of the achievement, and do not detract from its value.

So having non-difficult interludes doesn't matter for the value of an achievement. All that matters is that the whole process is difficult. So the consideration of our non-overlap case doesn't give us any reason to think that value tracks overlap. Thus there is no reason here to revise our original view that the unifying principle of achievements is co-location of process.

But co-location of process doesn't admit of degrees. So if co-location is the unifying principle for achievements, achievements cannot admit of degrees of unity in the way that matters for value. To be sure, the value of achievement can indeed vary with degree of unity in diversity, but only as a result of variation in diversity, not unity.

The Relative Value of the Will and Rationality

So far we have seen that achievements vary in value as a result of variations in degree of exercise of the will or rationality. The more the will is exercised, the more valuable an achievement is, and the more that rationality is exercised, the more valuable an achievement is. And we've also seen that the value of achievements comes from unity in diversity, and increases in diversity—as a matter of the exercise of additional perfectionist

capacities—make achievements more valuable. So, we might now wonder whether these various variations in the perfectionist capacities make
similar differences in the value of achievements. Is an achievement that
involves additional exercise of the will, say, just as valuable as an achievement that has an additional increase in any other capacity? What we need
is a trade-off schedule of the relative values of the various perfectionist
capacities.

A complete trade-off schedule of the relative values of the perfectionist capacities requires a project of its own, so here I will only consider the
relative value of the capacities that are essential to achievements. So the
question is this: is an increase in will as valuable as a comparable increase
in rationality? In other words, is an achievement better if it manifests the
excellent exercise of rationality, or is it better if it manifests an excellent
exercise of the will to a similar degree? Which, that is to say, is more valuable: the will or rationality?

The most basic answer to this question is that these perfectionist
capacities are *equally valuable*. This is indeed the position that I think
we should endorse. An increase of the will is as valuable as a comparable
increase of rationality. Other things being equal, it is just as valuable to
exercise the will as it is to exercise rationality. So the value of achievements
is determined by weighting equally the excellent exercise of the will and
rationality.

This might raise a skeptical eyebrow. Can we really make cross-type
comparisons? How much sense does it make to ask about "comparable
amounts" of the will and rationality? After all, the will is a matter of exerting effort, in units of eff-minutes, and exercising rationality is a matter of
weighted justified true beliefs. It seems ridiculous to suggest that, say, X
amount of eff-minutes would be worth Y amount of justified true beliefs.
If we can't compare degrees of excellence of exercise of the will and rationality, we can't make comparisons of assessments of value.

But I do indeed think that we can sensibly make comparisons about
degree of will and rationality. Compare, for example, the exercise of the
will in running a marathon with the exercise of rationality of adding two
three-digit numbers in your head. It seems fairly obvious to me that there
is a greater exercise of will in running the marathon than there is of rationality in adding the numbers.

This might do for rough comparisons, the skeptic might say—of course
it is obvious when there is so gross a difference, but this is no indication

that there is a common unit, so to speak, of excellence that we could use to compare the exercise of the two capacities.

Yet I don't see why there couldn't be—after all, if gross comparisons are possible, then it doesn't seem like it would be impossible to imagine a common currency of excellence that we are using to compare their excellence. So I proceed on the assumption that they are indeed comparable.

Even granting that they are comparable, you still might not be inclined to agree that the exercise of the will and rationality are just as valuable as each other. If they are, then it could be possible that doing something of *sheer difficulty*, but low rationality, if it were difficult *enough*, could be *more valuable* than a truly excellent exercise of rationality. For example, there could be a mountain so difficult to climb that doing so would be more valuable than proving Fermat's last theorem. This might seem implausible. It seems even to me, fan of difficulty that I am, that there is no mountaineering expedition so difficult, say, that the universe would be better off if we traded the proof for its success. Nothing of sheer difficulty, it seems, could be such that its difficulty was valuable enough to outshine the value of an achievement that manifested a significant amount of rationality. The will and rationality seem to be not as valuable as one another, unit for unit. Rationality is superior, and perhaps even lexically so. I share this intuition. Yet I think that my proposal is still correct: the will and rationality are each as valuable as the other.

Here is one reason why we might not be inclined to think that this is so. It is typically very difficult to do something that requires a high degree of rationality. As a result, achievements that involve a very high degree of excellence of exercise of rationality *also* involve a very high exercise of the will. So because solving Fermat's last theorem involves such a high degree of exercise of rationality, it's very difficult, so it could be as difficult as climbing a mountain. But I don't find this line of response sufficient. Of course it *could be*, but the thought here is that we are considering a mountain that requires *even more* effort to be climbed than the proof requires.

There is also the following consideration. Solving Fermat's last theorem, one might think, has an independently valuable product that is not simply tantamount to the exercise of rationality involved in its discovery. The proof itself has intrinsic value. Suppose that this is so, we will need to imagine an even greater mountain the climbing of which involves such a great exercise of will that it adds up to outweigh both the excellent exercise of rationality *and* the independent intrinsic value of the proof. Naturally, the proof might be thought to have a great deal of instrumental value as well, so we shall suppose the mountain is great enough to account for this too. Is it possible that climbing the mountain is more valuable than the proof and its discovery?

Admittedly, it may be unclear. There are problems that arise in making such comparisons. What if these two valuable things exhibit a kind of incommensurability? A mathematical proof may have the sort of value that can't accurately be compared with the value of achievements. Or the value of achievements may reach a certain kind of ceiling, where even the *most* valuable achievement might not be as valuable as some *other* thing. Now, in order for me to take a stand on this last question, I would have to go afield to further substantive theories of value. The proof of Fermat's last theorem, if it has intrinsic value, may have it in virtue of some other source of value.

But we have actually now strayed from the original question by introducing a further source of value. The original question was whether or not exercise of will could be more valuable than exercise of rationality. What we really need to compare is an exercise of will and an exercise of rationality *neither of which* result in an independently valuable product. So let us compare instead one individual's *understanding* Sir Andrew John Wiles' proof of Fermat's last theorem.

The product has no independent intrinsic value (it's already been proven; we already live in a world that is such that the proof is a part of it). So as far as the proof itself is concerned, we are not adding anything of intrinsic value to the universe; rather, we are not adding anything of intrinsic value to the universe apart from our own exercise of rationality. The question for comparison is this: could there be a mountain so high and difficult to climb that doing so is more valuable than one individual's personal comprehension of the (already proven) proof? Even if understanding the proof is very difficult, it is plausible that there very well could be a mountain the climbing of which was more valuable than one individual's comprehension of the proof. So it does indeed seem fair to say that the value of exercising the will is just as valuable as the exercise of rationality.

We may nonetheless find ourselves inclined to think that this isn't so, and that rationality is the superior of the two. I can think of two reasons that are worth mentioning why we might be pulled in this direction.

First, it may be typical of achievements that involve a very high exercise of rationality that they result in a product that has a high degree of independent intrinsic value. Perhaps even the comprehension of Fermat's theorem, and cases like it, really do have an independently valuable product—namely, one individual's comprehension—which is not identical to the individual's exercise of rationality. Exactly how this shakes out would be a very interesting question to pursue. Does an individual's single item of comprehension have independent intrinsic value apart from the act of rationality itself?

The second point reveals something interesting about the nature of our capacities. In short, the will is easier to max out than rationality. The rational capacity may seem better to exercise than the will because there is a greater upper bound for excellence of exercise of rationality than there is for the will. Given human beings as they are, the highest degree of excellence of exercise of rationality of which one is typically capable in a given instance is higher than the highest degree of excellence of exercise of the will. To be straightforward about it, there is only so much effort you can exert before you get really tired and have to stop, whereas exercising rationality can be done, even in a very valuable way, pretty much all day long.

Consider closely what it is to exercise the will excellently: to exercise the will excellently is to exert intense effort. Realistically, how much intense effort can we imagine even the most excellent human specimen exerting in a typical day? A lot, to be sure. But, even if you pace yourself, you're going to get tired and need to stop eventually.

Now consider what it is that we are doing when we exercise our rationality: having justified true beliefs. In other words, knowing things and thinking about them. And, on the view of excellence of rationality that we are adopting here, some kinds of justified true beliefs are more valuable to have than others; that is, having justified true beliefs that have a great deal of general explanatory power are worth a whole lot more than discrete, specific beliefs. So to comprehend all sorts of, say, scientific theories, or philosophical explanations, is to exercise the rational capacity very excellently. Our most excellent specimen, then, if he is exercising his rational capacity excellently on this sample afternoon, will, no doubt, be thinking about all sorts of wonderful expansive knowledge. It seems perfectly possible to learn, know, contemplate, and comprehend all sorts of wonderful knowledge all day long before you get too tired and need to stop.

As a result, the intuition is that it is better to exercise rationality than the will because you can get more bang for your buck, as it were. If you only have an afternoon, and want to exercise your perfectionist capacities with as much excellence as possible, it's likely that you will be able to have more excellent exercise of rationality than you would if you just exert the will. The point here is that, in a particular instance, it is often the case that you can exercise more rationality than you can the will. From this it does not follow that an increase of exercise of rationality is better than a comparable increase in exercise of the will, just that often we can get more value for our time with rationality. So perhaps Aristotle was on to something when he said that "we are more capable of continuous study than any continuous action."[11]

Now, you might want to object here that this observation about the relative limits of the will and rationality is merely contingent, since it's just a feature of how humans *happen to be* that our will has a lower upper limit than our rationality. It's possible to imagine a person with a capacity to will that is much greater—someone who is capable of exercising the will more excellently than the best exercise of rationality. So we can imagine a case of exercise of will that is better than rationality—we would have to say that there is indeed some sheerly difficult task that requires such exercise of the will that it is indeed better than comprehending Fermat's last theorem or even the grand unified theory of physics and philosophy. If the will and rationality are equally valuable, unit for unit, then this superhumanly difficult task could be more valuable than comprehending the very best of knowledge. And, the objection would go, this doesn't seem right.

While this might be meant as an objection to my view, I'm not sure that I myself have the intuition that this magnificent exertion of the will would *not* be better than solving Fermat's last theorem or comprehending the grandest of unified theories. So if this is indeed what perfectionism says, then I am open to this implication.

Yet it's not clear that this is indeed what perfectionism entails. As I discussed earlier, perfectionism values the characteristically human capacities. This capacity to exert an extraordinary amount of effort would *not* be captured by perfectionism as valuable, because it's not characteristic of humans. Quite literally it is superhuman. So in the end it's unclear whether or not perfectionism would have anything at all to say about a superhuman exertion of will and its value relative to genius-level comprehension.

[11] *Nicomachean Ethics*. Tr. Terence Irwin (Indianapolis: Hackett, 1999), 1177a23.

One further observation about the relative value of the will and rationality with regard to achievements: in order for something to be an achievement, it requires a much *higher* exercise of the will than it does of rationality. It doesn't take much exercise of rationality in order for a process to competently cause its product. But it may typically take quite a bit of exercise of the will for the process to be difficult. As a result, the value of achievements that comes from the excellence of exercise of the perfectionist capacities may often come from the exertion of the will in greater proportion than from the exercise of rationality. This also means that activities that are *not* achievements but involve a very high level of exercise of rationality could have more value sourced in the exercise of perfectionist capacities than an achievement. I point this out not as a problem with my view, since it isn't one, but rather as a noteworthy implication.

The Cure for Cancer and Other Valuable Products

Now, as I have said several times, it would be ridiculous of me to deny that having a product of positive value would augment the value of the achievement. Obviously it's far more valuable to *actually* develop the cure for cancer than it is to do something equally as difficult and equally as competent but which produces nothing of value beyond itself. So, since it wouldn't be reasonable not to, I hold the view that the product of an achievement adds value to the achievement overall.

The same is true of the process, since the process of an achievement could have value beyond the excellent exercise of the will and beyond the excellent exercise of rationality pertinent to competent causation. It's possible, as I intimated earlier, that the process could make use of some other perfectionist capacities—such as the physical capacity—and thus have value in this way too.[12] Moreover, the process may have other features that make it valuable, apart from involving an exercise of will or rationality, as we will see shortly.

---

[12] It turns out that it's actually more complicated than this. Later I discuss a highly plausible value-theoretic principle, which is that (in short) when given some intrinsically valuable thing, the active pursuit of this intrinsically valuable thing is itself of intrinsic value. Such a principle has implications for the value of achievements when the product has nonzero value, as we see shortly.

To be clear, the value at issue is the value that the product or process has independently of any value that comes from difficult or competent causation; that is, the value that the product has independently of being the excellent exercise of the will or rationality. Yet it is possible in a given achievement to exercise rationality independently of its contribution to competent causation. And in such a case, that exercise of rationality relevant for competent causation would be part of this further independent value of the process. In contrast, any exercise of the will in an achievement will be part of what makes the process difficult.

Apart from the exercise of perfectionist capacities, what could the sources of the value of process or product be? They are, to be straightforward about it, whatever value theory says they are. So far I have only explicitly affirmed perfectionism, as well as the value of unity in diversity. But, of course, this view can be supplemented with further theories of value and further value-theoretic principles. If pleasure is of intrinsic value, for example, as it is plausible to think, then if the process is especially enjoyable, it could have value from pleasure. Similarly if the product of some achievement involves pleasure, this too could be a source of value for the product. We can imagine a variety of ways in which the products or processes of achievements can have value—they could be very beautiful or have aesthetic value, they could involve a display of virtue, or the contemplation of some valuable knowledge.

More controversially, there are some axiological views that say that something can have intrinsic value in virtue of having *instrumental* value.[13] This is particularly relevant for achievements. For any achievement that has a product of intrinsic value, the *process* of the achievement could be said to have instrumental value. If it is indeed the case that instrumental value can be a source of intrinsic value, then achievements might sometimes be additionally intrinsically valuable in this way. And, of course, more straightforwardly, many achievements, no doubt, have products of instrumental value—such as the development of a vaccine, for example. This view would hold that these products have intrinsic value in virtue of their instrumental value, and this value would be incorporated in the intrinsic value of the achievement. This seems to me to be a highly plausible way of accounting for the value of achievements with products of instrumental value.

[13] Cf. Shelly Kagan, "Rethinking Intrinsic Value," *Ethics*, 2 (1998): 277–97.

In any case, the value of the process or product contributes to the value of an achievement. But how, exactly? The most straightforward approach would be *summative*. The additional value of the product or process of an achievement is simply summed with the rest of the value of the achievement's Essential Value. The total value of the achievement, then, is the achievement's Essential Value—namely, its value from the excellent exercise of the will and rationality and the value from unity in diversity—plus the value of the process and the value of the product.

Evil Achievements

The summative approach is appealing because it gives us a nice way of assessing what we might call *evil achievements*.[14] By evil achievement, I mean an achievement that has a product that is of negative value. In Chapter 1, I argued that restricting the value of the products had implausible and overly restrictive results. But this means that something that results in a product that is *very* evil—utterly heinous, even—can be an achievement, providing the process is difficult and competently causes the product. Insofar as it's an achievement, then, it's going to have the same essential features as any other achievement. According to what I have just argued, such an achievement will therefore have positive value insofar as it has the Essential Value common to all achievements.

Given the summative approach to incorporating the value of the product of an achievement into overall value, the value of the product is summed with the Essential Value of the achievement. Since evil achievements have products of negative value, the overall total value of the achievement can ultimately be *negative*, when the value of the product is of greater negative value than the Essential Value is positive.

However, it is also possible that an evil achievement be of overall positive value. The positive value of Essential Value could outweigh even a very bad product if the achievement was difficult and competent enough so as to have very high Essential Value.

This is deeply counterintuitive. An ingenious plan resulting in the murder of innocent people surely isn't of positive intrinsic value, even if it is

---

[14] In this section, I draw from my "Evil Achievements and the Principle of Recursion," in Mark Timmons (ed.), *Oxford Studies in Normative Ethics*, iii (Oxford: OUP, 2013), 79–97.

very ingenious, we might think. Yet note that such cases are rare. Typically, if the product is negative, there will also be elements of the process that are negative, such as desires to bring about evil in the world. So in a typical evil achievement the Essential Value will have to be so extraordinarily high that perhaps such a case might not seem too counterintuitive after all. Even still, this conclusion is hard to accept.

Additionally, there is concern about accidentally evil achievements. Suppose a team of brilliant doctors has been laboring arduously to develop a cure for cancer with enough effort and competence to potentially satisfy the achievement criteria. Unfortunately upon administering their cure to hundreds of patients, they discover that it instead causes horrific and painful death. Although the product here is clearly bad, we might be inclined to say that their endeavor was not, in fact, evil. It certainly isn't anywhere as bad as it would be had they intentionally brought about hundreds of painful deaths. So there may be some merit to the basic summative approach.

Indeed, contrasting our team of brilliant benevolent doctors with their brilliant malevolent counterparts brings to light something important that the basic summative approach fails to capture. This is the goodness of pursuing good goals and badness about pursuing bad goals. Pursuing a good goal is, plausibly, much better than pursuing a bad one. Moreover, doing so isn't simply better because of the additional value of the goal, but the pursuit of the good itself—independently from reaching the good goal—seems to be better than the pursuit of the bad. If we were to suppose that neither the benevolent doctors nor the malevolent doctors reached their goal, I think we would be inclined to say that the benevolent doctors' pursuit of the cure was *better*, intrinsically, than the pursuit of the malevolent doctors. This seems to be true intrinsically, since, if we suppose neither group attains their goal, their pursuits in this case don't have any instrumental value.

There is a philosophical tradition of honoring such intuitions with a principle. The general notion this principle captures is that *it is good to love the good*. Correspondingly, the principle also holds that is good to hate the bad, bad to hate the good, and bad to love the bad. Understood broadly, we can here take "love" and "hate" as pro- and con-attitudes and activities more generally, so "loving" can be a matter of desiring, wishing, enjoying, pursuing, preserving, appreciating, respecting, and so on; and "hating" can be a matter of disliking, avoiding, destroying, damaging, disrespecting. The notion is that, given some intrinsically good or bad object, a pro- or con-attitude directed toward the object *itself* gains a value of a certain valence as a result of being directed toward its object. There is no traditional name for the principle, although it has a distinguished history. I christen it the *amare bonum bonus*—to love the good is good.[15]

The philosophical tradition of this principle includes subscribers such as Aristotle, Brentano, Moore, Nozick, and others. Arguably, Aristotle holds a version of the notion, to the extent that he holds that at least some good things—activities—have a fitting or "proper" pleasure.[16] And, famously, that the pleasure "completes" a good activity, presumably thereby augmenting its value, as "the bloom on youths."[17] Chisholm attributes a version of the principle to Brentano, which is certainly in line with his definition of intrinsic value as that which loving is *correct*. Brentano, on Chisholm's reading, also holds that correct love of the good is also good.[18] G. E. Moore is often associated with this principle, since a great deal of his discussion of organic unities involves the positive value of wholes including loving the good or beautiful, or hating the bad or ugly.[19] Notably, Robert Nozick has an extensive discussion of the principle.[20]

---

[15] In "Evil Achievements and the Principle of Recursion," I followed Hurka in calling this principle "Recursion." To be clear, the principle covers not only that loving the good is good, but also the other corresponding values, including the goodness of hating the bad, and the badness of loving the bad, and the badness of hating the good.

[16] From *Nicomachean Ethics*:

[S]ince activities differ in degrees of decency and badness, and some are choice-worthy, some to be avoided, some neither, the same is true of pleasures; for each activity has its proper pleasure. Hence the pleasure proper to an excellent activity is decent, and the one proper to a base activity is vicious; for, similarly, appetites for fine things are praiseworthy, and appetites for shameful things are blameworthy. (1175b25–30)

It's unclear whether or not Aristotle's view is that the pleasures in the respectively good and bad activities are *intrinsically* good or bad. Hurka takes this to be an expression of Recursion (*Virtue, Vice and Value* (Oxford: OUP, 2001), 23) but also notes that there are differences between Aristotle's views in *Nicomachean Ethics* and fully formed Recursion. Moreover, it seems that Aristotle's view is that the pleasure that "completes" the activity is *caused* by the activity, when the activity is done the right way. He says it arises "as a consequent end" (1174b30), which seems slightly different from the relevant pleasure for Recursion. In any case, there is something of the spirit of the principle in Aristotle.

[17] e.g. see *Nicomachean Ethics* 1174b20–5, 1174b30.

[18] R. M. Chisholm, *Brentano and Intrinsic Value* (Cambridge: CUP, 1986), 63.

[19] *Principia Ethica* (Cambridge: CUP, 1971), 191 ff. Moore's view, on one reading, is that the value accrued in situations involving a pro-attitude toward a good is accrued by the *whole* comprised of the attitude and base good. He explicitly says that the mere existence of a beautiful object on its own is of very little value, and the pro-attitude, on its own, would have hardly any value (*Principia Ethica*, 190). In this respect, Moore's discussion departs from the *amare bonum bonus* as we understand it here, where the base indeed has significant positive intrinsic value.

[20] *Philosophical Explanations* (Cambridge, MA: Harvard University Press, 1981), 429 ff.

Thomas Hurka presents perhaps the most thorough development of *amare bonum bonus* in his account of virtue. He calls the principle *recursion*, after recursion in mathematics, which involves a similar pattern:

(1) For some base intrinsic good, G, loving G is itself of positive intrinsic value; hating G is of negative intrinsic value.

(2) For some base intrinsic evil, B, hating B is of positive intrinsic value; loving B is of negative intrinsic value.[21]

As in recursion in mathematics, Hurka's value-theoretic recursive principle concerns an operation performed on a base. We begin with a base intrinsic good, or a base bad, as the case may be. The operation is a particular attitude toward the base. The principle is such that that attitude itself accrues intrinsic value—good or bad—in accord with the value of the base, such that love of the good is good, and so forth.

The relevance of the *amare bonum bonus* to achievements is evident. Because of their process-product structure, achievements all involve a pursuit of a product. Pursuit is a pro-activity and as a result whenever it is oriented toward some object of positive or negative value, the *amare bonun bonus* is at play. Thus the *amare bonum bonus* tells us something about the value of the process of an achievement when it is in pursuit of a product of non-zero value. If the value of the product is positive, *amare bonum bonus* tells us the process has a positive value. If the value of the product is negative, *amare bonum bonus* tells us the process has a negative value.

As we have seen, features of the process of achievements ground much of the Essential Value of achievements. Difficulty, competent causation, and unity in diversity are all features of the process of achievements, and they are the ground of the Essential Value. Insofar as the process of achievements—of all achievements as such—is of positive intrinsic value, what *amare bonum bonus* tells us about the value of the process in a case with a positively valuable product isn't news. If the product is of positive value, *amare bonum bonus* tells us that the process has positive value, which we already know to be true. However, if the product is *negative* we now have something of a puzzle on our hands. What happens to the value of the process? Specifically, we want to know what happens to the value of

---

[21] This is a modified version of the principle of Recursion as presented by Hurka in *Virtue, Vice, and Value*.

the process when the *amare bonum bonus* pertains to achievements—evil achievements in particular.

A natural thought is that the *amare bonum bonus* operates summatively, such that the positive value of the process has some additional value added to it, in the case of a positively valuable product, and it has some value subtracted from it, in the case of a negative product. In other words, the value of the process is augmented when it is in pursuit of a positively valuable product, and it is diminished when it is in pursuit of a negative one. Presumably, *amare bonum bonus* responds to proportionality, so if the value of the product is of a large magnitude, the augmentation or diminishments of the value of the process would be correspondingly proportionately large. As a result, if the value of the product of an evil achievement is very large, then the value of the process might be diminished so greatly that the original positive value is completely obliterated, and its actual value is negative. So a summative approach to the *amare bonum bonus* would yield all-over negatively valuable achievements matching our intuitions.

However, if the *amare bonum bonus* governs the value of the process, we could have a case where the amount of value by which the process is diminished leaves precisely the same amount of positive value in the process as there is negative value in the product. To be precise, suppose that the value of the process apart from the considerations of *amare bonum bonus* is X, and the value of the product is some amount Y, which is negative. Suppose also that once *amare bonum bonus* is activated, the process is diminished by Z. The value of the overall achievement is thus $X - Z + Y$. It's perfectly possible that these could add to zero, say, if $X = 5$, $Y = -4$ and $Z = 1$.

Now, what's concerning here is that the very problem with the "basic summative approach" we were originally attempting to resolve by appealing to *amare bonum bonus* has reappeared once again. A summative construal of *amare bonum bonus* won't do, then. What I suggest might be considered a return to Moore—a proper organic unities approach.

A better way to understand the *amare bonum bonus* is such that it does not govern the value of the process. Instead, it governs the value of the overall achievement, as a whole. Moreover, I suggest that we also understand the *amare bonum bonus* to be such that parts of the achievement—the process and product—*retain* their original intrinsic value. Thus, the value of the whole, process and product, may *not be equal* to the sum of value of the process and the value of the product. As a result, the *amare bonum bonus* is a principle that yields an *organic unity*.

The idea is this. The *amare bonum bonus* is such that it governs the value of the *whole* of a pursuit-and-product. In contrast to the summative approach I considered a moment ago, according to which the *amare bonum bonus* governed only the value of the *pursuit*. On this construal, the value of the pursuit is untouched by the *amare bonum bonus*. Rather, the relevant entity whose value is shaped by *amare bonum bonus* is the whole of pursuit and product. According to the *amare bonum bonus*, when the product is of positive value, the whole will have positive value, and an achievement in which the product has negative value will have negative value as a whole.

However, you will recall from Chapter 1 my views about so-called *petty evil* achievements, such as practical jokes and art heists. Petty evil achievements, to be precise, are achievements with products that are of negative value, but of a relatively low level. In Chapter 1, I appealed to cases of petty evil achievements to motivate my *inclusive* account, that is, to motivate my position that achievements can indeed have products of negative value. If we are to exclude all achievements with negatively valuable products from being achievements, we will have to say that elaborate practical jokes and art heists are not achievements, which they surely are, and to deny this is unappealingly schoolmarmish. Similar considerations apply here as well. To deny that there is any positive value to petty evil achievement is also unappealingly schoolmarmish and overly moralistic. Surely there is something bad about practical jokes, but to say they are overall *evil* in every respect is a hilarious overstatement. The same applies to art heists. There is plenty of evidence that there is something of positive value in elaborate art heists in that their depiction in highly entertaining films seems perfectly fitting. To claim that an elaborate art heist is *evil* simply seems incorrect.

Now, *amare bonum bonus* as I have just described it on the proposed Moorean construal so far appears to fail to capture this. Rather, the Moorean construal entails that, *as a whole*, the value of an achievement with a negative product will be negative.

However, there is more to be said. We can avail ourselves of Moore's distinction between value *as a whole* and value *on the whole*.[22] The value *on the whole* is the total of the value of the whole as a whole, plus the sum

[22] *Principia Ethica*, 214–16.

of the values of its parts. The parts, as we know, retain the value that they would have independently from the whole. Thus we can add up the value of these parts, and then add this sum to the value of the whole itself as a whole. This gives the net value of all the entities—as it's called by Moore, the value of the whole *on the whole*.

In a petty evil case, we have a product with a small negative value, a process of high positive value, and a whole which is of small negative value. Added together, two small negatives and one large positive, we have a positive value on the whole. The positive value of the process is positive enough to outweigh the negative value of the product and the whole. Petty evil achievements thus have a positive value.

In the case of a significantly evil achievement, we would be hoping for the view to tell us that the achievement is of significant negative value on the whole. And it does. In a significantly evil case we have an achievement with a product of very large negative value, and a process of positive value, and a whole of negative value. Here, if the negative value of the product and whole are significantly negative, as they would be in a case of a very evil achievement, they outweigh the positive value of the process. Thus, the value of the very evil achievement is on the whole negative.

Nonetheless, there is still some *positive* value that is retained by the process in the evil achievement, and so there is still some respect in which the evil achievement is good. I'm inclined to say this is a plausible implication. After all, the evil achievement shares the very same good-making features that make non-evil achievements valuable. An incredibly ingenious and clever yet diabolical plan to commit the perfect crime is nonetheless ingenious and clever, and, assuming it is an achievement, it shares the other features common to all achievements, including those features that make them valuable. Yet *amare bonum bonus* tells us that the value of the very evil achievement on the whole is negative. So it is indeed overall bad, even though there is a respect in which it is good. This captures quite nicely what we might be inclined to say about very evil achievements.

But surely *amare bonum bonus* is subject to the very same objection that gave us grounds to reject the basic summative approach and the summative approach to the *amare bonum bonus* earlier. It appears that it is possible that an evil achievement with a very bad product could still be positive on the whole.

Such a case is indeed possible. If the positive value of the process, as a part, were so very large that it outweighed the negative value of both the evil achievement as a whole and the negative value of the product, then, on the whole, an evil achievement could have positive value.

However, what has been problematic about these cases for earlier summative approaches is not as problematic here. Even if the overall value of the whole is positive, the parts *retain their original intrinsic values*. The achievement as a whole retains its badness, the evil product retains its badness, and the Essential Value of the achievement retains its goodness. The earlier complaint with the summative approach to the *amare bonum bonus* was that, because the summative construal is such that the actual value of the *process* is determined by the *amare bonum bonus*, it is susceptible to cases where the value of the process is altered such that the overall achievement changes, meaning that an evil achievement is of positive value, full stop. But our understanding of the *amare bonum bonus* is not susceptible to this problem. The explanation is that the parts of the organic unities *retain* their values.

But what then do we say about the value of the achievement? What's the final value score, as it were? Presumably it's the value of the whole on the whole, since this is the ultimate bottom line. In the problematic case, then, the value on the whole of an evil achievement can be positive. So do we have to say that the value of this here achievement—this here ardent pursuit of a heinously evil end—has *positive* value? It seems that we do. But we still can reassure ourselves that even though this awful state of affairs has a positive value, some of its *parts* do not. The universe is *indeed* worse with the evil product and the evil achievement as a whole. Equally, the universe is indeed better with these valuable features of the achievement. And it turns out that this good thing and these bad things happen to occur in the same state of affairs. Simply because opposite values exist, does not mean that the universe isn't better for the existence of the good, and worse for the existence of the bad. This is so even when the opposite values occur in the same state of affairs.

And this is what's at play in evil achievements. The world is better for the good parts of the achievement and worse for its bad parts. There is the one funny bullet to bite, that overall the value of the achievement on the whole is positive, but it's not really so bad since we know that its components retain their various values nonetheless.[23]

---

[23] There is more to be explored here. A full treatment would involve a thorough excursion into deep questions of just how we go about tallying up value, and, more deeply, what it means for that value to matter, even if it is counterbalanced by an equal opposite value.

This concludes my discussion of the relative value of achievements. The Essential Value of achievements tracks their essential features—other things being equal, the more difficult the better, the more competently caused the better, and the more unity in diversity the better. But, as is often the case in philosophy, things are often unequal; the value of achievements can also be augmented or diminished by the value of their process or product.

6

Puzzles and Games

In this final chapter, I will reflect on some remaining issues, and open the door for discussion of some new intriguing puzzles that arise in light of my investigation. Since an entire chapter could easily be devoted to each of these puzzles, I will only entertain a few considerations and explore some of the space of possibilities, leaving the invitation open to develop new approaches and solutions.

The Value of Failure

Let's turn to the opposite of achievement: *failure*. What value might failure have? Obviously, failure can be bad. It can be instrumentally bad by causing the pain of disappointment, deprivation, and loss. Interestingly, however, closer inspection suggests that failure is not entirely bad, and can even be intrinsically good.

First, there is an obvious way in which failure can be instrumentally good—after all, we love to remind ourselves that we learn from our failures. But there is more to be said. To be precise, what's at issue here is a *failed attempt*, which is a matter of trying to achieve some product, but not bringing that product about. In other words, there is a process that is difficult and competent (i.e. involves many JTBs), but does not culminate in a certain product.

Yet a difficult process can competently cause *something*, even if it's just, say, last place in a race or a fallen soufflé, or simply the execution of the process itself. Coming in last place in a race might be just as difficult for the loser as coming in first place was for the winner. Does this mean, then, that *losing* a race can be an achievement? Can it be intrinsically valuable?

My account entails that it can be. Insofar as a process is difficult and competently causes some product or other, this fulfills my account for the so-called failure *itself* being an achievement. This might seem peculiar, but reflection indicates that we might welcome this implication. Consider running a race, such as the New York City marathon which thousands of competitors run every year. Of these thousands of runners, only a tiny handful considers anything less than winning to be a failure. In fact, even among the elite runners, crossing the finish line as closely behind the winner as possible is a success. For most of the thousands of runners, simply finishing the 26.2 mile distance is the achievement.

A surprising upshot is that, if a failed attempt is valuable, the failure has value *in virtue of* it being an achievement. Yet there is a strong sense that a success is *better* than a failure. How then are we to account for such a gap in value between a failed attempt and a success?

As far as achievements go, my view entails that there is *not* such a gap in value, other things being equal. Much of the pull to describe failures as less valuable from achievements comes from the notion that when we fail, we have failed *in our own eyes*. To the Olympic hopeful who had all the promise for achieving gold, a silver medal is a bitter disappointment. To be sure, the athletic performance and winning the silver medal are indeed achievements for the Olympian. But to her, she has failed to accomplish what she had aimed to. So here we have a very interesting ramification of my account of achievements: you can fail to accomplish your aim, yet what you have accomplished is nonetheless an achievement.

But surely accomplishing your aims is good, failing to do this is bad. But what I have shown is that this is not what's important about achievements. Of course, achievements often involve accomplishing one's aims, but often they do not. In many cases, what one achieves is not the same thing as what one had set out to do. But it is an achievement nonetheless.

It is an appealing idea that accomplishing a goal that one has set for oneself is valuable. I don't deny this. Indeed, it is plausible that accomplishing any goal is intrinsically valuable. However, as we have seen throughout the arguments of this book accomplishing one's goal is neither necessary nor sufficient for an achievement.

It may be worth pointing out that even those accounts that appeal to achieving aims as an element of wellbeing do not hold that it is achieving aims as such that is valuable. Raz, for example, holds that only the satisfaction of *rational* goals is relevant.[1] Even most desire satisfaction accounts of wellbeing reject an unrestricted view, suggesting that it is not the satisfaction of desires or aims per se that matters. Moreover, as we saw in Chapter 1, the target of these views is different from ours. These views are interested in aims that would be achievements in the broad, mundane sense of achievement, whereas this project is about "capital-A" achievements. Insofar as a "capital-A" achievement involves reaching one's aims, it could be said to be additionally valuable in the way that these competing views wish to claim.

One result of my view which philosophers may find particularly attractive concerns the nature of philosophical achievements. I say more about philosophical achievements later, but a plausible thought is that resolving a philosophical question is (or would be) an achievement. If this is the case, then there are no doubt *hundreds* of failed attempts in philosophy. Given the wide variety of interesting positions philosophers develop, the whole philosophical enterprise might be, in large part, made up of dozens upon dozens of failed attempts. An account that construes a failed attempt as an achievement and thus valuable as such should then be welcomed as a good way to account for the value of philosophical achievement, lest we cast away most of the philosophical work of the last 3,000 years as valueless failures.

A related question concerns the relative value of winning and losing. It's no secret that my account of achievements entails that losing can be a great achievement. But we do have an intuition that winning is *better* than losing. Can we validate this intuition axiologically?

Some of the value-theoretic material that I have drawn from in discussion of achievements might be helpful. One can say that winning is an instance of organic unity, in that it exemplifies unity in diversity. In winning, there is a certain matching that occurs between the aim of the process as defined by the rules of the game and the product, which does not occur in losing. This matching plays a unifying role. So winning is more unified than losing because the product matches the objective, and therefore is more valuable.

---

[1] *The Morality of Freedom* (Oxford: Clarendon Press, 1986).

Group Achievements

Throughout this book, I have only been discussing the achievements of *individuals*. But often we are not the sole authors of our accomplishments. Many achievements are the work of a group, where the members together engage in a difficult process that competently causes its product.

Consider the Houston Dynamo winning the semifinals of the Major League Soccer championship against DC United. Their win is an achievement, and it's a paradigmatic zero-value product achievement (actually, it probably comes with a big paycheck for each player, but let's leave that aside). *Whose* achievement is it? It is not the achievement of any one player, but of all of them.

Now here is an interesting question. How does the value of their achievement redound to the lives of each player? That is, how should we consider the value to be apportioned among the players? Does each share an equal amount in the win, or does the value vary, and if so, according to what factors?

In any group achievement such as these, there are many individual achievements. Each contributor does something difficult that culminates in a product for which he is responsible. Accordingly, each does something valuable. But together, all achieve something that we might reasonably say is greater than the sum of their individual achievements. How is the value of the overall group achievement apportioned among the various contributors?

First, what *is* this value? One thought is that it is the value of the product. But it can't simply be the value of the product that we are dividing, since many group achievements have zero-value products, including the soccer match. So it is the value of the achievement *overall* that we are considering, and how this value redounds to the lives of the individual players.

One thought is that each contributor gains only the value he generates and for which he is solely responsible—only his own exercise of rationality and will. It follows from the account I have given that each contributor does indeed garner this value. However, if this is the only value each contributor gains from the group achievement, that would mean *winning* the championship makes no difference in value, which doesn't seem right at all. The question is how the value of the *win* is apportioned to the lives of the players.

One thought is that the value is apportioned *equally* to all the contributors. Everyone who has a hand in the win earns an equal share of its value.

But we might think that some contributors have had more of a hand in contributing to the success of the product than others. Accordingly, we might want to capture that the win matters more for those who played a key role in the victory than it is for those who sat on the bench most of the time. In other words, the more of the *product* that is directly attributable to you, the more crucial your role in the achievement, and the more value you gain.

But just who plays a crucial role? This is a tricky matter, particularly in a championship match—players who may not have played in the final winning game nonetheless contributed throughout the season, and made possible the winning position. Their roles too are crucial, and without them, the product—the winning match—wouldn't exist. So perhaps we should return to the idea of apportioning value equally to all contributors.

Yet in other cases, equal apportionment seems less plausible. Consider a large-scale opera production. It would be peculiar if we held that the person whose sole job it is to open and close the curtains gains as much value as the artistic director of the production, or the concert master or the costume maker. An equal apportionment of value seems inappropriate in this case. So it's plausible that value redounds to contributors in unequal distribution. By what principles might the apportionment be governed?

We have already considered that crucialness matters. In addition, we might also consider that *effort* matters for apportioning value in group achievements. Perhaps the value of the achievement redounds to the lives of the contributors in proportion to the amount of effort exerted in their particular contribution. This approach has appeal, in that those who contribute more to the achievement by working harder gain more value in their lives than those who do not work as hard. A player who spends most of the time on the bench doesn't gain as much value as the players who are on the field throughout the winning match.

Yet effort, it seems, may be less important than crucialness. A player scoring the winning goal, for example, has a larger share of value than another player who may have exerted more effort but did not have a significant effect on the victorious outcome.

Yet consider a lazy striker. The lazy striker doesn't move far from her position near the opposing team's goal and more or less waits for the ball to be passed to her so she can score. This is an effective way to score a lot of goals, but in contrast to the midfielders who spend the entire game running at full tilt, strategizing and managing the ball, it seems the lazy striker, although crucial relative to the success of winning, doesn't deserve as much value credit as perhaps those who generate more output and exert higher effort. So effort, it seems, also matters.

Moreover, considering significance seems to weight too heavily the obvious contributions to success such as goal-scoring, and overlooks those who have less obvious but still important roles and generate a great deal of the output of keeping the ball in play during the game, such as midfielders and defense.

So an alternative approach looks at contribution to the *process* rather than contribution to the product. We might classify this as the "output" of the contributors' efforts—how many shots they blocked, assists, passes, and so on. In contrast to individual achievements, where "input," that is, the amount of effort expended is a main factor, in group achievements it is also relevant how much you actually contribute—how much of the process is the *output* of your efforts. It seems to matter for how much of the value you gain by way of contributing—your *actual* contribution matters. Of course, you still gain the value of the exercise of will, and each contributor has an individual achievement insofar as he exercises his will and rationality to competently cause some product. But as for the value gained from contributing to the group achievement, it matters how much of the process is the outcome of your efforts.

But we might think that output shouldn't come at the expense of crucialness—the player who scores the winning goal seems to deserve a large portion of the achievement's value, even if he didn't actually contribute as much to the process as others did. In short, goals scored get more value than missed shots. Similarly, the stagehand whose sole job is to open and close the curtains gains less value from his contribution than the artistic director or the soprano in the starring role.

Yet one might say that many of the contributions are crucial—after all, the striker wouldn't get the ball if it weren't for the midfielders, and the soprano can't have her solo if the curtains don't open. So many contributors may be crucial. Indeed, the difference between non-crucial and crucial output may be illusory, considering that a great deal of the activity of the midfielders, stage hands, second violins, and so on, makes possible the activities of those who have apparently more crucial roles, such as the striker and the soprano star. So perhaps there is in fact no distinction here. In any case, if there is a difference, just what matters for crucialness is a tricky matter.

So what can we say overall? None (or neither, if outcome and crucialness are the same) of these factors is irrelevant. Effort, outcome, and crucialness all matter for how much of the value of a group achievement an individual contributor gains from her contribution. Precisely how much they matter and how they interact with each other, however, is a question I'll leave to explore another time.

Aid in Achievements

While many achievements are group endeavors, most individual achievements are not entirely solo efforts. We often get a little help along the way in our achievements. And sometimes we help ourselves in ways that we shouldn't. In cases where other people help us, we might reasonably suppose that the value of the achievement is apportioned along the lines of what we have just discussed for group achievements. But sometimes we don't get help from other people, but we help *ourselves* to certain means—questionable means. Such means aid us in attaining a certain product, but cast a shadow on the achievement itself that wouldn't be there otherwise.

The sort of case I have in mind in particular is *cheating*. Consider Lance Armstrong who has, it would appear, fallen from grace. After winning the Tour de France seven consecutive times, he was stripped of his titles and banned from professional cycling, as a result of systematically making use of performance-enhancing drugs throughout his career. How does the use of questionable aid shape the value of an achievement?

The intuition is that doping in sports, as an instance of cheating, detracts from both the status of the achievement as such, and from its value. How might we explain this? There is a great deal of discussion in the philosophy of sports literature about the various pros and cons of performance-enhancing drugs.[2] I will just focus on one of the possible analyses of performance-enhancing drug use. I will suppose that it constitutes *cheating*. Cheating involves of breaking the rules of a sport or game, and since the performance-enhancing substances Armstrong was taking are

---

[2] One popular argument against the use of performance-enhancing drugs appeals to the harm they cause athletes. Another popular argument concerns the degrading of the spirit of sport or skill and virtue involved in athletic achievement (Cf. M. Andrew Holowchak, "Ergogenic Aids and the Limits of Human Performance in Sport: Ethical Issues, Aesthetic Considerations," *Journal of the Philosophy of Sport* (2002): 75–86).

banned by the regulations of the races in which he was a competitor, he was cheating.[3]

Cheating can detract from the value of an achievement in at least the following very straightforward way. It's plausible that cheating is of negative value, and accordingly when it is part of the process of an achievement, it detracts from its value. As we learned earlier, non-essential features of the process can shape the value of the achievement overall. We have seen that additional value in the process of an achievement contributes to the value of the achievement overall, just as a valuable product contributes to the value overall. Cheating, plausibly, has negative value. So a process involving cheating has a feature that has negative value that detracts from the value of the achievement overall. Presumably there are many plausible explanations to account for the negative value of cheating. For instance, cheating is morally wrong, and so might said to involve the exercise of a vice, and, in much the same way as we might say that exercising a virtue has positive value, exercising a vice has negative value. If a vice is exercised in the process of an achievement, it contributes negative value to the process of that achievement. So cheating, assuming it is an exercise of vice and therefore disvaluable, contributes negative value to the achievement. So the value of the achievement overall is *less* than it would have been in the absence of the vicious activity.

Holding onto our supposition that the exercise of vice is of negative value, this line of argument can be extended more broadly as well to other achievements that involve vicious activity in the process. Take as an example Hwang Woo-Suk, the South Korean scientist who gained celebrity after publishing results of his experiments that he had succeeded in producing stem cells from cloned human embryos. As it happens, he had not only fabricated some of his research, but also used human eggs that he had gathered by exploiting his female researchers. Interestingly, although Hwang had fabricated the result that he cloned human embryos, his experiments did, in fact, result in an extraordinary success. He succeeded in creating human embryos by parthenogenesis, that is, generation via an unfertilized egg.[4]

The value of Hwang's achievement seems to be thoroughly tainted by his vicious actions—the exploitation of the fellow researchers and the

---

[3] Although not all rule-breaking is cheating, all cheating involves breaking the rules in order to gain advantage over the opponent.

[4] <http://en.wikipedia.org/wiki/Hwang_Woo-suk>, retrieved December 2012.

deception of fabricating and misrepresenting his work. The negative value of these vices exercised in the process significantly diminishes the value of the achievement. Whether or not the achievement is of any positive value depends on just how bad the vicious activity is in comparison to the good of the exercise of will and rationality and the good of the actual results.

Alternatively, we might be inclined to think that Hwang's discovery does not, in the end, constitute an achievement. Because Hwang did not lay claim to the actual product of the putative achievement—namely generating embryos by parthenogenesis—it is unclear whether or not the product was caused competently. If Hwang did not accurately understand the nature of his activities, he may have had an insufficient amount of JTBs about his activities in order to satisfy the requisite measure for competent causation.

But one might be inclined to say that vicious means in general disqualify an activity from being an achievement—neither Hwang's nor Armstrong's endeavors, one might think, are really achievements.

Depending on the details of the case, my view just might accommodate this intuition. Here is how. If the achiever fails to have sufficient JTBs for competent causation, then his performance is not an achievement. One way he might fail to have sufficient JTBs is if he fails to understand that his method is a good method. Beliefs about method are very weighty toward competent causation, so if the cheater doesn't have the relevant beliefs about his method, he fails to cause competently.

There are some related variations on cases of this kind with interesting upshots.

What exactly are the structural beliefs that a vicious achiever might falsely believe? Since the general idea is that the vicious achiever uses a method that isn't good, let us start here: he believes that his method is *good*. The belief could concern the *practical* goodness of the process, that is, how well-suited the method is for attaining the desired product; or it could concern the moral goodness of the method, that is, whether or not the method is morally permissible. So there are two distinct beliefs about the goodness of the method at issue: one concerns its practical goodness, and the other concerns its moral goodness.

Supposing the vicious achiever is a reasonably good planner (morality aside), it seems plausible that he would be correct in believing that his method is a good one for attaining the desired product. Assuming the cheater is a reasonably good cheater, it might be a very effective way to attain the outcome, particularly if he is clever at outsmarting the competition (as both Armstrong and Hwang did—at least for a while).[5] So it's reasonable to conclude that the vicious achiever has structural JTBs about the practical goodness of his method.

Does the vicious achiever have true beliefs about the moral goodness of his process? We can consider two kinds of cases. First, there is a vicious achiever who falsely believes that his methods are morally permissible—a doping athlete may believe that doping doesn't constitute cheating, but if it does, his belief is false. Let's call such an achiever an *innocently vicious achiever*. On the other hand, a vicious achiever may know full well that what he is doing is morally wrong. Since Socrates there has been disagreement over whether someone can knowingly do wrong, but let's suppose for now that one can. Such a vicious achiever would be *knowingly vicious*—very vicious indeed.

Let's consider the innocently vicious achiever first since he has one of the candidate false structural beliefs—he falsely believes of his methods that they are morally permissible, that is, he falsely believes that it is permissible to cheat. Supposing that this belief is sufficiently general and therefore weighted, we can make a case that the innocently vicious achiever does not competently cause the product of his performance, and so his performance is not an achievement.

In contrast, the knowingly vicious achiever has the relevant true structural beliefs. So he succeeds in competently causing the product of the achievement. So vicious achievements, when knowingly vicious, are indeed achievements. But when unknowingly vicious, they are not.

So we have an interesting result. How funny that we are crediting the vicious achiever who is all the more vicious for knowing that he is, and yet denying credit to the innocently vicious achiever! But many people are inclined to think that innocently doing wrong is *better* than knowingly doing wrong, which certainly seems quite evil.

---

[5] Exception to this: cheating in a game with the object of winning. To win, one must be playing the game, and playing the game is a matter of engaging in the activity made possible by conforming to the rules, and choosing to do so just so one can engage in this activity. So winning is impossible if the rules are not followed, and so cheating undermines the goal of winning (see Bernard Suits, *The Grasshopper*, Toronto: Broadview Press, 2005). As a result, one could argue that Armstrong failed to have the relevant structural beliefs about the goodness of his process, if he thought that doping was a good way to *win* the Tour de France.

I don't disagree with this assessment. It does seem much worse to choose to do something morally reprehensible knowingly than it does to, say, have been innocently misled. But this by itself does not tell us anything about the status of the activities as achievements. As we have already seen, my account is such that an achievement can be of negative value overall. If the vices exercised by the knowingly vicious achiever are very bad, then plausibly the value of his achievement will be overall negative.

But we still have the peculiar result that the innocently vicious achiever does not in fact have an achievement, whereas the knowingly vicious achiever does. This contrast is interesting, and I don't think it is implausible once we consider the details. Bringing to mind the account of competent causation, the more that one knows what one is doing, the more competently one brings about the product of one's activities. The innocently vicious achiever does not have a good understanding of his activities. He is confused about just what it is that he is doing, and he is confused about morality. This detracts from the competence with which he engages in his activities. The knowingly vicious achiever, however, knows very well what he is doing.

To be sure, if we consider the incredible duplicitousness with which some vicious achievers pull off their daring schemes, it's hard not to be impressed with their ingenuity. If the allegations are correct about Armstrong, his doping was pervasive and systematic throughout his career. The USADA said of Armstrong's cycling team that it ran the "most sophisticated, professionalized, and successful doping program that sport has ever seen."[6] It was a duplicitous scheme, and knowingly so. Winning the Tour de France seven times without getting caught is truly a remarkable achievement. Duplicitous, but an achievement nonetheless.[7]

[6] "Statement from USADA CEO Travis T. Tygart Regarding the U. S. Postal Service Pro Cycling Team Doping Conspiracy," <http://cyclinginvestigation.usada.org/>, retrieved December 2012.
[7] But was Lance Armstrong even cheating? The answer to this question hangs on the relative strength of implicit versus explicit rules of a game. In the events where Armstrong was a competitor, no doubt there were explicit regulations forbidding doping, just as there were regulations about all sorts of other things. These regulations make up (at least in part) the constitutive rules of the game. But it's fairly clear that not all sports and games have all their rules and regulations spelled out explicitly. But one might question whether, even in highly regulated sports like cycling or the NBA, are *all* the rules of the game really spelled out explicitly. It's plausible that there are many significant elements of the game

Games

From language games to chess, games present an interesting source of philosophical fodder in many domains. As it happens, it has been argued that games are intrinsically valuable in virtue of achievement-like features.[8] Hurka's account of the value of games is parallel to his view of the value of achievements and difficulty: games achievements are characterized by difficulty, which is a matter of complexity, which also characterizes achievements and makes them valuable.[9] But we have seen now that difficulty is not a matter of complexity.

Presumably we should conclude from my account of achievements that games are valuable only in the case where they are indeed difficult for the person who plays. Truly difficult games—high-level chess, professional sports, and so on—are typically intrinsically valuable, but easy games such as tic-tac-toe or boggle, are not.[10] This is an unsurprising conclusion, and hardly worth mentioning.

But it turns out that there is more to be said. There is a certain degree of value-theoretic specialness about games in light of my discussion of

that are left implicit. Suppose that this is so, and thus there are details of the rules that are not in fact spelled out, but everyone knows very obviously that these are rules of the game. It stands to reason that these implicit rules are no less constitutive of the game than the explicit rules.

What, then, if implicit rules are in tension with some of the explicit rules? Indeed, in professional basketball, physical contact with members of the opposing team is explicitly forbidden by the rules, on pain of a foul call. However, as watching any NBA game will reveal, a great deal of physical contact is tolerated, while only a slim portion of fouls are called by the referees. In other words, there is an implicit rule that certain kinds of "fouls" and physical contact are *permitted*, while the explicit rules forbid *all* such contact. In practice, then, the implicit rule permitting certain kinds of physical contact trumps the explicit rule forbidding all kinds of contact. This supports the idea that widely accepted implicit rules that are in tension with explicit rules can carry the day in terms of which rules you are required to follow in order to count as playing the game. So breaking explicit rules that are overridden by implicit rules does not entail cheating. In the case of cycling, given the prevalence of the doping practices at the time, it's fairly clear that it was widely accepted that cyclists dope. In other words, it was a widely accepted implicit constitutive rule of the game. If all that is true, Lance Armstrong did not break any rules, and therefore did not cheat.

[8]   At an earlier stage before I started this project about achievements more broadly, I myself made similar arguments in "Kudos for Ludus."

[9]   Hurka, "Games and the Good," *Proceedings of the Aristotelian Society,* supplementary vol. (2006): 217–35.

[10]   As it happens, this is in line with Hurka's view which agrees that more difficult games are more valuable than less difficult ones ("Games and the Good," 220–1).

achievements. Games are special in that their very structure has something very close to the central elements of achievements built right in.

Let me here appeal to the marvelous discussion of the nature of games by Bernard Suits. On Suits' account, "to play a game is to engage in activity directed towards bringing about a specific state of affairs, using only means permitted by rules, where the rules prohibit more efficient in favor of less efficient means, and where such rules are accepted just because they make possible such an activity."[11] The general idea is this: in playing a game, such as golf, there is a goal, namely, to get the ball in the hole. But this goal is such that it can't be accomplished by any means necessary. Rather, there is a particular way of getting the ball in the hole—by hitting it with a club and playing it where it lies—stipulated by the rules of golf. These rules are such that they eliminate the most efficient and typically easier means. Thus games necessarily involve overcoming obstacles that stand in the way of reaching an outcome by easier means. As Suits puts it, games are the "voluntary attempt to overcome unnecessary obstacles."[12] In other words, one might say that games involve a certain degree of built-in difficulty.

Further, games require the "lusory attitude"—the rules of the game are accepted *just so* one can engage in the activity that they delineate. One may have other reasons to accept the rules and play a game, of course, but in order to play a game, it must be among the reasons to engage in the activity prescribed by the rules. If we did not choose to take the more difficult means just so that we could play the game; that is, if we do not have this among our reasons for engaging in the activity, then we are not, in fact, playing a game, although we may look as if we are.[13]

Taking Suits' account of games, Hurka's view of their value is that because games necessarily involve working toward a goal by taking on more obstacles than alternative means, games necessarily involve complexity and are therefore valuable. But although games involve the complexity of obstacles,

---

[11] *The Grasshopper*, 48–9.   [12] *The Grasshopper*, 55.

[13] Suits illustrates this with an example in which someone is running along with competitors in a race along the same route and toward the same finishing point, but only because there are no other ways to reach the finishing point safely, and he must reach the finishing point in order to diffuse a bomb before it explodes. This person is not running a race, even if he crosses the finish line first, because he has not chosen to run the route "just so" he can run the route; i.e. this is not among his reasons for running, and he would take a more efficient route were one available. This element—the lusory attitude—is necessary for playing a game.

surmounting these obstacles is not always effort-requiring. It doesn't take much effort for most people to play snakes and ladders or boggle.

Recall that I argued earlier that all exertion of effort has *some* intrinsic value—if the will is a special human capacity then its exercise is always going to have at least some intrinsic value. As long as games involve some exertion of will—which they do by definition—they have intrinsic value. This by itself isn't particularly interesting, since virtually all activity involves at least minimal exercise of the will and is therefore valuable in the same way. But the value of games in virtue of the exercise of will is interesting when combined with the lusory attitude.

The lusory attitude is the essential feature of games according to which we choose to accept the rules of the game just so we can make the activity they delineate possible. In other words, when we play a game, we choose to take the more difficult means to reach a goal rather than the more efficient means, just so that we can engage in the activity that taking these difficult means makes possible, such as playing golf. If we chose the easier means to get the ball in the hole, we would find ourselves not playing golf, but doing some other activity.

So the lusory attitude is a source of value in games—games by their very nature involve the *amare bonum bonus*. They involve by their very nature choosing to pursue a good, namely effort. The lusory attitude involves pursuing a more difficult means over an easier one, and therefore involves pursuing a good for its own sake. Then the *amare bonum bonus* is activated because games involve choosing exerting more effort than one otherwise could to reach the same goal.[14] Now, of course, the effort that's exerted may in many cases be slight, as it is in tic-tac-toe or boggle. However, the point is that in playing the game, one chooses to exert more effort to reach the same state than one otherwise could, and does this *just so* one can engage in this effortful activity. So games involve choosing effort for its own sake. Games have the *amare bonum bonus* as a necessary feature of their structure. Admittedly for many games, their value is very slight.

---

[14] This is assuming here that the "less efficient" means will be more effort-requiring than the more efficient ones, and therefore in fact more difficult for the particular person playing the game, but of course there could be scenarios where this is not the case—consider the helicopter flight to Mt Everest, for example, where it turns out that the apparently more efficient means are actually incredibly difficult.

But that is hardly surprising. What *is* noteworthy is that their structure is indeed value-theoretically special in this way. Games necessarily involve choosing to exert the will just for its own sake.

Philosophical Achievement

A philosophical investigation about achievements could hardly be complete without investigating philosophical achievements themselves. Let's not restrict our attention to the potential great philosophical masterworks of tomorrow, such as *Reasons and Persons*, but instead to the more plentiful achievements which fill *Philosophical Review* and get discussion in author-meets-critic sessions at the APA.

One is certainly inclined to say that these are indeed bona fide achievements. Doing philosophy is certainly very difficult and involves a great deal of exercise of rationality, and let's assume for now that this amounts to competent causation.

Just what is the product of a philosophical achievement? A paper, perhaps, or a book or a talk. But it's not the tangible book or paper that matters so much as the *content*. The content is typically a position that one ideally takes to be *true* or at least the most plausible, and defends with arguments. We could disagree about the nature of the philosophical product, but let's suppose that this is at least a plausible way of characterizing it. The product of a putative philosophical achievement is a position or a theory that one takes to be true, or at least plausible, and therefore supports with arguments.

But what if we're wrong? If our philosophical efforts culminate in a theory that's false, what does this mean for our achievement? A false theory might be of zero value, in which case this doesn't threaten the status of our endeavors as an achievement with some positive value. But, on the other hand, a false theory might not be of zero value, but of some *negative* value. Could, then, defending a false theory be an evil achievement? And if so, just how bad could it be? False beliefs alone might not be particularly evil, but a false moral theory might. Hitler, to be sure, subscribed to a false moral theory, and I think many people would be inclined to think this false theory was evil. When it comes to defending false theories, then, in at least some cases, the same philosophical considerations apply as for evil achievements. Yet, one doesn't devote one's career to defending a theory that one *knows* to be false. So if false theories are bad or evil, these cases are accidentally evil achievements.

On the other hand, you *know* as a philosopher that you might not be right because there are conflicting competing theories that other very smart people are just as convinced are correct. This would be equivalent to the vaccine-making scientist seeing that what she is making very well could be a toxin, yet proceeding to make the vaccine. Here we are running into the epistemological problem of disagreement. Given that many peers (or superiors, even) have considered the same evidence and come to believe that you are wrong, one might suppose that this gives you reason to doubt your belief. Or does it? It's controversial that we are truly epistemic peers in the relevant sense; moreover, it's also controversial that we actually have access to the same evidence in cases of philosophical disagreement. Some conclude from this that we ought to withhold our assent to our beliefs, but if our theory is correct, we might do something very bad by withholding our assent. However, among epistemological theories that address these questions there is disagreement too, so it hardly seems we could follow any advice without the problem reiterating itself. I'm not going to settle the issue of the nature of disagreement here, but we now see how my discussion adds a new level of concern to these debates. If we proceed to persist in beliefs that we should abandon, we risk doing something not only epistemologically wrong, but also possibly very bad. The stakes in philosophical disagreement are high. Defending a theory that is wrong might be very bad—evil, even. This is particularly troubling for theories that involve practical guidance and prescriptions for action, and for proponents of such theories that are very vociferous in propagation of their views. What such philosophers are doing could be quite evil indeed. So a great deal hangs on resolving these issues.

Let's put these considerations aside and suppose for the moment that philosophical achievement is *not* in fact evil, and perhaps even good. After all, even if we are defending an incorrect position, and therefore have a product of negative value, there may still be sufficient positive value in the exercise of will and rationality that the achievement is good overall.

Now we might wonder whether, in contrast to other considerations, it's a terrible waste of time. After all, an overwhelmingly huge portion of the world's population lives in poverty, suffering terribly from illnesses and privation of many of the simplest things that we take for granted. In one respect, this question concerns the relative urgency of moral claims, which is a topic I leave aside here. Instead, let's look at the value of philosophical achievements relative to other achievements.

Mirror, Mirror, on the Wall

It's interesting that it is an upshot of my view that philosophy is not the most supremely valuable achievement humans can undertake. This is interesting because that's the sort of thing we expect a philosopher to say—Aristotle said it, or something close to it. There is something of a philosophical tradition of endorsing philosophy as the highest form of human endeavor. Although the account of achievements that I have developed tells us that philosophical achievements might be very valuable, it's not particularly plausible that they are the most valuable.

What would make something the most supremely valuable achievement? Simply considering the value of the product, it seems far more plausible that there are other endeavors besides philosophy whose products are of far greater value than philosophy, so much so that this additional value seems likely to eclipse even the most difficult and competently caused philosophical achievement. It would be foolish to try to argue that philosophy is more valuable than achievements that have far-reaching life-saving ramifications, such as the development of treatment for diabetes or the vaccine for small pox. The products of these achievements seem far more valuable than even the most impressive works of philosophy.

But we can put aside achievements with valuable products and ask a different question. We can ask about candidates for achievements with the most Essential Value. These would be the most valuable achievements as such. So there are two questions to consider: what are good candidates for the achievement with the most overall value, and what are good candidates for the achievement with the most Essential Value?

But first let's be clear about the status of these questions. Since the *actual* amounts of effort and rationality exercised by the individual engaging in the achievement determine its value, we can really only speculate about candidates for the most valuable achievements of them all, and the answer will depend crucially on the nature of the activities of the achiever. And as far as the intrinsic value of the products is concerned, answers to these questions are bound up with further axiologies. I will simply help myself to claims about what things might plausibly have intrinsic value, noting that thorough answers depend on further theories.

Moreover, as we saw in Chapter 2, difficulty can be construed not just as a matter of effort exercised by an individual, but there is also a class-relative sense of difficult. When we say, for example, that climbing K2 is difficult what we mean is that it would be difficult for the typical member of the relevant class of mountain climbers. This could still suffice to make some endeavor an achievement. It would be an achievement for some member of the relevant comparison class, and in this respect we call it an achievement. Climbing K2 is an achievement, to be sure, even though we have not specified any particular person for whom it is an achievement. What makes it true is that climbing K2 is typically difficult, and typically an achievement, for those who typically do it.

However, these kinds of achievements with no specified achievers don't have any value. The source of value of achievements, after all, I have argued, is in the exercise and deployment of the will and rationality. Without actual exercise of these things, there is no actual value. So when we talk about the most valuable achievement of them all, this is properly a question looking backward at what achievements have been done, and an accurate answer to the question would look at what efforts and rationality have in fact been exercised. We can still ask of these achievements with unspecified achievers which of these would be a good candidate for the most valuable achievement of all. Indeed, one might even say that, since we may not have a good sense of just how much effort and rationality have been exercised in any particular achievement, this is really just the question we are asking, namely, what *would* be the most valuable achievement.

Let us then consider some candidates for the most valuable achievement overall. Good candidates will be very difficult, involve an excellent exercise of rationality, have supremely valuable products, and also have supremely valuable additional elements in the process. Obvious candidates are cures for fatal diseases and vaccines. Presumably, the products of these achievements include all the lives that they save. Thus the value of these products is great and, in certain cases, is continually growing as vaccines and medicines continue to save lives every day. Similar things could be said about important technological innovations, such as the development of electricity, the internet, air travel, cars, and so on, which have had such enormous and life-changing effects in enriching the lives of the world's population.

Now, this depends on our understanding of the products of vaccines, technology, and so on as including the lives saved and enriched. We might think that this is an inaccurate description of the product and in fact the product is restricted to just the medicine itself (or the formula for it). In that case, it would seem that the value of the medicine is instrumental, and not intrinsic. The value of achievements with which we are concerned here is their intrinsic value, so perhaps the intrinsic value of these achievements is actually not so enormous after all.[15] Moreover, many of these kinds of achievements have had very bad instrumental effects that they continue to have and many people would be inclined to argue outweigh the good that they have caused. Climate change, for example, caused by emissions from various innovations and achievements including cars, may eventually have unimaginably destructive outcomes. So the value of many of the most highly prized medical and technological achievements might not be so obviously supreme after all.

We might do better by concentrating our attention on achievements with products of less complicated and controversial intrinsic value. A good place to look would be artistic and cultural achievements, such as the ceiling of the Sistine Chapel, Wagner's Ring Cycle, or Angkor Wat.

But surely one might also put the works of Plato and Aristotle on this list, not to mention Kant, Wittgenstein, and so on. There is, it seems, a place for the great philosophical masterworks in this list of great achievements.

Yet there is a certain peculiarity to philosophical achievements in contrast to these other great works which we have already discussed, namely, that philosophical works argue for conclusions which they present as true, which leads us to complications about the value of false theories. But leaving these complications where we left them, at least we can say of the greatest philosophical masterworks, even if the positions defended are ultimately incorrect (after all, both Aristotle and Plato can't be right), as ways of looking at the world, or ideas or suggestions or proposals, they constitute something valuable. Or at least it wouldn't be implausible to suppose that this is true.

So at least we can make a case for the greatest works of philosophy belonging on the list of supreme achievements.

---

[15] One can make a compelling argument that instrumental value can generate intrinsic value. If that's so, then the value of the medical and technological achievements just considered becomes even more complex.

These conclusions are hardly surprising. And this, I take it, is a good thing. My account has successfully reached the conclusion that our intuitions endorse about what achievements are the most valuable. Perhaps, then, I can be satisfied, that I have succeeded in a small philosophical achievement in generating a highly plausible account that appears to capture intuitions.

Of course, since all the answers to these questions really depend on the actual details of how much effort and rationality in fact are exercised, there might, in the end, turn out to be some surprises. Perhaps we would find that an achievement with a superlatively valuable product was actually developed with little effort or rationality, or perhaps some achievements of only modestly valuable products involved such supreme effort and rationality that its value surpasses many others. So a more thorough understanding of these issues might generate some interesting upshots. But for the most part, the view captures what we hoped it would as far as overall value of achievements.

Now we also have the question of the achievements with the most Essential Value. This will be the achievement that involves the most effort and most rationality. What might this be? Nothing obviously pops up. Why might philosophy be a good candidate? It is very difficult, but it's not clear that it's the most difficult. It certainly does take high amounts of intense effort over longer periods of time, which, when added up over a career or over a project, might be extremely high. But other endeavors are similar, such as scientific inquiry.

One might say that the exercise of rationality is special in philosophy, in that it is pure, insofar as it is rationality being exercised for its own sake. I have to admit, I'm not entirely sure what this means, and it's not obvious to me that it's true. There is also another special way in which we exercise our rationality in philosophy, at least sometimes. It is often reflexive—rationality is exercised in the study of rationality itself. This has taken place to a certain extent in this book (as well as effort being exerted toward the study of the nature of effort itself). And one might wonder if such reflexive endeavors have additional value in virtue of their reflexivity. So let's consider these two candidates for special value in philosophy: purity and reflexivity.

First, what might we mean by the purity of the exercise of rationality in philosophy? We have in mind the notion that philosophy really *just is* nothing but an exercise of rationality. We don't need special equipment to do philosophy. It's pretty much entirely a matter of thinking about things in a careful, focused, and rigorous way. It's not clear, however, that this is unique to philosophy. Certain areas of scientific investigation and mathematics are also like this. Supposing that philosophy along with these other areas of inquiry involves a pure exercise of rationality, why might purity be especially valuable, and would it make the *rationality* especially valuable as such? It's not obvious why purity is a source of value, and one might even be inclined to say that intuitions that it is have led to great errors in value assessment (purity of race, for example). One might say, however, that purity is a way of gaining more unity, and we have seen from discussions of organic unity that an increase in unity generates an increase in value. This, I think, might be the best attempt at explaining any value unity might have. But increase in unity only adds value if it does not come at the expense of diversity, since it is unity in diversity that is the value of organic unity. It's not clear that purity does not come at the expense of diversity in philosophy.

Reflexivity is also a way of being unified, and it is a way of adding unity without sacrificing diversity. One might even say that it's a way that something can be even more unified with itself. So in this way philosophy might be more valuable than some other achievements. But the value of reflexivity isn't clearly part of the achievement's Essential Value, which stems solely from difficulty and rationality. Does reflexive exercise of rationality add to its own value as such? One could make a case that it does, because it makes these instances of rationality particularly valuable, and if the source of Essential Value of an achievement is additionally valuable, then the Essential Value of the achievement is greater. So we have a fairly promising way of defending the position that philosophy has a particularly high degree of Essential Value.

But one might say very much the same things about the study of poetry and literature (to an extent), mathematics, and perhaps psychology. All of these might involve at certain points and in certain ways a reflexive exercise of rationality. One might say that the reflexive investigation of rationality is properly the business of philosophy, in a way that it is not for these other fields of inquiry. This seems an unlikely claim, and perhaps we shouldn't try so hard to hog the spotlight.

There is a further interesting area of consideration, that philosophy is self-propagating. By its very nature, it is increasingly difficult and requires ever more exercise of rationality. As Aristotle says, it can be done "continuously" and although I don't think it's what he meant by it, it's certainly true that philosophy appears to be bottomless—or topless, depending which direction you're going—the more philosophical questions we investigate and putatively resolve, the more open themselves up to us. The boundary for completion continually pushes itself forward the closer we approach it.[16]

This strikes me as an exciting conclusion. There is really no good reason to think that our knowledge of the nature of all that is and all that there is to be contemplating is something finite. In this respect, philosophical achievement increasingly grows in value, as the exercise of will and exercise of rationality continuously expand.

Yet, once again, it's hardly obvious that philosophy is the only sort of inquiry that is self-expanding in this way. One might say the same thing of any kind of inquiry. The universe of possible things to learn and discover is perhaps even itself expanding, and so the more we know, the more there is to know. In any case, philosophy and all these other continually expanding areas of inquiry all have ever-increasing value.

A Puzzle about Philosophical Inquiry

Earlier I suggested that another puzzle arises which concerns the nature of philosophical methodology.

In doing philosophy, one might (naively, perhaps) think that one is genuinely working on solving the problems of philosophy. We might not in fact solve any of them, but we might think that solving these problems and generating accurate theories is indeed the ultimate aim, and philosophical inquiry is the way in which we try to solve these problems. Suppose that some philosophers do indeed have this optimistic outlook.

Other philosophers, however, might think that this is an impossible task. The problems of philosophy are impossible to solve. According to the pessimistic camp, the ultimate, true aim of philosophy is simply to engage in philosophical inquiry. According to the pessimists, what the optimists take themselves to be doing is impossible.

---

[16] Neil Levy has argued that activities of supreme value or meaningfulness are characterized by just this very structure of a self-expanding goal. There is certainly something very appealing about this notion. Levy, however, doesn't explain why this structure might be a source of value ("Downshifting and the Meaning of Life," *Ratio* (2005): 176–89).

Suppose that these pessimists (now realists) are actually right—that the problems of philosophy aren't in fact solvable. Let's further suppose that the optimists become *aware* that the problems of philosophy are impossible to solve. But it turns out that a very effective way to engage in philosophical inquiry is to *believe* albeit falsely that these problems really are solvable. It's very difficult, after all, to stay motivated if you are well aware that you are toiling away on an impossible task.[17] I will call this technique used by these enlightened optimists the PH method.

The technique, generally put, is this: there is an activity with a certain goal that the agent ultimately wants to attain. But it turns out that keeping this goal in mind is *not* the best way for the agent to attain the goal. Rather, it's better for the agent to have some *other* goal in mind. Let's call this other goal the *practical goal*.

For activities of this nature, having the practical goal in mind requires having some *false beliefs*. In the most basic case, the agent believes that the practical goal is truly the ultimate goal, which is false. In other cases, such as the one I'm about to discuss, using the PH method requires having even more false and some unjustified beliefs.

Now we see a puzzle. The PH method looks as if it presents problems for competent causation. The PH method involves having false beliefs, and unjustified beliefs, and it also involves having some false and unjustified beliefs about the overarching structure of the activity. So not only does it appear as if it may not do well in terms of number of JTBs, it also looks like it might not do so well in the one area where it looks as if content also matters.

But how bad is the damage? Does my view say that philosophers who use the PH method have a far lower level of competent causation than the realists? This seems implausible. The PH method seems to be a perfectly

---

[17] Many activities seem to be like this, in a more general way. Keeping the true nature or goal of the activity in the forefront of one's mind is a bad way to achieve the ultimate aim of these activities; rather, their ultimate aim is best achieved by keeping certain false beliefs about the nature of the goal in mind. Such activities resemble the paradox of hedonism. The best life, according to hedonism, is one with maximum pleasure. But it's virtually impossible to enjoy everything to the maximum when you are constantly *trying* to enjoy yourself as much as possible. Rather, a much better way to get the most pleasure is by focusing entirely on whatever it is that you wish to enjoy. For example, we might decide to play some pool in order to enjoy ourselves. But if we are constantly focused on enjoying the game, we're bound to enjoy it much less. Instead, we should pretend that our true aim is simply to win the game. This way, we enjoy the game much more than we would if we kept in mind our real true aim of playing, which is to enjoy ourselves.

reasonable method of doing philosophy, and it seems that PH-ers are competently causing their philosophical work just as much as the realists are.

But once we look closely, we will see that my view succeeds in capturing
all the intuitions about these different philosophical techniques.

First, let's suppose that it is true that the problems of philosophy are
impossible to solve. Imagine philosophers P and R. P uses the PH method.
She knows the problems are impossible to solve, and uses the belief that
the problems of philosophy are solvable as a "trick" to get herself to do
philosophy better; she knows that this belief is false, but believes it anyway
(via self-deception or some other similar technique). R is the realist. He
believes the problems are unsolvable, does not employ the PH technique.
R believes that, in doing philosophy, he is engaging in inquiry, nothing
more, nothing less.

To determine who is causing their philosophy more competently, on
my view, we tally the JTBs the philosophers have with respect to their
respective activities and products. Let's start with the realist, R. R has a
certain number of beliefs, all of which are true and justified.

P, who is using the PH method, has almost all the same JTBs as R does.
Except while R believes that his method is the best, P believes that the
PH method is the best. P has additional beliefs. She falsely believes that
the problems of philosophy are solvable, which is in tension with her
other JTB that the problems of philosophy are not solvable. Since these
beliefs contradict one another it seems plausible that at least one of them
is unjustified, by some standards of justification. Moreover, P has further
meta-beliefs about why she believes the problems of philosophy are solvable. These are beliefs about the PH method.

It seems that P, using the PH method, has *more* JTBs than R. P has all
the same JTBs as R, plus all the additional beliefs about the PH method.
Of course, P has more false and unjustified beliefs than R—these being
the beliefs about all the problems of philosophy being solvable that she
deceives herself into holding for the sake of the PH method.

Recall that only *true* JTBs count. The view does not discount competence if there are false or unjustified beliefs. In other words, the degree
of competent causation is a matter of all and only JTBs—only number of
JTBs counts, and all JTBs count positively. So if P has more beliefs than R,
P is competently causing her product to a greater degree than R is.

In the end, then, it seems to be the case that according to my view the relative competency of causation for P in contrast to R is that the PH method

results in a greater degree of competent causation. Because PH-ers have more JTBs about their process, they cause the product *more competently* than someone who does not use a PH method.

But what is it that is being competently caused? I have been speaking very loosely here. P is *competently causing herself to be engaged in philosophical inquiry by means of the PH method*. R is clearly *not* doing the same thing. Rather, he is doing something else, namely, engaging in philosophical inquiry by means of the straightforward method. Both are indeed engaged in philosophical inquiry, but is either one competently causing this to a greater degree than the other? It's hard to say, and I'm not quite sure what to say about the situation, if anything needs to be said at all.

Now, my view may not be particularly illuminating about the nature of the PH method. But it says exactly what I think it should. There is a sense in which there is a higher level of competent causation if the PH method is used (after all, the PH method is a very good one for many important activities), but there is also a sense in which one is engaged in a different activity if one is using a different method, so it's hard to say whether or not the achievement is more or less competently produced if the method is different—it's a different achievement, after all, if it's produced by a different method.

Whether or not *this* particular philosophical endeavor is an achievement of any particular value, I suppose, remains to be seen. I can report with genuine honesty that it has been difficult—but, like Betty the jogger—I have rarely found the effort bothersome. The degree to which I have competently caused this book is less clear—of course, I have many beliefs about achievement, but whether or not they are justified and true is another matter. The value of this project, as an achievement, or otherwise, I suppose, I leave for you to discover.

Works Cited

Aristotle. *Nicomachean Ethics*. Tr. Terence Irwin. Indianapolis: Hackett, 1999.

Bengson, John, and Marc A. Moffet. Eds. *Knowing How: Essays on Knowledge, Mind, and Action*. Oxford: Oxford University Press, 2011.

Betzler, Monika. "The Normative Significance of Personal Projects." In Michael Kühler and Nadja Jelinek (eds), *Autonomy and the Self*. Dordrecht: Springer, 2013, 101–26.

Bradford, Gwen. "Kudos for *Ludus*: Games and Value Theory," *Noesis*, 6 (2003): 15–28.

Bradford, Gwen. "Evil Achievements and the Principle of Recursion." In Mark Timmons (ed.), *Oxford Studies in Normative Ethics*, iii. Oxford: Oxford University Press, 2013, 79–97.

Bradford, Gwen. "The Value of Achievements," *Pacific Philosophical Quarterly*, 94 (2013): 204–24.

Bradford, Gwen. "Knowledge, Achievement, and Manifestation." *Erkenntnis*, published online, 2014: DOI 10.1007/s10670-014-9614-0.

Chisholm, R. M. *Brentano and Intrinsic Value*. Cambridge: Cambridge University Press, 1986.

Clarke, Maudemarie. *Nietzsche on Truth and Philosophy*. New York: Cambridge University Press, 1990.

Dorsey, Dale. "Three Arguments for Perfectionism," *Noûs*, 44 (2010): 59–79.

Dorsey, Dale. "First Steps in an Axiology of Goals," *International Journal of Wellbeing*, 1 (2011): 167–85.

Feldman, Fred. *Utilitarianism, Hedonism and Desert*. Cambridge: Cambridge University Press, 1997.

Gallwey, W. Timothy. *The Inner Game of Tennis*. New York: Random House, 1974.

Goldman, Alvin. "What Is Justified Belief?" In G. Pappas (ed.), *Justification and Knowledge*. Dordrecht: Reidel, 1979, 1–23.

Greco, John. *Achieving Knowledge*. Cambridge: Cambridge University Press, 2010.

Green, Barry, and W. Timothy Gallwey. *The Inner Game of Music*. New York: Doubleday, 1986.

Holowchak, M. Andrew. "Ergogenic Aids and the Limits of Human Performance in Sport: Ethical Issues, Aesthetic Considerations," *Journal of the Philosophy of Sport*, 29/1 (2002): 75–86.

Hurka, Thomas. *Perfectionism*. Oxford: Oxford University Press, 1993.

Hurka, Thomas. *Virtue, Vice and Value*. Oxford: Oxford University Press, 2001.

Hurka, Thomas. "Games and the Good," *Proceedings of the Aristotelian Society*, supplementary vol. (2006): 217–35.

Hurka, Thomas. "Nietzsche: Perfectionist." In Brian Leiter and Neil Sinhababu (eds), *Nietzsche and Morality*. Oxford: Clarendon Press, 2007, 9–31.

Kagan, Shelly. "Rethinking Intrinsic Value," *Ethics*, 2 (1998): 277–97.

Keller, Simon. "Welfare and the Achievement of Goals," *Philosophical Studies*, 121 (2004): 27–41.

Keller, Simon. "Welfare as Success," *Noûs*, 43 (2009): 656–83.

Korsgaard, Christine. "Two Distinctions in Goodness," *Philosophical Review*, 2 (1983): 169–95.

Kvanvig, Jonathan. *The Value of Knowledge and the Pursuit of Understanding*. Cambridge: Cambridge University Press, 2003.

Leiter, Brian. *Neitzsche on Morality*. New York: Routledge, 2002.

Lemos, John. *Intrinsic Value: Concept and Warrant*. Cambridge: Cambridge University Press, 1994.

Lemos, John. "Organic Unities," *Journal of Ethics*, 2 (1998): 323–4.

Levy, Neil. "Downshifting and the Meaning of Life," *Ratio* (2005): 176–89.

Moore, G. E. *Principia Ethica*. Cambridge: Cambridge University Press, 1971.

Nietzsche, Friedrich. *The Will to Power*. Tr. Walter Kaufmann and R. J. Hollingdale. New York: Random House, 1968.

Nietzsche, Friedrich. *Beyond Good and Evil*. Tr. Walter Kaufmann. New York: Random House, 1989.

Nozick, Robert. *Anarchy, State, and Utopia*. New York: Basic Books, 1974.

Nozick, Robert. *Philosophical Explanations*. Cambridge, MA: Harvard University Press, 1981.

Parfit, Derek. *Reasons and Persons*. Oxford: Clarendon Press, 1984.

Portmore, Douglas. "Welfare, Achievement, and Self-Sacrifice," *Journal of Ethics and Social Philosophy*, 2 (2007): 1–28.

Railton, Peter. "Alienation, Consequentialism, and the Demands of Morality," *Philosophy and Public Affairs*, 2 (1994): 134–71.

Raz, Joseph. *The Morality of Freedom*. Oxford: Clarendon Press, 1986.

Reginster, Bernard. "Happiness as a Faustian Bargain," *Daedalus* 133 (2004): 52–9.

Reginster, Bernard. *The Affirmation of Life*. Cambridge, MA: Harvard University Press, 2006.

Reginster, Bernard. "The Will to Power and the Ethics of Creativity." In Brian Leiter and Neil Sinhababu (eds), *Nietzsche and Morality*. Oxford: Clarendon Press, 2007, 32–56.

Richardson, John. *Nietzsche's System*. New York: Oxford University Press, 1996.

Scanlon, T. M. *What We Owe to Each Other*. Cambridge, MA: Harvard University Press, 1998.

Schopenhauer, Arthur. *Parerga and Paralipomena*. Tr. E. F. J. Payne. Oxford: Clarendon Press, 1974.

Sher, George. *Beyond Neutrality: Perfectionism and Politics*. Cambridge: Cambridge University Press, 1997.

Suits, Bernard. *The Grasshopper*. Toronto: Broadview Press, 2005.

Wiggins, David. "Truth, Invention, and the Meaning of Life." In *Needs, Values, Truth: Essays in the Philosophy of Value*. Oxford: Clarendon Press, 1998, 87–138.

Williams, Bernard. "Persons, Character and Morality." In *Moral Luck*. Cambridge: Cambridge University Press, 1981, 1–19.

Index